INDIA AND HER NEIGHBOURS

INDIA AND HER NEIGHBOURS

Towards a Proactive Partnership

Mohammed Badrul Alam

KALPAZ

A

ISBN: 978-93-5128-120-7
Price : ₹ 900

First Published, 2015

Published by

Kalpaz Publications
C-30, Satyawati Nagar,
Delhi-110052
Ph. : 9212142040
E-mail: kalpaz@hotmail.com

Laser Typesetting : Abhishek Mandal, Delhi
Printed at : G. Print Process, Delhi

Cataloging in Publication Data—DK

Courtesy: D.K. Agencies (P) Ltd. <docinfo@dkagencies.com>

India and her neighbours : towards a proactive partnership / Mohd. Badrul Alam.
pages cm
Contributed articles.
Includes bibliographical references (pages) and index.

ISBN 9789351281207

1. India—Foreign relations—South Asia. 2. South Asia—Foreign relations—India. I. Alam, Mohammed Badrul, editor.

DDC 327.54 23

Contents

List of Contributors

1. **Prof Mohammed Badrul Alam**, Head, Dept. of Political Science, Jamia Millia Islamia University, New Delhi.
2. **Dr Rajendra Kumar Pandey**, Center for Federal Studies, Jamia Hamdard, Delhi.
3. **Muzzaffar Ahemad Ganaie**, Doctoral Research Scholar, Dept. of Political Science, Jamia Millia Islamia, Delhi.
4. **Dr Amit Kumar Gupta**, Dept. of Political Science, Central University of Sikkim, Gangtok, Sikkim.
5. **Dr Biswajit Mohapatra**, Dept. of Political Science, North-Eastern Hill University, Shillong, Meghalaya.
6. **Reyaz Ahmad Ganaie**, Doctoral Research Scholar, Dept. of Political Science, Jamia Millia Islamia, Delhi.
7. **Sajad Husain Wani**, Doctoral Research Scholar, Dept. of Political Science, Jamia Millia Islamia, Delhi.
8. **Prof Veena Kukreja**, Dept. of Political Science, Delhi University, Delhi.
9. **Dr Sarish Sebastian**, Dept. of Political Science, I.P. College, Delhi University, Delhi.
10. **Dr Amulya Tripathy**, Dept. of Political Science, Science College, Hinjlicut, Odisha.
11. **Ms Roshni Kujur**, Dept. of Political Science, Berhampur University, Odisha.
12. Dr Veena Ravi Kumar, Dept. of Political Science, Lady Shri Ram College, University of Delhi.
13. **Dr Josukutty CA**, Dept of Political Science, University of Kerala, Trivandrum.
14. **Dr Anshuman Behera**, School of Social Sciences, National Institute of Advanced Studies, Bangalore.

15. **Dr Subhransu Sekhar Mishra**, Dept. of Political Science, National Defence Academy, Khadakvasla, Pune.
16. **Dr Avilash Roul**, Independent International Consultant, Society for the Study of Peace and Conflict, Delhi.

Preface

The primary purpose of this book is to analyse, examine, evaluate and critique and describe the emerging contours of India's foreign policy vis-a-vis its neighbours. India needs a closer relationship with its immediate neighbours as the small countries in the neighbourhood consider India as a viable partner which can facilitate intractable issues both in the South Asian region as well as beyond. India has never believed in the 'Big Brother Policy' and 'hegemony' and has emphasised on regionalism and institutionalism as the tools for effective strengthening of relationship between India and its neighbours. Focusing on the re-orientation of the Indian foreign policy in the context of its neighbours: Nepal, Bhutan, Bangladesh, Sri Lanka, Maldives and Pakistan, the book highlights the close historical, commercial, strategic and cultural relations with national interests as the central foci.

The book is likely to generate immense academic, scholarly and public debate on issues related to the shaping of foreign policy of India with particular emphasis on its dealings with her neighbours. By discussing the impact of important bilateral measures with regional and sub-regional ramifications, the book provides a new vista and a possible paradigm shift which may have long-term implications for the South Asian regional architecture and beyond.

Chapter One argues that South Asian regionalism is a product of reluctant handshake amongst its stakeholders presumably under compulsive motivations of forces operating both within and outside the region. Rajendra Kumar Pandey explains how a genuine change in mindset is imperative for regionalism to emerge in the South Asian scene.

Chapter Two explains and critically analyse the policy issues the littoral countries are faced with such as arms trafficking, narco terrorism, illegal migration. Biswajit Mohapatra summarises as to how these issues have assumed new proportions after their switch from land routes to sea routes and thus ensuring both regional and state security from all sources at large.

Chapter Three provides a balanced, objective as to how South Asia, which formed due to geophysical violence (plate tectonic movement), has been potentially, as many observers hypothesised, in risk of a probable water conflict among the sovereign countries.

Avilash Roul surmises that regular timely sharing of basic information on projects coming up would be the first step in right direction.

Chapter Four examine and evaluates how notwithstanding the commonalities and the central role played by India in the creation of Bangladesh, the relations between the two countries are characterised by mutual distrust and suspicion. Muzaffar Ahemad Ganaie elaborates how greater access to Indian market and removal of trade barriers on the part of India can help to create a conducive environment for Free Trade Agreement.

Chapter Five addresses the trajectory shift in the relationship as the security environment of a state is largely governed by its geographical location, which is closely linked to its domestic, regional and international setting. Subhransu Sekhar Mishra surmises that India, in the short-term, should continue to provide the resources required for the resettlement of Tamil population and invest in the economic development of the war-ravaged Northeast of Sri Lanka.

Chapter Six situates the India-Maldives relations from a historical context up to the contemporary times. Mohammed Badrul Alam dwells on how in spite of onerous challenges, India-Maldives relations has thrived well and looks promising in the intermediate to long term.

Chapter Seven examines how the history of both India and Pakistan impinge on each other so much that they impact the rest of the nations in the South Asian region. Veena Ravi Kumar discusses how on the part of India, suspicions and misperceptions need to be kept aside and a serious dialogue be initiated by treating the Muslims as an integral part of the Indian nation.

Chapter Eight examines and evaluates various confidence-building measures, military as well as non-military that were initiated between India and Pakistan. Mohammed Badrul Alam's chapter also addresses and delineates definition and conceptual notion as well as some of the pertinent aspects of ongoing peace process including Track-II diplomacy and nuclear risk reduction measures being undertaken by India and Pakistan.

Chapter Nine focuses on the continuous and cautious efforts of the heads of the nation and how those are germane for bringing peace into the sub-continent which is necessary for the betterment of both the nations. Amulya Kumar Tripathy and Roshni Kujur elaborate how India, under Prime Minister Manmohan Singh immediately after his election vowed that he would place top priority on carrying forward a nascent peace process with Pakistan and hold talks with all Kashmiri groups to resolve the vexed dispute.

Chapter Ten highlights how Indo-Pakistan relations have been riddled with conflicts – over a wide range of issues ranging from religion to water to territorial dispute in Kashmir. Veena Kukreja describes how this complex relationship has serious ramifications for national security of both the countries.

Chapter Eleven analyses the post-independence history of India and Pakistan which has largely been a history of conflict rather than cooperation. Sajad Hussain Wani summarises how despite several efforts at reconciliation, the two sides remain locked in an embrace of seemingly unending conflict.

Chapter Twelve looks at the India's post-2104 Afghan policy and how it should aim at mitigating the possibility of Afghanistan again becoming sanctuary for extremist outfits who, more often than not, take diktats from Pakistan's ISI. Reyaz Ahmad Ganaie explains the need for a stable and democratic Afghanistan which will serve India's interests within Afghanistan in the long run and can also limit Pakistan's manoeuvring of religious extremism as a state policy.

Chapter Thirteen discusses how the U.S. led intervention in Afghanistan was not only an effort to uproot terrorism from Afghan soil but also an attempt to cultivate democracy in the Af-Pak region. C.A. Josukutty surmises that the collaborative efforts by the World's oldest democracy (USA) and the largest democracy (India) could strengthen their bilateral relations and mitigate conditions of terrorism in South Asia.

Chapter Fourteen addresses the symbiotic relationship between India and Bhutan.

Sarish Sebastian analyses how Bhutan in spite of it being a land-locked country is committed to usher in Gross National Happiness for its own people and at the same time cement its relations with India on the basis of shared partnership.

Chapter Fifteen describes how despite strong cultural, emotional and historic links, India and Nepal have not been able to maximise their core interests. Anshuman Behera surmises that both the countries must think beyond popular sloganeering and move towards building a progressive partnership for a win-win proposition.

Chapter Sixteen discusses how the INOs (Indians of Nepali Origins) and the NIOs (Nepali of Indian Origins) despite their being internal tensions on the basis of language, religion, caste, class, ethnicity, have in fact emerged as a unified entity, fighting for one common demand of rights and respectful identity. Amit Kumar Gupta explains how assertive movements have important social processes which can be effectively harnessed not only to address the grievances of the competing groups but also to enhance social solidarity amongst the contending groups for upward mobility.

Mohammed Badrul Alam
Delhi

Acknowledgements

Mohammed Badrul Alam drew inspiration from teaching a wide range of students in India, USA and Japan over the past three decades. As for inculcation to foreign policy and American Studies discourse, it commenced long time ago in early 1980s in Jawaharlal Nehru University, New Delhi where he earned his M.Phil degree in American Studies at the School of International Studies. His professors, Dr B.K. Shrivastava, Dr M.S.Venkatramani and Dr R.P. Kaushik, taught him aspects and various nuances of foreign policy and American Studies and its implications. His long stint working at the Parliament Library, Teen Murti Nehru Memorial Library, American Center Library and ICWA Sapru House Library in New Delhi opened up his eyes to the scope and breadth of literature on almost all important facets of foreign policy, American Studies including strategic discourse.

In the United States, where Dr Alam attended Cornell University in Ithaca, New York, and earned his M.A. and Ph.D degrees in International Studies, many high profile professors such as Prof Mary Katzenstein, Prof Milton Esman, Prof Richard Polenberg, Prof Peter Katzenstein, Prof Lawrence Scheinman, Prof Geroge McKahin, Prof Benjamin Ginsberg, Prof Richard Rosecrance, Prof Water LaFeber, instilled in him the various intricacies and complexities of issues related to India's foreign policy with its immediate neighbours.

In Japan, where he has been teaching at Miyazaki International University in Southern Japan from 1998 to 2006, a number of colleagues such as Dr Kate Greenfield, Dr Getachew Felleke, Amanda Bradley, Dr Jeong Pyong-Hong, Dr Mika Mervio and Dr Yasu Izumikawa, helped Dr Alam in shaping his ideas and in bringing in the right focus on complex dynamics of India's foreign policy.

At Jamia Millia Islamia University, Delhi, where Dr Alam is presently a Professor of Political Science and its Head, all of his colleagues were of assistance in one way or the other. A number of his colleagues in the Department of Political Science including Prof Rumki Basu, Prof Furqan Ahmad, and Prof Shahid Ashraf, from the Economics Department and Jamia Millia's Registrar as well as Prof Mujtaba Khan, Director, UGC-Academic Staff College at Jamia Millia Islamia, were great source of inspiration and motivation. A number of doctoral research scholars including Reyaz Ahmad Ganie, Muzaffar Ahemad Ganaie, Akhilesh Tiwari, Digvijay Singh Sekhawat, Sarish Sebastian, Kuldeep Singh, Amit Gupta, were of immense help in collecting the source materials.

The greatest gratitude is owed to Dr Alam's mother, Mrs Hedatun Nisa and brothers: Dr Mohammed Shamsul Alam and Mohammed Aminul Alam, and sisters: Dr (Mrs) Swaleha Khatun, Mrs Rahima Khatun, Mrs Sofia Khatun, his wife: Mrs Gahartaj Rokeya and the children: Saira Alam, Zubair Alam, Sadaf Alam and Munawar Alam. Although quite demanding and at times frustrating, everyone allowed him the time and necessary emotional support he needed to complete his work. Much of Dr Alam's success is due to their love and affection at all times.

A special word of thanks to Shri Amit Garg, Director, Gyan Publishing House, New Delhi, India, for showing genuine interest in the manuscript and for its subsequent publication.

Prof Mohammed Badrul Alam

1

Changing Dynamics of Regionalism in South Asia

Rajendra Kumar Pandey

Regionalism has arguably been a hallmark of international relations in the post war times. Despite the inhibitory portents of the cold war, countries in different parts of the globe have been able to identify such commonality of interests that would propel them to forge some sort of regional cooperation. But South Asia apparently defied this global trend. Consequently, the idea of regional cooperation remained a distant dream for long owing to deep-rooted suspicions towards one another, on the one hand, and scepticism regarding ensuing benefits and loses from such cooperation, on the other. It was only in the early 1980s that serious arguments for some kind of regional cooperation in South Asia were advanced by Bangladesh in particular. Though the initial response of other countries was lukewarm, they agreed to ponder over the idea in due course. Thus, South Asian regionalism appears to be a product of reluctant handshake amongst its stakeholders presumably under compulsive motivations of forces operating both within and outside the region. Clearly, the disinclination of these countries seems to be rooted in their perceived futility of regionalism in the face of formidable, if not absolute, divergence of interests amongst some countries such as India and Pakistan. This is probably the reason that a few countries preferred to join global military alliances and forge strong ties with cold war groups instead of looking within the region to get their interests served. Further, in a way, regionalism in South Asia seems to be obfuscated by standing of India as the dominant power in the region. In the resultant complex scenario, while Pakistan traditionally sustains its animosity towards India, other countries are also weary of the relative advantages from a regional arrangement in which India is destined to be the pivot. So, regionalism in South Asia has not been an easy idea to dawn, and even if that has dawned, it has never been easy to take the idea to the levels attained by many other regional organisations in the world. What follows, therefore, is an attempt at critical analysis of the changing dynamics of regionalism in South Asia.

Regionalism in International Relations

International relations have been characterised by one or the other forms of regionalism ever since nations endeavoured to cooperate with one another. Even the finer stipulations of the Westphalian world order like balance of power and collective security had been contingent on regional cooperation amongst European principalities in seventeenth century. Yet, regional arrangements became distinct sub-level of global arrangements only after the First World War when the League of Nations was created.[1] Under the League system, regional organisations were not only granted legitimacy, they were also encouraged to act as bulwark against threats to international peace and security.[2] However, with the increasing number of regional arrangements, the theoretical landscape of region and regionalism became muddied with competing perspectives seeking to privilege one aspect of the idea or the other. Nevertheless, conceptually, a region has been defined as a group of states bound together by both a geographical proximity and a degree of mutual interdependence.[3] However, with the growing significance of non-governmental organisations in recent past, the idea needed to ordain a place for them as well along with the states. Accordingly, regionalism has been defined as 'cooperation among governments or non-governmental organisations in three or more geographically proximate and interdependent countries for the pursuit of mutual gain in one or more issue-areas.'[4] Within this conceptual framework, regionalism found its fullest manifestation in the decades following the Second World War with the United Nations Charter granting a place of prominence to regional organisations.[5] Arguably, strengthening of position of the regional organisations would expectedly not only reduce the potential points of dispute between the countries of the region, it would also enhance all round cooperation amongst the countries, thereby, advancing the goals for which the UN stands and exists.[6]

Hence, the decade of 1960s witnessed a 'regionalist wave' when regional organisations were established in many parts of the world.[7] In the subsequent decades, the march of regionalism spread to hitherto unchartered plains covering almost all parts of the world by 1980s.[8] This new regionalism sought to unclog the regional aspirations from the clutches of cold war, and provide a new vigour to regions like South Asia to go for regional cooperation braving both internal and external odds.[9] In the post cold war period, the inherent nature of regional organisations underwent a subtle transformation.[10] The core of regionalism now increasingly turned out to be overwhelmingly economic in comparison to their ambivalent focus in the past. Moreover, easing of political influence, if not control, on a large number of countries afforded them some operational leg space to be an active participant in the moribund regional organisations. Furthermore, with the diminishing political and strategic stakes in the regional organisations, they seemed poised for reinventing themselves in terms of becoming platforms for enhanced economic, social and cultural cooperation amongst the member states.[11] At this moment, a decisive push to reorient the nature and priorities of the regional organisations was given by globalisation.[12] That way, globalisation presented a dilemmatic situation before the regional organisations. It sought to enlist the support of regional organisations in extending the neo-liberal agenda of allowing free flow of goods and services across the regions in the world. At the same time, the regional organisations were also called upon to act as strident bulwarks against the exploitative nature of globalisation to protect the region from the vagaries of speculative and market-driven global economic risks.[13] Amidst these competing claims on regional organisations, many of them has continued to be marred by internal dissensions and political manoeuvring by member states. As a result, a comparative assessment of the working of regional organisations presents a mixed bag of successes and failure. While a few regional organisations like European Union (EU), Association of South East Asian Nations (ASEAN), North American Free Trade Area (NAFTA), among others, are scaling new heights towards mutual cooperation, others such as South Asian Association for Regional Cooperation (SAARC), Organisation of African Unity (OAU), Arab League etc., are still struggling to find an incontrovertible purpose for their continued existence as regional organisations.

South Asian Regionalism

The sub-continent of South Asia presents an interesting study in the discourse on regionalism and regional cooperation, and has drawn the attention of researchers for quite long.[14] Conceptually, four hypothetical models of regional structure in South Asia have been identified to critically analyse aspects of conflict and cooperation in the region.[15] Nevertheless, it has often been described as a region without regionalism in subtle recognition of the inherent divergence of interests amongst the countries of the sub-continent.[16] This euphemism is reflective of the relative absence of cherished traditions of meaningful regionalism despite the region being a compact geographical landmass with seamless spatial contiguity amongst the countries of the subcontinent. At the same time, it also brings out the complexity of physical standing and psychological perceptions of the countries vis-a-vis one another that tend to mar than make the success of regionalism in this part of the globe.[17] What has, therefore, been argued to be the *fait accompli* of regionalism in South Asia is a symbolic rather than substantive cooperation amongst the member countries given multitude of conflicts existing in the region.[18] The reasons for such a lacklustre performance of South Asian regionalism are not far to be found.

Conventionally, national security and economic development are the foreign policy goals of the South Asian nations.[19] In their conceptualisation and concrete realisation of the twin goals, majority, if not all, of the countries in the region seem to be ambivalent towards their individual as well as collective posturing with India. As far as national security is concerned, great asymmetry in power configuration of the region has apparently tended to dissuade the nations to go for regional cooperation. Instead, they sought to look for the extra-regional powers to provide fillip to their national security aspirations that could well have been fulfilled by regional cooperation amongst them. Unsurprisingly, therefore, a submission made about thirty years back prophetically holds true even today: The involvement of extra-regional powers in South Asia was facilitated by four prevalent factors: the dire need for economic aid; differences in the political system, with narrow and intense nationalism; widespread instability in most states within the region; and finally, general suspicion of both the core and the periphery – India and its neighbours – against each other.[20]

The thrust for regional cooperation in South Asia, therefore, has always sought to be rooted in the economic considerations than political or strategic.[21] That way, urge for cooperation amongst the nations of the region dates back even to the days when the political texture of the region had not yet been clear. For instance, stray thoughts on regional cooperation in South Asia were expressed in the Asian Relations Conference at New Delhi in April 1947.[22] Similar sentiments marked the ambience of the Baguio Conference in the Philippines in May 1950, and the Colombo Powers Conference in April 1954 where regional cooperation was argued to be the way for peace and prosperity in the region.[23] However, these references to regional cooperation remained at best pious wishes of a few individuals without any proper conceptualisation of the idea based on wider consultation or a concrete blueprint to attain the objective. So, once the echo of these international meets tapered off, the idea of regional cooperation also dimmed away, and there was no talk of regional cooperation for a long time to come. This situation, however, seemed poised for a change with the birth of Bangladesh as an independent nation in 1971. Interestingly, Bangladesh is considered as the pioneer of regional cooperation in the sub-continent. But the contexts of Bangladeshi initiatives in this direction were quite perplexing. Undoubtedly, the tumultuous circumstances of the creation of Bangladesh put the nascent nation in a quandary to find a dignified place for it in the comity of nations. This pitch was further queered by military coup in the country sooner than expected, and the new military leadership's urge to enlist support of various countries to legitimise the *coup d'état* regime.[24] Furthermore, the failure of Bangladesh's attempts to get membership of ASEAN prompted it to be more serious with its efforts for regional cooperation in South Asia. Subsequently, in its parleys with other leaders of the region, Bangladesh became increasingly forthcoming on regional cooperation in South Asia. It found support from the countries like Nepal who stood to gain much from regional cooperation in the areas like water resources. The final push to concretise the proposals of regionalism in South Asia was provided by the meetings between the leaders of Bangladesh and Sri Lanka in 1979 at Colombo in which they agreed to broaden the ambit of consultations and move towards realisation of regional cooperation in South Asia.[25] This was followed by numerous meetings and consultations amongst the foreign secretaries and foreign ministers of various countries with Bangladesh drafting the desirable proposals and agendas for such meetings. Finally, with the decision to make a beginning with the non-political and non-bilateral issues, SAARC was set to herald a new phase of regionalism in South Asia with the summit meeting of leaders of the member states on December 7-8, 1985 at Dhaka.

South Asian Association for Regional Cooperation

Establishment of SAARC was undeniably the glorious moment of regionalism in South Asia, for, it was for the first time that the member countries agreed to make collective forays in ameliorating the conditions of the people of the region to the best possible extent. However, its onward march has been fraught with multifarious challenges because 'the issues that are facing the successful regional integration of South Asian countries are more daunting than one finds in other regions.'[26] Clearly, the ominous portents underpinning this historic development have been obvious right from the contexts and persuasions of formation of the group. For instance, no meaningful and vastly beneficial regionalism can possibly be visualised for South Asia in the absence of proactive and enthusiastic cooperation from India and Pakistan. But the fact of the matter is that these two powerhouses of South Asia were not only reluctant towards such a regional formation, they appeared cautiously thoughtful regarding the probable cons to be warded off rather than the pros they could draw from the formation of SAARC.[27] In other words, regionalism in South Asia has been thrust on the two countries by the smaller states of the region in order to make them partners rather than spoilers in advancing the peace and prosperity in the region. India and Pakistan's unenthusiastic joining of the group was presumably under the consideration of not being left out of association formed in their neighbourhood.

Yet, despite becoming members of SAARC, the two countries never seemed convinced of its viability and vitality as the powerful engine of regional cooperation in South Asia. India's first impression would ever be to see it as an instrument in the hands of the smaller neighbours to gang up against the foreign policy pursuits of the country. Similarly, Pakistan would never be able to perceive SAARC more than an extension of Indian hegemony in the region that would invariably hurt its national interests. Above all, be it through the instrumentality of bilateralism or multilateralism, Pakistan in no case would venture into a course of action whose direct or indirect benefits might accrue to India. In these circumstances, the journey to be chartered by SAARC was likely to be full of thorns than roses. As a result, it seems to have more failures than successes to its credit. It even failed to act upon those issues on which member countries has expressed their avowed faith. Illustratively, 'the lack of a common human rights mechanism for South Asia must be regarded as an anomaly considering that each member country forswears a commitment to democracy and rule of law.'[28]

Nonetheless, epitomising institutionalisation of regionalism in South Asia, SAARC has been able to move forward in a slow but steady fashion defying all scepticism and initial inhibitions in the course of its almost three decades of existence. The stipulated annual summit meetings of the heads of governments of the member countries provide the most propitious opportunity for the leaders to meet and deliberate on the ways and means to carry forward the charter-based objectives of SAARC. Otherwise, given their routine relations and low priorities for bilateral cooperation, many of the leaders would not have been able to meet their neighbouring counterparts for many months and years to come. Hence, if these summit meetings have not been able to achieve path-breaking results, their outcomes have neither been so disappointing. Enhancing the pace of socio-economic development in the member countries is the basic purpose of SAARC.[29] And, its progress has been remarkable in this field.

In the face of non-conducive circumstances, the achievements of SAARC have been quite prominent in three particular areas of mutual interest. One, like other regional organisations existing in other parts of the globe, SAARC has been able to foster a good degree of economic cooperation and collaboration in the region despite certain odds, 'due mainly to the forces of globalisation and economic liberalisation within many of the SAARC countries.'[30] The most remarkable success story in this regard has been that of South Asian Free Trade Area (SAFTA) agreement signed in 2004 and operationalised in 2006. In conjunction with other economic measures such as Agreement on Avoidance of Double Taxation, Agreement on Custom Matters, Agreement for establishment of SAARC Arbitration Council, Agreement on the establishment of South Asian Regional Standardisation Organisation (SARDO) and establishment of SAARC Development Fund (SDF), SAFTA has been expected to bring about an turnaround in the trade and commerce amongst the countries of the region. With the greater economic integration of the region, free flow of goods and services along with people might go a long way in paving the way for permanent peace and tranquillity even if the bilateral issue areas between two nations defy the attempts for their amicable resolution.[31] Next, the social sector cooperation engineered by SAARC has also been quite significant. In the wake of the SAARC Social Charter signed at Islamabad in 2004, alleviation of poverty emerged as another focus area of cooperation.[32] Additionally, a number of steps have been taken or visualised to be taken in the areas of population stabilisation, empowerment of women, universal primary education, human resources development, promotion of health and nutrition of the children, apart from poverty eradication and cultural development. While Agreement on establishment of SAARC Food Bank is a giant leap in securing health and nutrition of the people, SAARC Convention on Combating and Prevention of Trafficking in Women and Children for Prostitution, and Convention on Promotion of Welfare of Children are landmark instruments aimed at altering the dismal social profile of the region. Similarly, Convention on Mutual Assistance on Criminal Matters and SAARC Convention on Narcotic Drugs are good examples of cooperation and assistance in weeding out these menaces from the region. Moreover, for the countries like India that are marred by scourge of terrorism, SAARC Regional Convention on Suppression of Terrorism, and the Additional Protocol on Terrorism provide valuable framework in which the cooperation of neighbouring countries may be solicited in uprooting the tentacles of terrorism from the region. Finally, SAARC has embarked also on a comprehensive plan of institutionalising cooperation in the fields of education, disaster management etc., by establishing centres of excellence in the related field. In brief, thus, SAARC has come of age to act as the pivot of regionalism in South Asia despite all the fissures and divergences amongst the countries of the region.

These encouraging achievements notwithstanding, SAARC as an archetype of South Asian regionalism has failed to take off. In comparison to other regional arrangements such as NAFTA, EU and ASEAN, the standing of SAARC is so dismal that many would call it more a symbolic than substantive example of cooperation and eventual integration of South Asia to present a distinct South Asian identity. Evidently, many of the decisions taken at the summit meetings are either not implemented or implemented in a half-hearted manner. For instance, despite the implementation of SAFTA, Pakistan has not been able to grant the most favoured nation (MFN) status to India for the purposes of trade and commerce. To put it differently, irrespective of the multilateral decisions taken at the forum of SAARC, many countries prefer to be guided by their bilateral considerations when it comes to put those decisions into practice. Further, due to the long years of integration of their economies with the extra-regional economies, they have not been quick to find commonality of economic interests with other countries of the region in which further cooperation and collaboration may be facilitated. Above all, most, if not all, of the countries in the region are obsessed with their misplaced security concerns that eventually go to hold SAARC hostage to such concerns.[33] In a way, the politico-strategic dimensions of these countries dominate relations with one another, and amidst such environment, the talk of economic considerations amongst them appear to be meant more for public consumption than become a formidable area of cooperation. In the meanwhile, increasing institutionalisation of cooperation amongst the countries of the region may also tend to induce a bureaucratic culture in the functioning SAARC that may not prove to be helpful in evolution of regionalism in South Asia. Still, these issues and challenges are not insurmountable given a political will for that. On its own, SAARC needs to reinvent itself with the changing times. As one of the brains behind the idea of SAARC put lucidly: 'The construct of a vision for SAARC in the twenty-first century must impart a face to SAARC – a set of values, norms and cultural attributes that means more than geography and boundary, a face that means a way of life, and an intellectual space called home. A sense of belonging must be infused in the hearts of the peoples as much in the heads of policy-makers.'[34]

Problems and Prospects of Regionalism

Conflicts are common challenge to probably all the regional organisations which many of them have overcome to ordain a successful model of regional cooperation.[35] The complexity of changing dynamics of regionalism in South Asia has been a conundrum whose proper explanation can probably neither be offered in a unilinear fashion nor with reference to the prevailing circumstances only. In other words, apparently insurmountable stumbling blocks to the emergence of successful model of regionalism in the sub-continent are both multidimensional and rooted in the painful colonial past of the region. So, the problems lying at the root of regionalism find their locale in politico-strategic, socio-cultural and economic aspects of public life across the countries. What is more heartening is that the seeds of most, if not all, of these discords had been sown by the colonial masters in vigorous pursuance of their divisive policies in India. "The most significant were the 'denial of self-esteem' and also the aggravation of ethnic conflicts amongst different ethnic groups due to the 'divide and rule' policy."[36] For instance, within a short span of just few decades, the British did not only drive an irreparable wedge between the hitherto friendly communities of Hindus and Muslims, they brazenly pursued this agenda so much so that a section of the two communities became sworn enemies of each other that eventually resulted in the partition of the country. The succession states of India and Pakistan endured that colonial discord and even till date they consider each other their enemy number one. Paradoxically, however, they experience a great deal of similarity in the issues and challenges of economic development in their two countries. Thus, 'for almost all the developing nations engaged in the pursuit of regional cooperation, their common colonial legacy unites them economically but divides them politically.'[37] Unfortunately, in South Asia, nations seem to have preferred to pursue political objectives than pushing for economic cooperation.

Precarious situation in the region is further complicated by asymmetrical standing of various states of the region vis-a-vis India. Sharing borders with many of them, India has one or another problem with these countries that make them suspicious of the latter. What is more intriguing is that instead of showing some degree of ambivalence and flexibility in its dealings with the smaller neighbours, India has characteristically been rigid with them and quite often pursues a policy of tit for tat in case of any unilateralism on their part. Nevertheless, vigorous endeavours of the smaller states for regionalism in the sub-continent succeeded in bringing about a thaw in the frozen landscape of cordial bilateral as well as multilateral interactions amongst these countries. Indeed, through the South Asian regionalism, the smaller states presumably seek to serve both their politico-strategic as well as economic interests. While securing a better global positioning through South Asian collectivism, they also erect a formidable collective line of defence vis-a-vis their bigger neighbours. Thus, regionalism in South Asia is beset with myriad of challenges whose successful overcoming becomes *sine qua non* for its survival in the long run.

Persisting problems of regionalism in South Asia, as referred to earlier, owe their roots to colonial times. But, shockingly enough, instead of fading away in the course of last more than six decades, these problems have not only subsisted, they became redoubtable with the passage of time. Hence, in the realm of politico-strategic matters, India and Pakistan have already fought three devastating wars and probably are ever prepared for another in case situation warrants, with Kashmir as the flashpoint. As regards the other countries, their persisting issues with India always make them suspicious of Indian strategic moves in the region. Thus, there exists a high degree of trust deficit amongst the states of South Asia which undeniably holds them back from moving in the direction of closer regional cooperation. The democratic polity of India is also perceived by certain neighbours as a threat to their regimes given their authoritarian regimes, on the one hand, and dissidence activities against them from the Indian soil as India becomes safe havens for such democrats, on the other.[38] Collectively these factors tend to create a scenario in which each and every country seems to privilege politico-strategic concerns over all other imperatives of international relations.

Deep-seated politico-strategic distrust amongst the states apparently percolates down to the level of non-state, voluntary and commercial organisations also, apart from the common populace in the course of time. Ethnic roots of a group of people are schematically highlighted to widen the social divide between the two groups.[39] Religious differences between the people of different countries are so much underscored that one gets pitted against the other in such a fashion as if there is a score to settle. In other words, vested interests in all the countries fanatically arouse sectarian cleavages as a counterbalance to any talk of regional cooperation. In the face of these well-organised countervailing forces to regionalism, the only plausible common cause left is the necessity of economic development. However, the appreciation of this phenomenon also gets bogged down when it comes to assessing the relative gains likely to accrue to the rival nation. Consequently, at the end of the day, it happens to be the politico-strategic considerations that prevail, and the economic concerns are relegated to the background. This vicious circle debilitates the march of regionalism in South Asia from all sides and at all times that eventually reduces regionalism to be more symbolic and less substantive.

In spite of discomforting platitudes, prospects for more and more regional cooperation in South Asia cannot be undermined. As father of Human Development Index (HDI) Mahbub ul Haq argues, we need to 'bury deep the bitter legacy of the past and cultivate a new harvest of hope.'[40] However, for that to fructify, a change of attitude and mindsets amongst the states of the region becomes *sine qua non*. A fine balance has to be worked out between the requirements of strategic interests and imperatives of regional cooperation. The political issues that seem irresolvable need to be left then and there only without seeking their resolution through conflict and wars. 'At the end of the day, intransigence fosters alienation, and the use of force creates festering hostilities before, during, and after the conflict.'[41] In a way, the traditional rivals of the region have to take a leaf from the centuries old intense rivalry between prominent European powers like Germany and France that had been the cause of a number of wars and violent clashes in that continent from seventeenth to twentieth century. But in response to the transformed realities in time and space, the two sidelined their age old animosity to make EU a matchless success story in regional cooperation and eventual integration. Likewise, South Asian rivals would also have to ward off internal as well as external pulls and pressures in order to bypass the contentious issues and focus on the core areas of trust and cooperation amongst them, at least for the time being on a trial basis. The ensuing positive results would definitely act as the catalyst for perpetuation of such regional cooperation that might ultimately become the way of life for them.

Undoubtedly, in making South Asian regionalism a substantive venture, the onus of responsibility seems to lie on India more than any other country of the sub-continent given their relative stakes. Indeed, 'any movement towards regional cooperation in South Asia in inconceivable without India's active participation because South Asia is predominantly an Indo-centric region.'[42] India has to prioritise its foreign policy objectives and make a conscious decision whether it wants to remain entangled in the region or seeks a global status for itself. Given the indisputable choice for the latter, 'it needs to disentangle itself from regional problems in order to stake a solid claim to a global standing. Attempts to control its neighbours can only enmesh it locally and detract from its global image and interests.'[43] Further, India needs to shed its apprehensions towards SAARC as an organisation to work against its national interests. Next, it needn't remain overwhelmingly preoccupied with Pakistan and move over to the other neighbours to make the regional apparatus a vibrant entity. At the same time, in accordance with its relatively colossal status in comparison to its small neighbours, India should also exhibit certain degree of munificence in addressing the concerns of the former. It should 'offer a progressive reduction and elimination of controls on the movement of peoples, and sports and cultural exchanges.'[44]

Indeed, India has to be the shepherd to steer SAARC towards unchartered fertile domains in order to allow it to reap a good harvest of peace and prosperity in the region. However, Indian magnanimity needs to be reciprocated by majority, if not all, of the states of South Asia to make holistic efforts towards reinvention of regionalism in the sub-continent. Clear and careful identification of the areas of boundless cooperation must not only help them to put regionalism grow by leap and bounds, the contentious issues need also be put aside lest they play spoilsport in the whole endeavour. Once the positive outcomes of such cooperation begin to transform the lives of the people, states might gradually be relieved of their onerous responsibility of stewardship of regional cooperation, for, the people would become indomitable flag bearers of regionalism in the sub-continent.

Concluding Observations

South Asian regionalism is a classic example of deliberate denigration of an idea which all the stakeholders purport to stand by. Geographical compactness of the region and anticipated benefits likely to accrue from the cooperation amongst the countries has failed to make much impact on the deep seated distrust and animosity with one another. Theoretical arguments, global waves of regionalisation, and concerted efforts on part of a few countries have undoubtedly compelled the reluctant partners to join hands together to erect the edifice of SAARC, but when it came to make the organisation the harbinger of development, peace and prosperity in the region, the countries took no time in lapsing back to their old habits of mutual bickering and manoeuvring. This is precisely the reason that in its functioning of over around three decades, SAARC has not even been able to achieve the modest goal of establishing free trade area in the region in full and substantial measure. What can be a more sad commentary on the state of regionalism in the sub-continent than the fact that it is easy for the citizens of some SAARC countries to secure a visa for rest of the world than to travel to their neighbouring country. Amidst such a gloomy scenario, a silver lining can be visible only with the change in the mindsets and attitudes of the countries towards each other. Unless that happens, South Asian regionalism will remain a mirage for its proponents to chase.

References

1. Louise Fawcett, "Exploring Regional Domains: A Comparative History of Regionalism", *International Affairs,* Vol. 80, No. 3, May 2004, p. 430, Available at: http://www.jstor.org/stable/3569018, Accessed on 19/09/2014.
2. See, Russet M. Bruce, *International Regions and International System,* (Chicago: Rand McNally, 1967).
3. Joseph Nye, *International Regionalism,* (Boston: Little Brown, 1968), p. vii.
4. Muthiah Alagappa, "Regionalism and Conflict Management: A Framework for Analysis", *Review of International Studies,* Vol. 21, No. 4, October 1995, p. 362, Available at: http://www.jstor.org/stable/20097422, Accessed on 19/09/2014.
5. See, Michael Pugh and W. P. S. Sidhu (eds.), *The United Nations and Regional Security: Europe and Beyond,* (Boulder, CO: Lynne Rienner, 2003).
6. Rajendra Kumar Pandey, "United Nations: Political Strengths and Weaknesses", in Tapan Biswal (ed.), *International Relations,* (New Delhi: Macmillan, 2009), p. 382.

7. Andrew Hurrell, "Explaining the Resurgence of Regionalism in World Politics", *Review of International Studies,* Vol. 21, No. 4, October 1995, p. 331, Available at: http://www.jstor.org/stable/20097421, Accessed on 19/09/2014.
8. Cf. Paul Taylor, *International Organisation in the Modern World: The Regional and Global Process,* (London: Pinter, 1993).
9. See, Norman D. Palmer, *The New Regionalism in Asia and the Pacific,* (Lexington, Massachusetts: Lexington Books, 1991).
10. A succinct account of regionalism in post-cold war period is given in, Richard Rosecrance, "Regionalism and the Post-Cold War Era", *International Journal,* No. 46, 1991, pp. 373-93.
11. Insightful discussions, though dated, on select regional systems are presented in, Werner J. Feld and Gavin Boyd (eds.), *Comparing Regional Systems,* (New York: Pergamon Press, 1980).
12. Complex relationship between globalization and regionalism has been critically analysed in, Stefano Zamagni, "Globalization and New Regionalism: Implications for Development and Peace", *Society and Economy in Central and Eastern Europe,* Vol. 17, No. 5, 1995, pp. 19-32, Available at: http://www.jstor.org/stable/41468243, Accessed on 19/09/2014.
13. Ajay Gudavarthy, "Globalisation and Regionalization: Mapping the New Continental Drift", *Economic and Political Weekly,* Vol. 44, No. 24, January 13, 2009, p. 93. Available at: http://www.jstor.org/stable/40279111, Accessed on 19/09/2014.
14. One of the early researches on South Asian regionalism are presented in, Robert I. Crane (ed.), *Regions and Regionalism in South Asian Studies: An Exploratory Study,* (Durham: Duke University Monograph and Occasional Paper Series, Monograph No. 5, 1967).
15. Citha D. Maass, "Four Models of South Asia's Regional Structure", *Pakistan Horizon,* Vol. 55, No. 1/2, January-April, 2002, pp. 121-130. Available at: http://www.jstor.org/stable/41404010, Accessed on 19/09/2014.
16. There exists a wide spectrum of authors who argue that regionalism cannot be a successful saga in South Asia owing to inherent cleavages in the region. See, Norman D. Palmer, "The Changing Scene in South Asia – Internal and External Dimensions", *Orbis,* Fall, 1975; Chitra K. Tiwari, "South Asian Regionalism: Problems and Prospects", *Asian Affairs,* Vol. 12, No. 2, Summer, 1985: R. P. Anand, *South Asia: In Search of a Regional Identity,* (New Delhi: Banyan Publications, 1991); *Michael Brecher,* The New States of Asia, (London: Oxford University Press, 1963); and Devi Dutt (ed.), *The Himalayan Sub-continent,* (New Delhi: Metropolitan, 1972).
17. Cf, Partha S. Ghosh, *Cooperation and Conflict in South Asia,* (Missouri: South Asian Publications, 1989), Kishore C. Dash, *Regionalism in*

South Asia: Negotiating Cooperation, Institutional Structures, (London: Routledge, 2009), and Zahid Shahab Ahmed and Stuti Bhatnagar, "SAARC and Interstate Conflicts in South Asia: Prospects and Challenges for Regionalism", *Pakistan Horizon,* Vol. 61, No. 3, July 2008, pp. 69-87. Available at: http://www.jstor.org/stable/23725986, Accessed on 19/09/2014.

18. This aspect of South Asian regional cooperation has been well articulated in, Bhabani Sen Gupta (ed.), *Regional Cooperation and Development in South Asia,* (New Delhi: South Asian Publisher, 1986) and, Bhabani Sen Gupta and Urmila Phadnis (ed.), *Domestic Conflict in South Asia,* (New Delhi: South Asian Publisher, 1986).
19. Tiwari, *op. cit,* p. 10.
20. *Ibid*, p. 7.
21. For a comprehensive discussion on political aspects of regional cooperation in South Asia, see, V. Kanesalingam (ed.), *Political Dimensions of South Asian Cooperation,* (New Delhi: Macmillan, 1991).
22. Sisir Gupta, *India and Regional Integration in Asia* (Bombay: Asia Publishing House, 1964), p. 36.
23. Michael Haas, *The Asian Way to Peace* (New York: Praeger, 1989), p. 276.
24. Kishore C. Dash, "The Political Economy of Regional Cooperation in South Asia", *Pacific Affairs,* Vol. 69, No. 2 (Summer, 1996), p. 187. Available at: http://www.jstor.org/stable/2760724, Accessed on 19/09/2014.
25. S.D. Muni and Anuradha Muni, *Regional Cooperation in South Asia* (New Delhi: National Publishing House, 1984), p. 30.
26. Sumitra Chisti, "Regionalism and Globalisation in South Asian Countries", in S.D. Muni (ed.), *Understanding South Asia,* (New Delhi: South Asian Publishers, 1994), p. 232.
27. For a lucid discussion on complexities of regional cooperation in South Asia, see, Atiur Rahman, *Political Economy of SAARC,* (New Delhi: Sterling Publishers, 1986), and Rehman Sobhan, "Political Economy of South Asia cooperation", *South Asia Journal,* Vol. 1. No. 3, 1988.
28. Garimella Subramaniam, "Writing SRRAC's incomplete chapter", *The Hindu* (Delhi), 15th September 2014, p. 9.
29. Q.K. Ahmad, "SAARC: Some Comments and Elements of a Future Agenda", in Ponna Wignaraja and Akmal Hussain (ed.), *The Challenge in South Asia,* (New Delhi: Sage Publications, 1989), p. 349.
30. Ananya Mukherjee Reed, "Regionalization in South Asia: Theory and Praxis", *Pacific Affairs,* Vol. 70, No. 2, Summer, 1997, p. 235, Available at: http://www.jstor.org/stable/2760774, Accessed on 19/09/2014.
31. Prospects of economic cooperation amongst the countries of South Asia has been critically assessed in a number of research studies, including, Mukesh K. Kayathwal, "SAARC and Economic Cooperation",

Indian Journal of Asian Affairs, Vol. 5, No. 1/2, 1992, pp. 48-62, Available at: http://www.jstor.org/stable/41950369, Accessed on 19/09/2014, and Nitish Sengupta and Arindam Banik, "Regional Trade and Investment: Case of SAARC", *Economic and Political Weekly,* Vol. 32, No. 46, November 15,1997, pp. 2930-2931, Available at: http://www.jstor.org/stable/4406062, Accessed on 19/09/2014.

32. Nisar-ul-Haq, "Regional Cooperation in South Asia: A Theoretical Perspective and Prospects under SAFTA", *Indian Journal of Asian Affairs,* Vol. 17, No. 1, January, 2004, pp. 75-76, . Available at: http://www.jstor.org/stable/41950440, Accessed on 19/09/2014.
33. Muchkund Dubey, "SAARC and South Asian Economic Integration", *Economic and Political Weekly,* Vol. 32, No. 14, April 7, 2007, p. 1239. Available at: http://www.jstor.org/stable/4419435, Accessed on 19/09/2014.
34. C.M. Shafi Sami, "Vision of SAARC for the Twenty-First Century", in Dipankar Banerjee (ed.), *SAARC in the Twenty-First Century: Towards a Cooperative Future,* (New Delhi: India Research Press, 2002), pp. 16-17.
35. A theoretically- informed analysis of conflict and cooperation in regional organisations is offered in, Joseph S. Nye Jr., *Peace in Parts: Integration and Conflict in Regional Organisations,* (Boston: Little Brown, 1971).
36. Saman Kelegama and Kirit S. Parikh, "Political Economy of Growth and Reforms in South Asia", in Isher Judge Ahluwalia and John Williamson (ed.), *The South Asian Experience with Growth,* (New Delhi: Oxford University Press, 2003), pp. 84-85.
37. Ramesh Dadhich, "Understanding SAARC: Regional Cooperation in Neo- Colonial Context", *Indian Journal of Asian Affairs,* Vol. 18, No. 1, June 2005, p. 59. Available at: http://www.jstor.org/stable/41950453, Accessed on 19/09/2014.
38. Manorama Kohli, "India and South Asian Regional Cooperation", *Indian Journal of Political Science,* Vol. 49, No. 3, July-September, 1988, p. 307, Available at: http://www.jstor.org/stable/41855876, Accessed on 19/09/2014.
39. K. Raman Pillai, "Tensions Within Regional Organisations: A Study of SAARC", *Indian Journal of Political Science,* Vol. 50, No. 1, January-March, 1989, p. 22, Available at: http://www.jstor.org/stable/41855404, Accessed on 19/09/2014.
40. Cited in Frances Stewart and Taimur Hyat, "Conflicts in South Asia: Prevalence, Costs and Politics", in Khadija Haq (ed.), *The South Asian Challenge,* (Karachi: Oxford University Press, 2002), p. 108.
41. Swarna Rajagopalan, *State and Nation in South Asia,* (Boulder, Colorado: Lynne Rienner Publishers, 2001), pp. 186-187.
42. Rajen Harshe, "South Asian Regional Cooperation: Problems and Prospects", *Economic and Political Weekly,* Vol. 34, No. 19, May 8, 1999, p. 1100. Available at: http://www.jstor.org/stable/4407929, Accessed on 19/09/2014.

43. Rajesh M. Basrur, "Global Quest and Regional Reversal: Rising India and South Asia", *International Studies,* Vol. 47, Nos. 2-4, April, July and October, 2010, p. 267.
44. Eric Gonsalves, "South Asian Cooperation: An Agenda and a Vision for the Future", in L.L. Mehrotra, H.S. Chopra and Gert W. Kueck (ed.), *SAARC 2000 and Beyond,* (New Delhi: Omega Scientific Publishers, 1995), p. 41.

2

Maritime Security in India's Neighbourhood and Indian Ocean: Challenges and Strategies

Dr Biswajit Mohapatra

The multidimensional and multifaceted problem of maritime security has now captured the imagination of all policy-makers as the littoral countries are now faced with new challenges like arms trafficking, narco terrorism, illegal migration, which have now assumed new proportions after their switch from land routes to sea routes and the increased attacks by pirates on the ships carrying petroleum and other vital resources which have not come down despite several talks of international cooperation amongst several countries.

This points out to the greater need for not only some focused regional cooperation but also for involvement of more state actors and non-state actors in this enterprise as state security, as regards its territory is no more a concern to the state, only since populations both inside and outside the territory are also involved in the multifarious economic activities for their survival and increased economic prosperity.

Further in the post cold war era, with the fast moving pace of globalisation, the volume of goods being exchanged in the context of international trade, in particular in case of economic globalisation, has brought in the issue of maritime security to the centre stage of policy debate today.

As such the Indian Ocean the Straits of Hormuz, Straits of Malacca, Lombok and the Sunda Straits have acquired great importance as far as the global trade is concerned. It goes without saying that any disruption in traffic flow through these points, be it through acts of sabotage, subversion, or terrorism, has the potential to destroy the growing economic prospects of the countries in the region and others at large. The disastrous consequences of any disruption of energy flows in particular is a considerable threat to the littoral states, as a majority of their energy supplies are now through the sea routes. Further as scarce energy resources is now a critical factor in the geo-political strategies of any country, any kind of disruption surely can prove to be serious security consequences. It is inevitable that these countries have to be highly sensitive to the security of the sea lines of communication (SLOCs) of the region. Countries like India, China as the powerhouse of economic growth are likely to be affected more as they not only require the sea routes to be more effectively secured but also for the fact that in the region they are competing with each other for a larger political role.

Security Framework

Maritime peace and security issues have arose recently with the emergence of new forms of transborder crimes which greatly pose threat to the security of countries and also its large population. These activities, viz., illegal drug trafficking like narcotics, enormous rise in the trafficking of arms and humans, entry of terrorists through sea route, and rise in terrorism as was evident in 26/11 Mumbai episode, besides number of piracy and kidnapping of workers from the various vessels and armed robbers and pirates in the sea, are now considered to endanger not only the security of states and human beings in the sea and over land within national borders as well but also threaten the smooth flow of navigation, maritime trade, thereby destabilising the prevailing socio-economic scenario within the states and also in the region.[1,2,3]

Given the transboundary nature of such above noted maritime crimes, and the fact the perpetrators of these crimes are often in a position to cross the respective national jurisdiction of the coastal countries, immediately after committing various offences, the task of bringing them to justice and meting out severe punishment by way of deterrence has proved to be very difficult entailing a number of years of pursuit and risk of further complication of bilateral relations as these criminals and terrorists have been reported to be the subjects of neighbouring countries.

To meet this daunting task of curbing these new kinds of threats, states have been making colossal efforts to voluntarily form some kind of regional and international community to deny any kind of safe haven to these new kinds of criminals and terrorists. Besides a number of international conventions and instruments have also been signed authorising the various States Parties to rigorously implement measures within their domestic arena for prescribed law enforcement action to bring them to book. At the international level, efforts have also been made to put in place some kind of universally ratified international instruments, e.g., United Nations Convention on the Law of the Sea to ensure maritime security.[4] But such objectives are yet to be fully achieved and hence the States have not been able to strengthen their capabilities either for enforcement of law or launching of strong action including use of force against the perpetrators of such crimes having transboundary effects both at the international and national level, to the utter dismay of many a concerned security analyst.

As such the objective of development of some strong legal and procedural framework within which States can have the assured strength to combat maritime threats faced by them and the wherewithal to prevent such maritime threats in future within an environment of mutually assisted maritime security enforcement has assumed greater urgency today. Further the response of the international community will have to be commensurate with the nature of various international threats being posed to several states from outside their respective domestic boundaries. In these contexts it is seen that states have been vigorously experimenting and also have often become successful in pursuing the mechanism of regional cooperation as supplementary efforts to boost global cooperation for tackling the issues of maritime threats and maritime security and for expeditious implementation of international instruments framed for the purpose through the regional machinery effectively.

The formation of Indian Ocean Rim Association for Regional Cooperation (IOR-ARC) to boost economic cooperation amongst its member states, as Indian Ocean Region which accounts for eight per cent of world GDP and 12 per cent of world trade, has been a step in this direction. The setting up of the economic community comprising Bangladesh, India, Myanmar (Burma), Sri Lanka, and Thailand, known as BIMSTEC, which accounts for less than three per cent of global trade, and the vigorous effort to vitalise the South Asian Association for Regional Cooperation (SAARC), have also been appreciated. All these initiatives have however proved to be inadequate since by their limited working, they have only demonstrated that without much proactive participation of these countries and sufficient amount of trust and cooperation amongst them, there can be no assurance of any maritime security, an important cornerstone of national security for littoral countries including India.

It is being said that this can only serve as the best bet in the enhancement of political cooperation and overall security amongst these countries, besides being the locomotive in ensuring maritime security for these countries and also the world community as a whole. In this context it is important to consider the IOR-ARC in details and examine if IOR-ARC can be justifiably play its role in the Emerging Regional Comprehensive Economic Partnership besides ensuring maritime security.

Indian Ocean Rim-Association for Regional Cooperation (IOR-ARC): Role and Regional Security

The Indian Ocean Rim-Association for Regional Cooperation (IOR-ARC), which was christened earlier as the Indian Ocean Rim Initiative, was established as an international organisation with the coming together of 20 member states on March, 1995 in Mauritius. And later its formal launch took place on 6–7 March 1997. Undoubtedly one of the main motivator is the sharing of common historical bonds over the millennia among the peoples of the Indian Ocean Rim besides the late realisation that given their diversity, in the Indian Ocean region, they can very well take advantage of the available opportunities to engage in mutually beneficial activities leading to a deeper economic interaction and co-operation over a wide range of issues in a spirit of equality.

The Governments of Australia, Bangladesh, India, Indonesia, Islamic Republic of Iran, Kenya, Madagascar, Malaysia, Mauritius, Mozambique, Sultanate of Oman, Singapore, South Africa, Sri Lanka, Tanzania, Thailand, United Arab Emirates and Yemen, decided to come together for the creation of an effective Association and establish the practical modalities of some form of viable and stronger economic co-operation as they realised they may be passed over in the days of rapid globalisation and swift economic changes taking place all around, if they fail to take bold initiatives to ensure the welfare of their peoples and to improve their standards of living and quality of life, befitting the human dignity. Consequently, they also decided to have a quick revision for amending the Charter of the Indian Ocean Rim Association for Regional Co-operation (IOR-

ARC), adopted at the first Ministerial Meeting on 5-7 March, 1997 in Mauritius, and adopted a set of broad objectives, such as, inter alia:

(a) To promote the sustained growth and balanced development of the region and of the Member States, and to create common ground for regional economic co-operation;

(b) To focus on those areas of economic co-operation which provide maximum opportunities to develop shared interests and reap mutual benefits with a view to formulating and implementing projects for economic co-operation, particularly in the areas of trade facilitation and liberalisation, promotion of foreign investment, scientific and technological exchanges, tourism, movement of natural persons and service providers on a non-discriminatory basis; and the development of infrastructure and human resources inter-alia poverty alleviation, promotion of maritime transport and related matters, co-operation in the fields of fisheries trade, research and management, aquaculture, education and training, energy, IT, health, protection of the environment, agriculture, disaster management;

(c) To explore all possibilities and avenues for trade liberalisation, to remove impediments to, and lower barriers towards, freer and enhanced flow of goods, services, investment, and technology within the region, without prejudice to obligations under other regional economic and trade co-operation arrangements;

(d) To strengthen co-operation and dialogue among Member States in international fora on global economic issues, and where desirable to develop shared strategies and take common positions in the international fora on issues of mutual interest.

Further to boost cooperation within the IOR-ARC, attempts were made to prioritise six substantive areas of co-operation, in 2011. These include: Maritime Safety and Security, Trade and Investment Facilitation, Fisheries Management, Disaster Risk Management, Academic and Science and Technology Cooperation, and Tourism and Cultural Exchanges.

IOR-ARC – Structural Dynamics

When we look into the structural factors, one sees that the Charter very well emphasises that the IOR-ARC need to focus on building an expansive understanding and a mutually beneficial co-operation amongst the member states with emphasis on evolution of a consensus. To facilitate the fulfillment of this, it has rightly adopted the principles, what is popularly known as Panch Sheel (though evolved in the context of India-China Relations), i.e., respect for the principles of sovereignty, equality, territorial integrity, political independence and non-interference in internal affairs, peaceful coexistence and mutual benefit. In order to provide for a durable order of cooperation, the IOR-ARC not only remains anchored to the principle of open regionalism, but also does not seek to bind the rights and obligations of the Member states to co-operate within the regional group nor tries to restrict the member states rights to engage with other countries beyond this group within any other framework of other economic and trade cooperation arrangements. The larger goal of this group has been rather conceived to be very intelligently so as "to be complementary to and consistent with the bilateral, plurilateral and multilateral rights and obligations of Member States." The only self-imposed limitation in case of the states willing to join the group has been rather a modest one, as it requires the states, within the framework of the Association, "to pursue measures to promote the achievement of its objectives and not to take any action likely to prejudice its objectives and activities". In fulfillment of the objectives, routine meetings are regularly held at the level of Heads of Missions of IOR-ARC countries, in Pretoria. Further the Working Group of Heads of Mission (WGHM) in its thirteen meetings have made efforts to keep a close eye on the group's progress on several issues and also suggested necessary ideas for the way forward of this group. However, even after all these developments the progress so far achieved within the group has been rather dismal given the fact of a wide consensus amongst the member countries.

Constructive Engagement through Dialogue Partners - Mechanisms for Cooperation and Assistance

It appears as if such a problem was already forethought of and hence the Charter while providing for all sovereign States of the Indian Ocean Rim to be eligible for membership following their willingness to adhere to the principles and objectives enshrined in the Charter of the Association, it also incorporated a provision to the effect that the Council of Ministers (COM) may grant the status of Dialogue Partners or Observers to other States or Organisations, having the capacity and interest to contribute towards the growth of IOR-ARC. This provision though can be seen as a positive step, yet with the expressed desire of various global and regional power to join this kind of regional group, a worldwide trend being seen in case of many such regional groupings, many commentators have expressed apprehension that these regional groups, given the fact that they were conceived out of the economically weak developing countries, to achieve a spirit of collective self- reliance and mutually beneficial economic growth along with social stability, can turn themselves into theater of global and regional conflicts, with the entry of the advanced countries such as US, UK, France, Japan and other members of G8 countries and also regional powers like China, Egypt, etc.

It's true that the provision of Dialogue partners is primarily meant to get other countries interested in cultural and economic co-operation with the member countries to appreciate the complementarities and hence to intensify these forms of co-operation on either bilateral or multilateral basis. The practice came to be started in 1974 with the ASEAN when Australia became ASEAN's first Dialogue Partner. Today, ASEAN has ten Dialogue Partners with diverse countries like Australia, Canada, China, EU, India, Japan, New Zealand, ROK, Russia and the United States, having the opportunity to interact with it on a more substantive basis. In 2007, even Australia has entered into an agreement with ASEAN and signed the Partnership. The Plan of Action expressly provides for implementing the Comprehensive Partnership in the areas of political and security, economic, socio-cultural and development co-operation, to strengthen the framework for engagement, to boost the possibility for a Regional Comprehensive Economic Partnership (RCEP), as announced by Australia.

As far as Indian foreign policy objectives are concerned, India is now focused upon intensifying its economic co-operation with the South East Asia through its announcement of Look East Policy as it believes such intensification would make available various avenues for faster economic development for the people in the region. Further the policy objective of development of India's Northeastern states and the need to curb insurgency activities along the border with Myanmar is also accorded high priority with the strong belief that the economies of India, China and the ASEAN could be centred on the states of the region as this region can play a contributory role in propelling the economies of the sub-continent and the ASEAN countries simultaneously. The present thaw in the bilateral relationship between India and China is also expected to facilitate concrete co-operation not only between India and the SE Asian countries, but also between India and China as closer co-operation can be concretised with improvement of trust as can happen in their participation in the various meetings of regional grouping as IOR-ARC. The presence of other G8 countries like UK, Japan and France etc., can also provide the group with necessary economic incentives by way of liberal technical, technological and financial assistance to help the member states to undertake rapid economic developmental initiatives, besides presenting them with expanding opportunities for regional integration through substantial increase in the intra-regional trade.

Regional Comprehensive Economic Partnership (RCEP) - Emerging Scenario

While as talks are on amongst the ASEAN leaders since 2011 about forming a mega-regional trade deal in the form of earlier mentioned, a Regional Comprehensive Economic Partnership (RCEP). This is aimed at creating probably the world's largest trading bloc, which will undoubtedly have significant implications for the world economy, as it seeks to combine both the East Asian Free Trade Agreement, that includes ASEAN, China, Japan and South Korea, and the Comprehensive Economic Partnership, taking Australia, India and New Zealand on board.

This attempt at Regional Comprehensive Economic Partnership (RCEP), as will bring together three of the world's largest economies in the world, i.e., China, India and Japan is a significant development as they together constitute 49 per cent of the world's population and also accounts for about 30 per cent of world's present level of GDP. They also make up 29 per cent of world trade and 26 per cent of world FDI inflows, to say the least. It is also claimed that when this partnership is implemented, the world economy would stand to gain between $260–644 billion as additional income in a decade or so. Further the RCEP will be helpful in the promotion of easier FDI flows and technology transfers by willing multinational corporations to these countries and reduce trade barriers, besides being consistent with WTO agreements. It will further help them in their cherished goal of achieving a free trade area of the Asia Pacific making them very significant actors in the emerging regional trade architecture in the region and the world.

It is well known that to realise these expected goals, negotiations with large countries such as G8 countries and other regional power blocs like China in Asia and Egypt in the African context, would certainly be very difficult as these nations are also competitors in the present day world economy. Further they may also not appreciate the idea of according a central role to ASEAN and other Asian Countries, like India, given its Look East Policy, to be likely beneficiaries within the context of RCEP, at all. However, the provision of dialogue partners in this trading bloc and more precisely the presence of G8 countries and China etc., can be expected to smoothen over these difficulties over a period of time and not exacerbate the divergence between these countries. The closer contact among these countries in the IOR-ARC meetings and other international for a would surely be useful not only in the narrowing down of political differences but also would increase opportunities for regional infrastructure financing with prevention of overlap among the various Asian FTAs. It has to be remembered that technical cooperation and dispute settlement mechanisms do also receive boost by the several high level meetings of political leaders, which also facilitates the conclusion of comprehensive agreement for liberalisation of trade, resulting in greater benefits to world population, and ensuring both regional and state security from all sources at large.

3

Water Security: India's Hydro Diplomacy in Neighbourhood

Avilash Roul

'Too much and too little water destroys the creation', this age-old Oriya proverb is true to represent physical situation of freshwater in South Asia. While the water encompasses all religions, culture, socio-economic strata, it is also highly emotive political in nature within a sovereign country and beyond. The South Asia, which formed due to geophysical violence (plate tectonic movement), has been potentially, as many observers hypothesised, in risk of a probable water conflict among the sovereign countries. The history so far has not coincided with these observers hypotheses. However, inter-state conflict, intra users conflict within the countries in the region has been on rise. A decade ago, due to transboundary nature of major perennial rivers, India has been in the cog of all river sharing arrangements which are explicitly bilateral in the region. However, increase of China's demand for energy and water from rivers originated from Tibetan Plateau has changed the strategic thinking on transboundary rivers. Due to geographical character of rivers, any unilateral measures on transboundary rivers are potential to trigger perpetual tension or apprehension between or among the countries. A shift of hydro politics is being foreseen in the region with global environmental change. As vital riparian country, India needs to accommodate such gradual shift in managing water resources.

Water Security in South Asia

The definitions of security have moved beyond a limited focus on military risks and conflicts. The concept of 'environmental security' of 1980s and 1990s has moved beyond the causal relationship between environmental degradation and conflict to a more inclusive concept focusing on the intricate relationship between environment and society or environment and livelihood—human security and ecological security. As water transcends political boundaries - their scarcity, distribution, and quality – have been an important issue to be addressed immediately. The concept of water and security is restricted in terms of management of transboundary river (Dinar 2000: 375-407). Water has been considered to be an essential ingredient for human survival and development throughout history. Currently water resources are facing tremendous and ever-increasing pressures throughout the globe, particularly daunting to developing countries because the rates of population growth and urbanisation both are high and per capita water availability is already low. The global water crisis is likely to witness in the next 25 years far-ranging and far-reaching consequences of several orders of magnitude higher and more complex than what have witnessed during the past 25 years (Biswas, 2005). As water is a finite resource, with its spatial and seasonal variations, and having no substitute, has attracted both conflict and cooperation over shared rivers. However, the access to and availability of water within a sovereign country is becoming highly threatening. From a strategic resource to value commodity, water is being called as the 'oil of the 21st century' or 'liquid gold' or 'blue gold'.

In the world of natural resources, the most sensational headlines are being dedicated to the scarcity of fresh water in all over the world. During the last decade media reports are being written in bold and loud in the lines of 'water wars' regarding water disputes between inter-state or intra-state and among the various users within the country. Such striking news has attracted attention of not only environmentalists and water managers but researchers, hydrologists and international relation theorists (Alam, 2002). The conceptualisation of 'hydro politics' is being sought in the western literature mostly on the West Asia and Middle East situation, to deal with interaction of politics with the use and management of fresh water, at a national and international level. When the hydro politics within intrastate spill over to neighbouring countries, consequently it becomes 'hydro-diplomacy.' In South Asia, the politics of water has been contested among the various actors including national, international, non-state entities on the issue of demand and supply, management, ownership and distribution and of late, river ecology.

Despite the urgency of addressing highly political and emotive issue as water, the conceptualisation and theory building for policy implication on water security had not been attempted until 2013 (Roul, 2010). Despite first ever official declaration of water security cropped up in 2000 Second World Water Forum (WWC, 2000), it took more than a decade by the UN to pronounce and promote a 'working definition' on water security in 2013. The UN-Water, the United Nations' inter-agency coordination mechanism for all water-related issues, says water security should be defined as, "[T]he capacity of a population to safeguard sustainable access to adequate quantities of and acceptable quality water for sustaining livelihoods, human well-being, and socio-economic development, for ensuring protection against water-borne pollution and water-related disasters, and for preserving ecosystems in a climate of peace and political stability" (UNU, 2013). However, the working definition falls short of approval by countries with its inherent vague propositions. However, the conceptual clarity must go beyond the traditional security principle of state controlled notion in achieving water security (Roul, 2010). The water security remains a subject for further research and elaboration especially in the context of South Asia. It must be looked into the prism of environmental security and human security perspectives in dealing with water resources both surface and underground.

Water in South Asia is a prime mover of individual livelihood as well economy of the country. In South Asia, while water encompasses the cultural, social, religious, economic and political fabric in the lives of one sixth world's population, it is the key to development of the region. In South Asian context, most of the glaciers-fed rivers originate from beyond borders in Tibetan Plateau, which is under the autonomous administrative unit of China. At the same time the Monsoon or depending precipitation from Monsoon to fill the rivers in the region is beyond any countries' control. Additionally, the climate change has disrupted both pace of glacier melting and erratic rainfall which attributed to natural disasters like flood and droughts thereby affecting both depending life support system and economy across the region.

Managing Inter Basin Transfer of Water with Neighbours

Grand water schemes are not new in the world. Indian government has also developed a scheme to tackle its peculiar climatic contradiction of drought and flood situations by linking rivers. The Inter Basin Water Transfer (IBWT) that proposes to transfer water from surplus water basin to deficit water basin in India, which was initiated and accelerated by the then NDA government and briskly followed by both UPA I and II, has again brought into the attention of neighbouring countries by the present BJP-led NDA government. This Indian unilateral proposal has created much criticism and apprehensions not only in domestic arena but also spilled over to neighbouring riparian countries.

The IBWT or (hereafter ILR as interlinking river) proposal has emerged in a strange manner backed by the three organs of the Indian political system-executive, legislature and judiciary.[1] The President's National Address on August 14, 2002, the filling up of Public Interest Litigation (PIL) to clean up Yamuna River in Delhi in late August, and a hearing on the Cauvery dispute by Supreme Court on October 31, led the union government to issue a statement in Parliament in December for the interlinking of rivers. The ILR proposal has two components: (a) Himalayan Rivers and (b) Peninsular Rivers (Roul 2006; Iyer 2003 and NWDA, 2003). As the proposal includes the Himalayan Rivers, which are transboundary in nature; the other South Asian riparian countries have conveyed apprehensions to India. However, the National Commission for Integrated Water Resource Development Plan in its September 1999 report did not discuss the proposed Himalayan links in detail because the data are classified as confidential.

Concerns of Bangladesh

While the 'Terms of Reference for the Detailed Project Report (DPR)' states that the water assessment studies shall be carried out within the ambit of the Memorandum of Understanding (MoU) between the Government of India and the participating State Governments (NWDA, 2003), there is no mention of consultation with the regional riparian countries regarding any water or infrastructure assessments. "The idea of linking these (Ganga and Brahmaputra) rivers is very dangerous. It could affect the whole of Bangladesh and be disastrous," said Hafiz Ahmad, the Bangladesh Water Resources Minister (Vidal, 2003). The Bangladesh scientists estimated that even a 10 per cent to 20 per cent reduction in the water flow to the country could dry out great areas for much of the year. (Khalequzzaman *et al.*, 2004). Even Bangladesh was mulling to approach the International Court of Justice at The Hague if India went ahead with the river-linking project unilaterally (Anon, 2003).

Bangladesh expressed the fear that the 'project might trigger a mass migration destroying the social fabrics of both the countries'.[2]

As the pressure from the public mounted, Bangladesh as the first country lodged formally its apprehension about the project to India in August 2003 through diplomatic channel. Indian government reacted in general to the protest by saying that Bangladesh should 'need to address these complex issues in a mature manner'.[3] On the other hand, India without responding to the complaint maintained official silence till both the government delegations met in Delhi for the Joint River Commission (JRC) talks in September 2003. A parliamentary committee in Bangladesh has decided to seek details of a renewed initiative for ILR through its Water Resource Ministry (*Times of India*, 2014).

Nepal: Silent Spectator

It was believed that Nepal had maintained a diplomatic silence on the Indian ILR project. As Nepal has bitter memories of previous Indian water projects, Nepal Water experts believe that Nepal should be extra cautious on ILR (Pant, 2003). Nepal perceived that the construction of dams in the upstream Nepal will not solve the water problems in India both during summer and during flood in time, but it will create the socio-economic problems in both the countries (Gwayali, 2004).[4] One of the main reasons for Nepal's guarded silence is the due importance of Nepal in the whole project design. Welcoming the Indian ILR proposal, some argued that this was a significant shift in India's policy, which would help to bridge the wide gap that exists in the perception of Nepal and India on the development of the large water infrastructure in general and the Karnali High dam in particular. At the scholarly level, concerns have already been enunciated in Nepal that India should have invited it to join in feasibility studies of the project. The major concerns of Nepal are the resulting social and environmental costs of the huge storages that India plans to construct on the shared rivers. The Indian government appointed a special envoy in Ministry of External Affairs to coordinate bilateral relations with neighbouring countries on ILR during the NDA government.

Engaging Bhutan

A landlocked Himalayan country, Bhutan is largely dependent on river diversion for the source of water for all irrigation schemes (except in the Geylegphug lift irrigation scheme) in Bhutan. For the exploitation of its massive hydropower resources, Bhutan is fully dependent upon India. Besides being the largest aid donor to

Bhutan, India has also assisted a number of development projects in the country ranging from electricity sector to irrigation and road development. Cooperation, particularly in the hydro-power sector, represented a win-win situation for both countries with India receiving an assured supply of cheap and clean energy and Bhutan receiving a significant revenue stream. The tributaries of Brahmaputra- Manas and Sankosh - are included in ILR. Earlier, Bhutan government agreed for a DPR on the Sankosh River in the late 1980s. For Manas River, the Indian government has been engaging in dialogue with Bhutan. On Manas River the storage construction had rejected by the Ministry of Environment and Forests under the forest clearance act 1980.[5] However, given the degree of relationship between India and Bhutan, one cannot expect any criticism or disapproval to the Indian ILR from the Bhutanese side. Recently, Indian Prime Minister's first foreign visit to Bhutan has consolidated Bhutan's unopposed support on ILR by adding financial support for hydropower generation. The other upper riparian country of Brahmaputra, the China has never responded on Indian ILR proposal.

India-Bangladesh Relation on Sharing Water Resources

'As a lower riparian country, water is a question of the life and death for Bangladesh,' once said the Bangladesh Minister for Water Resources Hafiz Uddin Ahmad, at the United Nations while addressing the high-level meeting of the UN Commission for Sustainable Development (CSD) at its 13th Session (MOWR (GOB) 2005). From this statement the India-Bangladesh water relations can be measured. This may be a political statement at the highest level, but the general public mood on relation with India regarding water, which spanned nearly 42 years, have been no different either. This public posturing as well as government's sensitivity have influenced all the bilateral water issues between two countries. The latest addition is the Teesta River Agreement which has been on hold since 2011.

The concern for sharing of rivers water and the birth of Bangladesh are inseparable twins for India. "Water is central to the way of life in Bangladesh and the single-most important resource for the well-being of its people" (MOWR, 1999). As commonly accepted, there are 54 rivers including three large ones, the Ganges, Brahmaputra and Meghna, are shared between India and Bangladesh with Bangladesh being the lower riparian for all the rivers. The dispute over Ganges erupted as a result of India's decision to construct a barrage in West Bengal in 1951, known as the Farakka Barrage, about 10 miles from the borders with then East Pakistan. Emergence of Bangladesh from Pakistan had put the Ganges water sharing issue into a political and immediate issue to be resolved by both the countries. Besides, Ganges water mentioned in the early pacts between India and Bangladesh, both governments established Joint River Commission (JRC) - an institutional mechanism to address the rivers water sharing issue between India and Bangladesh (MOWR GOB; Bhasin 1996 and Abbas 1984). Frustrated with India's delaying tactics to come to negotiating table, Bangladesh internationalised the Farakka issue by raising the issue at the Istanbul Islamic Foreign Minister's Conference (May, 1976), Non-Aligned Movement (NAM) Summit at Colombo (August, 1976) and the UNGA (September, 1976). It is interesting to note that the 'Farakka problem' had become 'Farakka dispute' soon after Bangladesh raised the issue in the UN. Even, the Bangladesh government had tried for third party mediation to resolve the deadlock.

During the internationalisation process, the pressure mounted on both countries to negotiate for an outcome. With change in government in Delhi, an agreement was signed in 1977 followed by two ad-hoc solutions (Salman and Uprety, 2002). The change in political establishments had created the friendly atmosphere for further negotiations on permanent sharing of Ganges water. The Gujaral Doctrine put forward by the Indian government in 1996 was well accepted by the India-friendly Awami League led government in Bangladesh. At the end involving West Bengal Chief Minister, which was a departure from previous negotiations, the Sharing of Ganges water treaty was signed by India and Bangladesh on December 12, 1996 (MOWR, 1996). The success of the Treaty are the result of several factors: the patient efforts of the Indian Ministry of External Affairs and the high priority attached to the resolution of the Ganges water by the same ministry, the wisdom and courage of the Prime Minister of Bangladesh; the constructive and sagacious role played by the chief minister of West Bengal and his finance minister and last but not least, facilitatory efforts at non-official levels (Iyer, 1999).

The conclusion of the treaty was generally welcomed in both countries. Because of longstanding emotional attitudes towards India and the absence of official information about the operation of the treaty, experts argue that it may lead to a perception of India being a culprit (Iyer, 2003). However, the National Water Policy of

Bangladesh envisages: "Although the 1996 Treaty with India has brought some relief to the drought-prone area of the southwest, the water shortage problem during the dry season is likely to aggravate in the Ganges and other basins with rising demands of the increasing population. It is, however, encouraging to note that the relevant provision of the treaty will provide the basis in the future for discussion on sharing of waters of the common rivers" (MOWR, 1999). The smooth functioning of the Treaty depends on, however, the flow of in the river which literally depends on seasonal monsoon and glacier melt which is already changing due to climate change.

Teesta River Agreement Impasse

While inclusion of bordering state government within the bilateral water sharing treaty framework by India has proved to be a success previously, the same state government has vetoed a near agreed sharing of Teesta River. Initially, Dhaka proposed equal sharing of Teesta water, keeping 20 per cent for river flow and equal sharing by both countries of remaining water. Further, two sides agreed that India would get 42.5 per cent of water and Bangladesh 37.5 per cent than the earlier agreed equation. (*The Daily Star*, 2012). The proportion of agreed water was vehemently opposed by West Bengal Chief Minister whose government demanded retaining 75 per cent of Teesta river water while Bangladesh would receive 25 per cent. A near possible signing of Teesta Agreement during Indian Prime Minister's visit to Dhaka in 2011 was stalled. Since, the hope of an amicable solution of sharing of Teesta water has been taken up by high level meetings between the countries for reaching at an interim agreement (*The Telegraph*, 2013; *Bangla News*, 24 2014; *The Economic Times*, 2014).

India-Nepal Bilateral Water Resources Development

India-Nepal water sharing issue has been altogether a different one from other bilateral water issues as far as India and other South Asian countries are considered. Although the potential for joint endeavours is considerable as several experts believe (Vergese, 1990; Banskota, 1981; Biswas and Uitto, 2001), the co-operation between these two countries on the water resource development issues has been strange one. For some analyst India-Nepal water issues is not that of a major one as there has not been any conflict involved (Iyer, 1999), while other categories the relation over water as 'resource conflict over environment and development' (Gyawali, 2000). Despite some breakthrough has been achieved, the dominant controversies due to differences in perception and lack of trust between citizens and governments have marred the further improvement of relations over water resources (Salman and Uprety, 2002). The water issue has and will be in future, political and social connotation whenever there is a human intervention that occurs in the natural river regime. Nepal's perception on water has changed from under-rating its water resource wealth in 1920s to zealous overvaluation (hydropower potential) in the early 1990s.[6] This states the bilateral strange relation between India and Nepal over water resources. The Energy Policy of Nepal has focused on developing the country's large, economically exploitable hydropower potential as a renewable source of energy for domestic use and for exports.

The cooperative arrangement for the economic benefit of the shared water system was negotiated between British India and Nepal in 1920 on Sarada River (Mahakali in Nepal). Subsequently, for the purpose of meeting the demand for industrialisation, irrigation and electricity production and flood control, India had entered into two major agreements on development of water resources on the shared international Rivers, known as the 1954 Kosi Project Agreement and the 1959 Gandak Irrigation and Power Agreement with Nepal (MEA 1966 and MEA, 1959). Both the water treaties were vehemently opposed by the public and subsequently amended.

Tanakpur Barrage: The Phase of Mistrust

The Kosi and Gandak Agreements set the perception of mistrust on water sharing issue between India-Nepal. Besides Nepalese belief of India's control over the headwork on Nepali territory and at the operational level, Nepal authorities were not comfortable with India's refusal to allow independent assessment of downstream benefits (Gyawali, 2000). Under these circumstances, the Nepal government had taken the best possible and available strategy in stalling the negotiation on various projects and minimising dependence on India for technical study of various projects. With strong Indian interest in developing and benefiting from Nepal's water resource, as well as Nepal's unfavourable balance-of Payments position with India, the tactics of delay or stalling could not be sustained for long by Nepal.[7] The unilateral intervention in the Mahakali River by India in Tanakpur barrage issue brought India-Nepal bilateral relation into its lowest nadir. The MoU on Tanakpur Barrage project between Nepal and India on December 1991, which commonly referred to as the Tanakpur Agreement, was fought politically, legally and socially in Nepal with its ramification felt on subsequent India-Nepal bilateral relations. The framers of the new constitution, abided by the general mood, had incorporated a new provision in the 1990 Constitution of Nepal which provides guidelines for the international treaties especially on international river water.[8] However, the way in which Tanakpur Agreement brokered and later its political, legal and social ramifications have altogether strained the India-Nepal bilateral relations on water.[9]

The Mahakali River Treaty

The attempts to validate the past activities in Sarada Treaty in 1920 and more recently the Tanakpur Agreement, both countries entered into a comprehensive development of water resource of the Mahakali River in 1996 as the Mahakali Treaty. Considering the concerns of both the countries on the Tanakpur Barrage issue, it took five years of negotiations to initiate a treaty for the 'integrated development of water resources on the Mahakali River' (MOWR, 1996). The Mahakali Treaty deals with three projects related to water resources: the Sarada Barrage, the Tanakpur Barrage, and the Pancheswar Multipurpose Project-the centrepiece of the Treaty. The Mahakali Treaty subsumes all other Indo-Nepalese agreements relating to downstream projects on the Mahakali River, thus, it absorbs the regime established by the Sarada Treaty, validates the Tanakpur Agreement, and endorses the idea of multipurpose Pancheswar Multipurpose Project. With the Indian Prime Minister's first visit after 19 years by any Indian Prime Minister, the Term of Reference of Pancheswar Multipurpose project has agreed (*The Indian Express*, 2014).

India-Pakistan Relation on Sharing Water Resource

The joint management of Indus River water resources was vociferously discarded by the governments just after the partition between India and Pakistan. After 54 years of the Indus Water Treaty (IWT) signed between India and Pakistan, there have been hardly any instances of joint management or efforts for such initiative by both the countries. The intriguing rivalries between India and Pakistan have guided the international claims on the Indus basin as the most successful resolution of water resources (conflict) against the water war hypothesis (Alam, 2002). The IWT has been regarded not only as a remarkable example of successful resolution of conflict between two sovereign countries but also as a landmark in the role of the World Bank as an international mediator (Kirmani and Rangeley, 1994 and Kirmani and Moigne, 1997). The western analysts always appreciate the IWT for its survival on the face of full scale wars and limited war between the parties.

However, the Subcontinent's expression has gone, off late, to scrutinise the IWT. Since India's 9/11 i.e., Parliament attack by terrorists in December 2001, the rational of IWT has been questioned by the Parliamentarians, policy-makers, security analysts and of course the Indian media at large. The then BJP-led NDA government's immediate response by cutting all the bilateral relation with Pakistan and execution of 'Operation Parakram' had aggravated the situation where, some argued, abrogation of IWT was certain. To make the situation worse, the Jammu and Kashmir (J & K) Assembly members demanded to invoke the IWT. Recent outburst of members of Pakistan's National Assembly to re-negotiate IWT with India has made the situation more complicated. While for the first time the arbitrator clause in the IWT invoked by Pakistan on Indian Baglihar hydro-power project in 2005, the IWT has also drawn into International Court of Arbitration (ICA) by Pakistan in 2010. The Indus River - the cradle of the oldest civilisation in South Asia, is, indeed the 'life blood of Pakistan' and is 'divine' and 'symbol of strength' for India. The Indus river system, one of the largest in the World, has shared by India, Pakistan, Afghanistan and China (Gulhati, 1973).

The Baglihar Dispute

When the Secretary level talks between India and Pakistan regarding the construction of a 450 MW Baglihar hydro-electric project on the Chenab River failed in 2005, Pakistan resorted to seek arbitration by the World Bank. Although India is allowed under the IWT to make such arrangement as run-of-the river project in the western river as Chenab is, Pakistan alleged that the project would store water and control the flow of the Chenab River. The deadlock appeared with India suggesting continuation of discussions on the project's technical issues but Pakistan demanding an immediate halt on construction at the project site as a pre-condition for doing so. The issues raised by Pakistan on the design of the project were discussed in eight meetings of the Permanent Indus Commission (PIC) under IWT between March 2000 and May 2004 and in two meetings at the level of the concerned Secretaries of the two governments held in June 2004 and January 2005, but no agreement could be reached.

On 18th January, 2005, Pakistan submitted a request to the World Bank to appoint a neutral expert as it claimed that a difference had arisen between India and Pakistan. According to the IWT, when asked to help resolve a dispute, the World Bank can appoint a neutral expert, in consultation with both the countries, and also establish a trust fund for the expert (Roul, 2005). After holding five meetings in neutral venues– Paris, Geneva, London, Paris and Washington; visiting the project site in Doda district in Jammu and Kashmir including its hydraulic model at Roorkee University and examining the written and oral submissions made by both parties, on 12th February 12, 2007, the neutral expert released his recommendation at Berne to representatives of India, Pakistan and the World Bank by suggesting overall design of the Baglihar dam being built by India has been upheld.

Kishenganga Project and International Court of Arbitration

India's 3600-crore (INR) worth 330 MW (Megawatt) Kishenganga project is designed to generate power by diverting water from a dam site on the Kishenganga to the Bonar Nallah, another tributary of the Jhelum, through tunnels in north of Jammu and Kashmir. Pakistan had opposed the construction in view of reduction of flow in downstream at Neelam in Pakistan in violation of IWT. Pakistan demanded that natural flow be maintained all the time with 100 cubic metres per second (cumec) of flow. As India moved on with the project, Pakistan formally lodged a case for arbitration against India under the provisions of the IWT against the project on 17th May , 2010.

In a Press Release, the Ministry of External Affairs of India said that the "Partial Award" delivered in February 2013, the Court of Arbitration already upheld India's main contention that it has the right to divert waters of the western rivers, in a non-consumptive manner, for the optimal generation of power (*The Hindu*, 2013). Subsequently, the Court of Arbitration has allowed India to go ahead with construction of the project in its final order in December 2013. The Court also directed that India shall release a minimum flow of nine cumecs into the Kishenganga river (known as Neelam in Pakistan) below the project at all times to maintain environmental flows.

Changing Water Scenario

With a view in mid 1980s that water was a scarce and precious national resource to be planned, developed and conserved in an integrated and environmentally sound basis. Since, three National Water Policies have been formulated to govern water resources. While water governance comes under State under the Constitution of India, the Union Government formulates the national water policy. The first NWP (1987) and Second NWP (2002) maintained that 'water is a prime natural resource, a basic human need and a precious national asset' (MOWR 1987 and 2002). Interestingly, both NWPs didn't mention about international aspect of water resources especially transboundary rivers. However, the 2012 NWP which states that water as a 'scarce natural resource, is fundamental to life, livelihood, food security and sustainable development, has envisaged bilateral cooperation on transboundary rivers. The notion of water as 'national asset' has substituted with a 'scarce resource' (MOWR, 2012).

The global environmental change especially climate change has predicted to substantially and fundamentally change hydrological systems in the region including both source of water-glacier melting and monsoon rainfall. In recent memory, the floods of Uttarakhand in 2013 and Jammu and Kashmir in 2014 are the indication of such variability which may be a recurring phenomenon in future. In addition to environmental problems, the demand for energy and irrigation and satisfying growing urban needs, increasing pollution and supplying safe drinking water to all under international pledges above all with preserving river ecology and protecting people and facilities from water related disasters, India and its neighbouring countries are facing daunting task in managing water resources.

Of late, the China factor has dismantled the apple cart for India. Many analysts in India have postulated China as 'water hegemon' due to its arbitrary unilateral interventions as well as hosting the source of major Asian rivers. Decades ago Nepal, Bangladesh, Pakistan have similarly implicated India in this role. When China has started intervening in Yarlang Zangbo (Brahmaputra in India), the apprehension of India is similar to apprehensions of Bangladesh of India's unilateral intervention in transboundary rivers (Roul, 2013). In many occasions both Nepal and Bangladesh had proposed for a multilateral agreement, as a strategic bargaining chip against India, for harnessing transboundary rivers. Ironically, both India and China are not signatory to the 1997 UN Convention on Non-Navigational Use of Watercourse which has recently been came into force. It must be noted that China is the largest supplier and financier of water related projects and equipments in South Asia.

Conclusion

With new government in Delhi that has emphasised the neighbourhood policy as first priority with developmental overtone, it is expected that India's hydro diplomacy will be one of the major cornerstone of robust foreign policy. The revival of and faith in

South Asia Association for Regional Cooperation (SAARC) by the new government must open an avenue for forging a co-operation mechanism for water resources. Track-II efforts have been existing since late 1980s especially on water resources and many are being created to support the government co-operation. By accepting the differential perception of each country to its water resources, the SAARC must begin with regular Ministerial meeting to build confidence and trust among riparian countries. The transboundary rivers which evade the national sovereignty are best managed as a Unit or basin approach. It is difficult to concede ownership of water by the countries especially India, but the environmental challenges are forcing to consider river basin management under integrated water resource management (IWRM).

India is willing to consider IWRM as it has drafted a national law in 2013 which is waiting for approval in Parliament with state units consent. As New Prime Minister is suggesting to create border states unit with all western States of India sharing international border or mountain states unit, India must take lead on creating basin countries forum to talk on particular river basins. With new aspects are evolving and practising like river flow, ecological flow, climate change, India should extend its magnanimity to invite basin countries to review existing agreement with good intention to accommodate such concerns. A step forward would be to share the prospective plans on all shared rivers among riparian countries. The perspective plan must include all past, present, and reasonably foreseeable future projects or activities on the river by countries. A cumulative impact assessment study on shared rivers should be taken by jointly all riparian countries. The bilateral suspicion on sharing water has always been the norm of river bank politics. To minimise such suspicion, regular timely sharing of basic information on projects coming up would be the first step in right direction. Water binds people and country, not divides.

END

Dr Avilash Roul (Ph.D.) is an environmental policy analyst specialising on environmental negotiations, currently with SSPC as a Senior Fellow.

Notes

1. The idea of linking the rivers of India is an old one. The linking of rivers was first mooted by Arthur Cotton in the mid-nineteenth century to link rivers in southern India for inland navigation. Though partially implemented, the idea was later abandoned

because inland navigation lost ground to the railways under British Raj. The similar idea was subsequently proposed again by C P Ramaswamy Aiyer in 1926. After nearly half century, the 'Ganga-Cauvery Link' proposal was mooted by the then irrigation minister, K L Rao in 1972. The proposal was examined and found impracticable because of the very large financial and energy costs involved. Subsequently, the 'Garland Canal' idea put forward by airline pilot Captain Dinshaw Dastur in 1977 was rejected as technically unsound.

2. The apprehension was put forward by Bangladesh Foreign Minister Morshed Khan at the BIISS Seminar on *Bangladesh Foreign Policy: Vision and Achievement*, October 2001-October 2003 at Dhaka 25 October 2003.
3. As quoted in "Interlinking of Rivers: Contradictions and Confrontations", A report on the Electronic debate at riverlink@yahoogroups.com, 2004.
4. Mr Deepak Gwayali was Minister of Water Resources in HMG Nepal from 2002 to 2003.
5. NWDA Presentation on ILR at Bigyan Bhavan, New Delhi, March 22, 2003.
6. As per the Nepal's Ministry of Water Resources, the immense quantity of water available in the country and its potentiality to generate hydro based power and irrigate significant percentage of the total agricultural land, provide the opportunity of overcoming the barriers of economic development in this beautiful Himalayan country.
7. *Ibid.*
8. According to Article 126 of the 1990 Constitution of Nepal, ratification of, accession to, acceptance of, or approval of treaties or agreements regarding natural resources and the distribution of their uses are to be approved by a two-thirds majority of the members present at a joint sitting of both houses of the Parliament. See Article 126 (2) (d) of the Constitution of Nepal.
9. The Chisapani Multi-purpose Project, the largest single project in the Karnali basin has been a subject of controversy between India and Nepal despite being found feasible.

References

Abbas, B.M. (1984), *The Ganges Water Dispute*, Dhaka: University Press Limited.

Alam, Undala Z. (2002), "Questioning the Water Wars Rational: A Case Study of the Indus Waters Treaty", *The Geographical Journal*, 169 (4): 141-151.

Anon (2003), "River-linking project: Bangladesh Threatens to Move International Court at The Hague", *The Indian Express* (Delhi), November 1, 2003.

Anon (2012), "Teesta Water Issue: A Few Hard Facts", *The Daily Star* (Dhaka), 11 January 2012, URL: http://archive.thedailystar.net/new Design/news-details.php?nid=217791, (Accessed on 12 August 2014).

Anon (2014), "India, Nepal sign 3 deals, put off power pact", *The Indian Express* (New Delhi), 4 August 2014, URL: http://indianexpress.com/article/india/india-others/india-nepal-sign-3-deals-put-off-power-pact/ (Accessed on 12 August 2014).

Anon (2013), Breakthrough Possible in Teesta River Agreement, *The Telegraph* (Kolkata), 8 November 2013, URL: http://www.telegraphindia.com/pressrelease/prnw/enin201311070292_ indiapublic.html (Accessed on 12 August 2014).

Anon (2014), "Bangladesh concerned over India's river linking project", *Times of India* (New Delhi), 17 July 2014, URL: http://www.timesnow.tv/Bangladesh-concerned-over-Indias-river-linking-project/articleshow/4459568.cms,(Accessed on 10 August 2014).

Anon (2014), "External Affairs Minister Sushma Swaraj speaks to Mamata Banerjee ahead of Bangladesh visit", *The Economic Times* (New Delhi), 25 June 2014, URL: http://articles.economictimes.indiatimes.com/2014-06-25/news/50856043_1_teesta-water-sharing-treaty-land-boundary-agreement-bangladesh-visit (Accessed on 12 August 2014).

Anon (2014), "Teesta Deal Framework Finalized", *BanglaNews 24* (Dhaka), 2 September 2014, URL: http://banglanews24.com/en/fullnews/bn/97882.html (Accessed on 10 September 2014).

Bakker, Karen (2012), "Water Security: Research Challenges and Opportunities", *Science*, Vol. 337, no. 6097, pp. 914-915.

Banskota, N.P. (1981), "Nepal: Toward Regional Economic Cooperation in South Asia", *Asian Survey*, 21 (3): 342-354.

Bhasin, Avtar Singh (1996), *India-Bangladesh Relations, 1971-1994*, Documents, Vol. I, New Delhi: Siba Exim Private Ltd.

Biswas, Asit K and Juha I. Uitto (eds) (2001), *Sustainable Development of the Ganges-Brahmaputra-Meghna Basins,* Tokyo: United Nations University Press.

Biswas, Asit K. (2005), "An Assessment of Future Global Water Issues", *International Journal of Water Resources Development*, 21 (2): 229-237.

Crow, Ben, Alan Lindquist and David Wilson (1995), *Sharing the Ganges-The politics of Technology of River Development*, New Delhi: Sage Publication.

Dinar, Shlomi (2000), "Negotiations and International Relations: A Framework for Hydropolitics", *International Negotiation*, 5 (2): 375-407.

Gaan, Narottam (1998), *Environmental Degradation and Conflict: The Case of Bangladesh*, New Delhi: South Asian Publishers.

Gaan, Narottam (2000), *Environment and National Security*, New Delhi: South Asian Publishers.

Gulhati, N. D. (1973), *Indus Water Treaty: An Exercise in International Mediation*, Bombay: Allied Publishers.

Gyawali, Dipak (2004), "Nepal's Perception of River Linking in India", Paper presented at a seminar in the School of Environmental Studies, JNU, March 22, 2004.

Gyawali, Dipak (2000), "Nepal-India Water Resources Relations" in Zartman, I. William and Rubin, Jeffrey Z (ed), *Power and Negotiation*, US: University of Michigan Press.

Gyawali, Dipak and Ajaya Dixit (1999), "Mahakali Impasse and Indo-Nepal Water Conflict", *Economic and Political Weekly*, 34 (9): 553-564.

Iyer, Ramaswamy R. (1999), "Conflict-Resolution: Three River Treaties", *Economic and Political Weekly (EPW)*, 34 (24): 1510-1512.

Iyer, Ramswamy R. (2003), *Water: Perspectives, Issues, Concerns*, New Delhi: Sage Publication.

Joy, K. J. et al. (ed) (2007), *Water Conflict in India: A Million Revolts in the Making*, New Delhi: Routledge.

Khalequzzaman, Md. et al. (2004), "The Indian River-Linking Project: A Geologic, Hydrologic, Ecologic and Socio-economic Perspective", in M. Feroz Ahmed et al., (eds), *Regional Cooperation on Transboundary Rivers: Impact of the Indian River-Linking Project*, Dhaka: Bangladesh Poribesh Andolon.

Kirmani, Sayed and G. Le Moigne (1997), *Fostering Riparian Cooperation in International River Basins,* World Bank Technical Paper No. 335, Washington, DC: World Bank.

Kirmani, Syed and Robert Rangeley (1994), *International Inland Waters: Concepts for a More Active World Bank Role*, World Bank Technical Paper No. 239, Washington DC: World Bank.

MEA (1959), Agreement between His Majesty's Government of Nepal and the Government of India on the Gandak Irrigation and Power Project, Kathmandu, 4 December 1959, New Delhi: MEA (GOI).

MEA (1966), "Annexure - Agreement between the Government of India and the Government of Nepal on the Kosi Project, Kathmandu, April 25, 1954", in Revised Agreement between the Government of India and His Majesty's Government of Nepal Concerning the Kosi Project, Kathmandu, 19 December 1966, New Delhi: MEA (GOI).

MOWR (1999), *National Water Policy-1999*, Ministry of Water Resources, Dhaka: Government of Bangladesh.

MOWR (2005), *Press Release*, Dhaka: Ministry of Water Resource (GOB).

MOWR (1987), *National Water Policy-1987*, Delhi: Government of India.

MOWR (2002), *National Water Policy-2002*, Delhi: Government of India.

MOWR (2012), *National Water Policy-2012*, Delhi: Government of India.

MOEN (2005), *National Water Plan-Nepal*, Ministry of Energy, Government of Nepal, URL: http://www.moen.gov.np/pdf_files/national_water_plan.pdf (Accessed on 15 September 2014).

Mustafa, Daanish (2007), "Social Construction of Hydropolitics: The Geographical Scales of Water and Security in the Indus Basin", *Geographical Review*, 97 (4): 484-501.

NWDA (2003), Presentation on Inter Basin Water Transfer, National Water Development Agency, Bigyan Bhavan, New Delhi, March 22, 2003, New Delhi: Government of India.

Pant, Suvecha (2003), "Nepal has no official knowledge of mammoth Indian Project", *The Kathmandu Post*, July 29, 2003.

Parsai, Gargi (2013), "ICA Gives Go Ahead to Kishenganga Project", *The Hindu* (India), 22 December 2013.

Roul, Avilash (2005), "Clear As Mud", *Down To Earth* (New Delhi), February 15-28.

Roul, Avilash (2006), "India's Water Future: Are Inter-basin Water Transfers a Solution," EcoWorld, 14 March 2006, URL: http://www.ecoworld.com/home/articles2.cfm?tid=383 (Accessed on 13 August 2014)

Roul, Avilash (2010), *Negotiating Water Security: International and Regional Dimension with Special Reference to South Asia*, Unpublished Doctoral Thesis, School of International Studies, Jawaharlal Nehru University.

Roul, Avilash (2013), "India-China Hydro Diplomacy: Beyond Information Sharing MoUs", *SSPC Analysis*, 22 March 2013, URL: http://www.sspconline.org/opinion/IndiaChinaHydroDiplomacy_22032013 (Accessed on 12 September 2014).

Salman, Salman M. A. and Kishor Upreti (2002), *Conflict and Cooperation on South Asia's International Rivers*, Washington DC: The World Bank.

UNU (2013), "Water Security": Experts Propose a UN Definition on Which Much Depends, *Press Release*, 26 March 2013. URL: http://unu.edu/media-relations/releases/water-security-a-proposed-un-definition. html#info (Accessed on 10 July 2014).

Vergese, B.G. (1990), *Waters of Hope: Himalaya-Ganga Cooperation For a Billion People*, New Delhi: Oxford IBH.

Vidal, John (2003), "Troubled waters for Bangladesh as India presses on with plan to divert major rivers", *The Guardian*, July 24.

Wirsing, Robert G. (2007), "Hydro-Politics in South Asia: The Domestic Roots of Interstate River Rivalry", *Asian Affairs*, Vol. 34, No. 1, pp. 3-22.

World Water Forum (2000), *Final Report: From Vision to Action*, 17-22 March, 2000, The Hague, Netherlands: WWC.

4

India and Bangladesh: Issues in Bilateral Relations

Muzaffar Ahemad Ganaie

Introduction

India and Bangladesh are two close neighbours sharing a common history, common language and common culture. Notwithstanding these commonalities and the central role played by India in the creation of Bangladesh, the relations between the two countries are characterised by mutual distrust and suspicion. Narrating the downward trajectory of India-Bangladesh relations Farooq Sobhan, former Foreign Secretary of Bangladesh observes that: "... if we look back over... last 37 years, we can only conclude that India-Bangladesh relations have been a source of disappointment and frustration for the people of both countries."[1] The relationship between the two countries took off smoothly after the liberation war of 1971. In 1972, two sides signed the Treaty of Friendship, Cooperation and Peace for a period of twenty five years which *inter alia* obligated the contracting parties to "refrain from giving any assistance to any third party taking part in armed conflict against the other party. In case either party is attacked or threatened with attack, the High Contracting Parties shall immediately enter into mutual consultation in order to take appropriate effective measures to eliminate the threat and thus ensure the peace and security of their countries."[2] The relationship, however, lost momentum in the post-1975 years because of the assassination of

Sheikh Mujibur Rahman, first president of Bangladesh and replacement of a civilian regime by successive military regimes. In the words of Prakash Nanda, "the pro-Indian sentiment of liberation war evaporated quickly and an anti-Indian movement surfaced—particularly after the assassination of Mujibur Rahman in 1975. Bangladeshi nationalism asserted itself against India's cultural domination and economic penetration."[3] The anti-India postures adopted by successive military regimes and the failure on the part of India to win over changed administrations further led to dilution of bilateral relations. Marked by the lack of trust and hostile stands taken on bilateral issues, two sides continued to experience strained relations until 1996. In 1996, Sheikh Hasina, daughter of Sheikh Mujibur Rahman came to power in Bangladesh. The new political dispensation in Dhaka showed a keen interest to improve bilateral relations with India. During her tenure two landmark agreements were signed which greatly helped to improve the relations between two sides. First was the agreement on sharing the waters of Ganges River, signed in 1996 and second was the Chittagong Hill Tracts Peace Agreement signed in 1997 which paved the way for the return of the refugees of Chittagong Hill Tracts. The relations, however, nosedived in 2001 when Bangladesh Nationalist Party (BNP) led by Begum Khaleda Zia came to power. The period between 2001- 2006 has been described as a "worst phase" in India-Bangladesh relations. During this period, there were not only "limited high level contacts and exchanges, each side also freely levelled charges against the other and at times Bangladesh openly took an openly hostile stance."[4]

An attempt to restore normalcy to the relations was made during 2006-2008 when a caretaker government was at the helm of affairs in Dhaka. During this period, a formal invitation was extended to the retired Indian army soldiers who had taken part in Bangladesh's liberation war to participate in "Victory Day" celebrations, the chief of the Bangladeshi army visited India and two sides also held a joint exercise in 2009.[5] The real transformation of bilateral relations, however, started when Awami League led by Sheikh Hasina returned to power in 2008. The new regime in Dhaka will take a different approach towards improving the relations with India became evident during 2008 election campaign, as the election manifesto of Awami League noted that:

"Friendly relationship will be maintained with India, Nepal, Bhutan and Myanmar, our neighbouring countries, in the context of further strengthening cooperation with all. Regional and sub-regional cooperation will be further strengthened including relationship with member countries of SAARC, BIMSTEC and D-8."[6]

A new phase in India-Bangladesh relations started in 2010 when Prime Minister Sheikh Hasina accompanied by a delegation of 123 members visited India. During her visit several key agreements pertaining to security, international terrorism and transit facilities were signed. A great achievement of the Hasina regime was the action taken against anti-India terror outfits operating from Bangladeshi territory. Responding positively to the India's security concerns, two sides also signed an extradition treaty in 2013 paving the way for the return of high profile ULFA leader Anup Chetia. Under the treaty, "two countries can request extradition of criminals detained in each other's jails and will be able to exchange criminals or prisoners convicted for over a year at each other's request."[7]

To take this momentum forward and to elevate bilateral relationship to newer heights, Indian Prime Minister Dr Manmohan Singh visited Bangladesh in September 2011 on the invitation of Prime Minister Sheikh Hasina. During his visit several important agreements including a Framework Agreement on Cooperation for Development and Protocol to the Agreement concerning the Demarcation of Land Boundary between India and Bangladesh and Related Matters were signed. The implementation of this agreement will resolve decades old boundary dispute between India and Bangladesh.

In past several years, leaders of the two countries have shown a deep resolve and commitment to improve bilateral relations, but there are a number of outstanding issues between the two countries which continue to plague the relationship. It is, therefore, imperative for the leaders of the two countries to seek an early settlement of these issues to make this relationship one of the defining relationships of 21st century.

Contentious Issues in Bilateral Relations

Water Sharing

India and Bangladesh share fifty four rivers. Sharing the waters of these rivers on fair and equitable basis has always been contentious issue between the two countries. The origin of the dispute pertaining to water sharing can be traced back to 1951, twenty years before the emergence of Bangladesh when Bangladesh formed a part of federation of Pakistan. The issue first surfaced in 1951 when India decided to construct a barrage across Ganges River at Farakka in Murshidabad district of West Bengal. The objective behind the construction of the barrage as cited by India was to keep Hoogli River silt free and Calcutta port operational. The construction of seventy-five foot high barrage was started in 1962 and was completed in 1972.[8] The Indian decision to construct a barrage at Farakka, however, made Pakistan to raise objections against the project on the grounds that it could have an adverse impact on the agriculture and ecology of East Pakistan. Downplaying these concerns Indian Prime Minister, Jawaharlal Nehru declared in Indian Parliament that, "It is our view that there should be no real injury caused to Pakistan by this scheme."[9] But strong objections from Pakistan ultimately made India to discuss the issue with Pakistan. Between 1961-1970, several meeting at different levels were held, but the parties failed to reach to an agreement.

In 1971, crises in East Pakistan erupted and a new country Bangladesh came into existence. All this added a new dimension to Farakka issue. India now faced a weak but a pro-Indian regime across negotiating table. With this intention to resolve the Farakka dispute, both the countries expressed their strong commitments to find a permanent solution to the problem. However, divergent interests and differing perceptions regarding the augmentation of Ganges flow eluded the solution to the problem for next four years. Ultimately with the intervention of Bangladeshi Prime Minister an agreement on Farakka was reached and signed on 18 April, 1975. Under the agreement India was to receive 11,000 cusecs of 55,000 cusecs during the first ten day period of the lean season, leaving the balance for Bangladesh. Towards the last part of the lean period, Indian share was to be increased to 16,000 cusecs of the 65,000 cusecs leaving the remaining flow for Bangladesh.[10] The agreement signed on 18 April, 1975 was valid for one lean season only i.e., from April 21 to 31 May 1975 and before it could be replaced with another agreement political crises erupted in Bangladesh due to the assassination of Sheikh Mujibur Rahman. The new regime in Dhaka under Major General Ziaur Rahman showed a keen interest to resolve the issue but got a poor response from New Delhi, thus forcing Bangladesh to raise the issue at different international forums. The attempt on the part of Bangladesh to seek international intervention made Indira Gandhi to harden her stand over the issue which further exacerbated the situation.

In 1977, parliamentary elections were held in India which led to Indira Gandhi's ouster from power. The new non-Congress government in New Delhi under Morarji Desai took a special interest in resolving the Farakka dispute. Strong political determination shown by the two parties finally paved the way for a five year agreement on sharing the Ganges waters at Farakka.

The agreement was signed on 5th November, 1977. The new agreement defined the lean period from 31 January to 31 May. Under the provisions of the agreement, "the amount of water for Bangladesh was to be calculated from recorded flows of the Ganga at Farakka from 1948 to 1973."[11] A notable feature of the new arrangement was the "guarantee clause" which guaranteed 80 per cent of the stipulated share for Bangladesh even if flows at Farakka decreased below 55,000 cusecs during the leanest period i.e., 21 April to May 31.[12] The 1977 agreement expired on 4th November, 1982. However, before its expiry an interim Memorandum of Understanding (MOU) was signed on 7th October, 1982 for next two dry seasons. The interim arrangement was drawn mainly on the provisions of 1977 agreement, but unlike 1977 agreement it missed the "guarantee clause", main feature of the 1977 agreement.[13] Another MOU was signed in 1985. This agreement also followed the provisions of 1977 agreement. It expired in 1988 after several extensions and after that no progress on the issue could be made until 1996 because of differing positions adopted by the concerned parties.

In 1996, Sheikh Hasina Wajed came to power in Bangladesh which greatly raised the hopes of finding a permanent solution to the Farakka dispute. With this intention to improve relations with India, talks over Farakka issue were resumed and after several rounds of high profile talks a settlement on sharing the Ganges waters at Farakka was reached. The agreement was signed on 12th December, 1996. Expressing his satisfaction over the agreement, Indian Prime Minister Dev Gowda said that:

"I wish to record my profound satisfaction at the agreement on the sharing of the Ganges waters... It is a tribute to your wisdom and leadership that we succeed in resolving an issue that had defied our efforts in the past."[14]

The treaty established a new formula for sharing the Ganges waters at Farakka. Under the new arrangement if the flow of water at Farakka is 70,000 cusecs or less, then the parties will share the flow equally. If the volume of water is between 70,000-75,000 cusecs then Bangladesh will receive 35,000 cusecs and India rest. If the flow is 75,000 cusecs or more, then India will receive 40,000 cusecs and the balance will go to Bangladesh (Annexure I).[15] An "indicative schedule" for sharing the waters at Farakka between January 1 to 31 May given in Annexure II of the treaty is as under:

Like 1977 agreement, the 1996 treaty also contains a guarantee clause under which India cannot reduce Bangladesh's share at Farakka except for "reasonable uses" (Article III). If the flow of

Period	*Average of total flow 1949-88 (cusecs)*	*India's Share cusecs*	*Bangladesh's Share cusecs*
Jan			
1-10	107,516	40,000	67,516
11-20	97,673	40,000	57,673
21-31	90,154	40,000	50,154
Feb			
1-10	86,323	40,000	46,323
11-20	82,859	40,000	42,859
21-28	79,106	40,000	39,106
March			
1-10	74,419	39,419	35,(xx)
11-20	68,931	33,931	35,(xx)*
21-31	64,688	35,000*	29,688
April			
1-10	63,180	28,180	35,000*
11-20	62,633	35,000*	27, 633
21-30	60,992	25,992	35,(xx)*
May			
1-10	67, 351	35,000*	32,351
11-20	73,590	38,590	35,000
21-31	81,854	40,000	41,854

(*Three ten day periods during which 35,000 cusecs shall be provided)

Source: Treaty between Government of the Republic of India and the Government of the People's Republic of Bangladesh on Sharing of the Ganga/Ganges Waters at Farakka.

water at Farakka falls below 50,000 cusecs, the treaty obligates the parties to "enter into immediate consultations to make adjustments on emergency basis."[16]

Though 1996 treaty has put an end to a long running dispute between the two countries on sharing Ganges waters but the controversy on sharing the waters of Teesta River and Tipaimukh dam continues to bedevil the relations between the two countries. Currently, two countries share 75 per cent water of Teesta River on 39 and 36 per cent basis as per the agreement signed in 1983. During the visit of Prime Minister Manmohan Singh to Bangladesh, two countries were supposed to sign an agreement on sharing the remaining 25 per cent waters on 50:50 basis. But strong opposition from Chief Minister of West Bengal prevented India from singing the agreement.[17] Holding back the agreement on Teesta provoked Bangladesh to withdraw from signing transit agreement with India.

India's intention to build Tipaimukh dam on river Barak is also acting as an irritant in bilateral relations. The project has given rise to widespread protests in Bangladesh. Bangladesh fears that the project could have catastrophic consequences for Northeast Bangladesh.[18] Commenting on the adverse consequences of the dam, an Australian environmentalist writes that, "the dam would cause the Surma and Krishna (rivers in Bangladesh) to run dry from November to May... A detailed study by the World Dam Commission published in 2000 states that the adverse impacts of any large dam are irreversible for the lower riparian region."[19] Though Indian Prime Minister has assured Bangladesh that "India would not take any step regarding their planned Tipaimukh dam that might affect the bilateral relations between Bangladesh and India",[20] but the controversy continues to prevail.

Trade Imbalance

India-Bangladesh trade relations are marred by persistent and chronic trade imbalance. Bangladesh is experiencing a large trade

	05-06	*06-07*	*07-08*	*08-09*	*09-10*	*10-11*	*11-12*
India's exports	1864.7	2268.0	3364.0	2841.06	3202	4586.8	4743.3
India's imports	241.96	289.42	358.08	276.58	305	512.5	498.4
Total trade	2106.70	2557.40	3722.08	3117.64	3507	5099.3	5241.7

Source: www.mea.gov.in/Portal/foreignRelation/Bangladesh_Brief.pdf. (Original source: Bangladesh Bank/EPB)

deficit in her bilateral trade vis-à-vis India which is more than $ 4 billion and is increasing at an alarming rate of 9.5 per cent annually.[21] The figures of last six years clearly show that the trade between the two countries is highly tilted in India's favour. In financial year 2011-2012, bilateral trade stood at $ 5.242 billion with exports from India accounting for $ 4.743 billion while imports accounting for $ 0.498 million only.[22]

This trade imbalance has largely been attributed to the liberal access that Indian goods have to Bangladesh market and restrictive trade regime followed by India till late 1990s.[23] In Bangladesh, trade deficit with India has been largely ascribed to various tariff and non-tariff barriers imposed by India which act as great impediment in improving trade relations and narrowing down the trade deficit and for long Bangladesh has been urging India to remove these barriers. If India removes these trade barriers, it will not only help to reduce the trade gap, but it will work as a catalyst in improving the downward trajectory of India-Bangladesh relations as was noted by H.E. Tariq A. Karim, Bangladesh High Commissioner to India:

"...if India were to facilitate Bangladesh's export to India by completely removing all tariff and non-tariff barriers, then the loss in revenues to India from duties or levis would be insignificant, while in return huge goodwill will be created..."[24]

A positive step in this direction was taken in 2011 when India granted duty free access to all products exported from Bangladesh barring twenty five liquor and tobacco items.[25]

Apart from trade barriers, there is a very large illegal trade taking place between the two countries which adds to the trade deficit. Like the legal trade, in illegal trade India is also enjoying a trade surplus which is a cause of concern for Bangladesh. The goods which are being imported illegally from India are about 1.2-1.5 times higher than legal imports.[26] The illegal trade which is greatly encouraged by the easy across the border takes place mainly through neighbouring North Eastern region of India and comprises mainly of live animals, food items and consumer goods imported from India and synthetic yarn, electronic goods and spices imported from Bangladesh to India.[27]

To reduce the trade deficit, India has offered a Free Trade Agreement (FTA) to Bangladesh. India has signed such an agreement with Sri Lanka and it has worked positively in reducing the trade asymmetry between the two countries and there is no reason to believe that why same cannot happen in the case of India-Bangladesh bilateral trade. However, keeping in view Bangladesh's limited export base and volume of goods exported to Bangladesh from India, FTA can work towards reducing the trade deficit if "Bangladesh has a very extensive 'negative list', while India has a very small one, and Bangladesh reduces trade restrictions very slowly over a long period, where as India liberalises very rapidly within a very short period."[28]

Indian investment in Bangladesh can also play a critical role in reducing the trade asymmetry. India has been investing in Bangladesh from a long period but this investment is minuscule confined to few sectors. In 2007, India was the 12th largest investor in Bangladesh. Between 1971-2006, country has invested $389.206 million in Bangladesh.[29] To encourage bilateral investments two sides have signed a Bilateral Investment Promotion and Protection Agreement. To boost Indian investment in Bangladesh, recently India's Tata Group has announced to invest $ 2.5 billion in Bangladesh in fertiliser and power sectors. India's pharmaceutical companies have also started their operations in Bangladesh. Recently India's Sun Pharmaceuticals has set up a pharmaceutical unit in Bangladesh and Apollo Group has opened a state-of-art modern hospital in Dhaka as a joint venture.[30]

Illegal Migration

Among the issues that have dogged the relations between India and Bangladesh, illegal migration from Bangladesh to India is the most crucial one with serious security implications for India. According to Sanjoy Hazarika, huge influx of people from Bangladesh into neighbouring states of India is "(V)isibly reshaping and transforming the demographic, ethnic, linguistic and religious profile of large parts of the population in these areas, it stirred a potent brew of hatred, suspicion and fear."[31] The problem of illegal migration has been equated to the terms like "demographic aggression"[32] and "silent invasion".[33]

The phenomonon of illegal migration from Bangladesh to India is not new. It has a long history and started in latter part of 1940s with the emergence of Pakistan as a sovereign state. A number of factors have contributed to the large scale immigration from Bangladesh into India, ranging from socio-economic factors to religious persecution. The period between 1947-1971 witnessed the greatest influx of immigrants, comprising mainly of Hindus fleeing religious persecution. During this period over 4.7 million Hindus migrated to India. This trend continues even today leading to considerable decrease in Hindu population in Bangladesh.

"Since 1947, Hindu population in Bangladesh has been reduced from 30 per cent to less than 10 per cent."[34] The large scale migration, however, is not only confined to Hindus, large number of Muslims are also making their way to India in search of better economic opportunities. There are about 15-17 million Bangladeshi nationals living in India and it is estimated that about three million people from Bangladesh annually migrate to India.[35]

Among the areas which have witnessed the large scale infiltration of Bangladeshi nationals, Assam is the most affected one. It is estimated that there are about six million illegal immigrants from Bangladesh living in Assam.[36] In a report submitted to the President of India in 1998, Lt General Sinha, the then Governor of Assam warned that "the influx of illegal migrants is turning the lower Assam districts into a Muslim-majority region."[37] To prevent the influx of illegal migrants, an agitation was launched in 1975 by All Assam Students Union which ultimately culminated in Assam accord of 1985. The Accord provided that anybody who has come from Bangladesh and settled in Assam after March 25, 1971 is not an Indian citizen but an illegal migrant.[38] Earlier in 1983, the central government had passed Illegal Migration (Determination of Tribunals) Act to check illegal migration from Bangladesh into Assam. The Act set 25th March, 1971 as a cut off date for acquiring Indian citizenship. The Act, however, proved ineffective to check illegal immigration from Bangladesh because of its severe drawback to make "complainant rather than accused responsible to prove latter's citizenship status."[39] Ultimately the Act was scrapped by the Supreme Court of India in 2005. A three judge Bench of the Supreme Court observed that the Act "created the biggest hurdle and is the main impediment or barrier in identification and deportation of illegal migrants."[40]

Recently state cabinet has approved a proposal to rehabilitate the Hindus who have migrated to Assam even after March 25, 1971 because of religious persecution and communal violence. The number of such immigrants is about eighty five lakhs.[41] Guided by the narrow political interests, such a policy could encourage large scale immigration of Hindus living in Bangladesh. It could also flare up religious tensions because not only Hindus but Muslims in large numbers are also entering Assam on regular basis in search of better economic opportunities. Accommodating only one community along the religious lines could prove detrimental to the peace and security of the state.

As mentioned earlier, there are a number of social, economic, political and religious factors which facilitate illegal migration from

Bangladesh to India. Apart from these factors, there are a number of other factors like pours and poorly managed borders, lack of a comprehensive immigration policy, corruption among border guards and narrow political interests which greatly encourage illegal migration.[42] To minimise the magnitude of the problem, there is an urgent need to work on these issues. So far, Bangladesh has followed a lackadaisical approach to address India's concerns. It has even denied that such a migration has been taking place at all. There is only one incidence when in 1991, during the visit of Begum Khaleda Zia to India two sides agreed to check illegal migration. But this understanding has remained a non-starter. Failure on the part of Bangladesh to recognise the issue has forced India to take unilateral measures to stop illegal migration from Bangladesh. It has started fencing of 4000 km border which it shares with Bangladesh. But Bangladesh has raised its objections to the fencing of the border by citing 1974 Land Boundary Agreement which states that "no defensive structure be built within 150 yards of the Indo-Bangladesh border."[43]

The issue of illegal migration as a national issue was first time raised by Bharatiya Janata Party (BJP). Presently, we have BJP government at the centre headed by Prime Minister Narendera Modi. During an election rally at Ramnagar, Narendera Modi said that:

"As soon as we come to power at the centre, detention camps housing Hindu migrants from Bangladesh will be done away with ...We have a responsibility towards Hindus who are harassed and suffer in other countries. Where will they go? India is the only place for them. Our government cannot continue to harass them. We will have to accommodate them here."[44]

If present government pursues such a policy, it will hurt India's national interests and secular credentials. It must find a permanent and an equitable solution to the problem and for this engagement on the part Bangladesh is critical. The issue of illegal migration is acting as a great impediment in bilateral ties, the two sides must discuss the issue pragmatically to seek a mutually acceptable solution to the problem.

Border Dispute

India shares 4095 kilometre border with Bangladesh. Out of this an area of 6.5 km has not been demarcated yet. This boundary which was drawn haphazardly by British official Sir Cyril Radcliffe has left in its wake several contentious issues between India and

Bangladesh. It has created enclaves of one country located in the territory of other country and lands in "adverse possession" which often leads to clashes between the border guards of two countries. In 2001, India lost 16 BSF personnel in an attempt to take control of the Boraibari village which India claims its own territory but is under the adverse control of Bangladesh. Indian action was provoked by the occupation of Pyrdiwah village by BDR. Bangladesh claims Pyrdiwah its own territory but is occupied by India.[45]

There are about 51 Bangladeshi enclaves inside India and 111 Indian enclaves in Bangladesh. The population of these enclaves is said to be 51,000 with 34,000 living in Indian enclaves in Bangladesh and 17,000 living in Bangladeshi enclaves located in India. The quality of life in these enclaves is appalling and people continue to live in "squalid conditions amid lack of adequate employment opportunity, infrastructure, educational institutions, electricity and medical facilities."[46] Besides this, there are about 3000 acres of Indian land which is in adverse control of Bangladesh and about 3345 acres of Bangladeshi land in adverse possession of India.[47]

An early attempt to settle the boundary dispute was made in 1958 when Indian Prime Minister Jawaharlal Nehru and his Pakistani counterpart Feroz Khan Noon signed an agreement known as Nehru-Noon Agreement which provided for the exchange of enclaves without any consideration for territorial loss or gain. In order to implement Nehru-Noon understanding, Indian constitution was accordingly amended in 1960 (9th Constitutional Amendment Act) but exchange of enclaves could not take place. Another attempt was made in 1974, when Indian Prime Minister Indira Gandhi and Bangladeshi Premier Mujibur Rahman signed an agreement known as Indira-Mujib Land Boundary Agreement of 1974. This agreement among other things provided for expeditious exchange of enclaves. Under the agreement India was also supposed to give a corridor on lease in perpetuity to Bangladesh to ensure access to Dahagram and Angarpota enclaves. Bangladesh on her part ratified the agreement and handed over Berubari enclave to India but India failed to ratify the agreement, leaving the issue unaddressed. Thereafter, in 2001, two Joint Boundary Working Groups (JBWGs) were constituted to look into the issue of enclaves and adverse possessions, but not much progress on the issue could be made due to political instability in Bangladesh. The JBWGs could only meet three times from 2001-2006.[48]

The latest in the series of attempts to settle the boundary dispute and issue of enclaves is the Protocol to the Land Boundary

Agreement signed during the visit of Prime Minister Manmohan Singh to Dhaka in 2011. The protocol *inter alia* provides for the exchange of enclaves, transfer of lands under adverse possession and demarcation of 6.5 km un-demarcated border. The 2011 deal, however, has faced a vehement opposition from different political parties on the grounds that India would loss thousands of acres of land because of the deal. 111 Indian enclaves, that are under the adverse possession of Bangladesh are spread over 17,160 acres of land and 51 Bangladeshi enclaves that are under the adverse control of India are spread over 7,110 acres of land. If exchange of enclaves takes place as 2011 agreement provides for, then net loss of land for India would be 10,050 acres.[49] The opposition, however, must recognise the fact that the land which India has to cede to Bangladesh if 2011 deal comes into effect is already under the control of Bangladesh and India has no access to it. The 2011 protocol only "converts de facto reality to a de jure one."[50] The 2011 agreement must not be seen in the context of gain or loss of land for one country or other, but it must be seen as a historic move to settle decades old boundary dispute between the two countries. Former Indian Prime Minister Dr Manmohan Singh rightly noted in Rajya Sabha that: "This agreement will ensure peace and tranquillity along the borders with Bangladesh and peace and order in both countries."[51] So, in the interest of thousands of people living in these enclaves and in the interest of elevated India-Bangladesh ties, India must work towards the swift implementation of 2011 Land Boundary Agreement.

Conclusion

India and Bangladesh are two close neighbours having cultural and civilisational links. These two neighbours as rightly said by Khalida Zia are destined to live with each other and they cannot "mean ill to each other".[52]

References

1. Farooq Sobhan, (May 2008), "India-Bangladesh Relations: Past, Present and Future," *ORF Discourse*, Vol. 3, Issue No. 3, p. 2.
2. Cited in Choudhury M. Shamim, "The Bangladesh-India Friendship Treaty: A Critical Analysis," p. 6. Available at: www.fairbd.net/Files/jbs3.1_1. pdf, accessed on 12/8/2014.
3. Quoted in S.A. Zafar, (July-October 1993), "Indo-Bangladesh Relations: Problems and Prospects," *Pakistan Horizon*, Vol. 46, No. 3/4, p. 100.

4. Sreeradha Datta, "Indo-Bangladesh Relations: An Enduring Partnership?," *IDSA Issue Brief*, p. 4.
5. "India-Bangladesh Relations: Towards Convergence," (September 2011), *IDSA Task Force Report*, p. 12.
6. Cited in *ibid*. p. 29.
7. "India-Bangladesh Treaty Raises Hopes of Chetia Extradition," (October 26, 2013), *The Times of India.*
8. Ishtiyaq Hossain, (November 1981), "Bangladesh-India Relations: Issues and Problems," *Asian Survey*, Vol. 21, No.11, pp. 1117-1118.
9. Quoted in Shaista Tabasum, (July 2003), "Indo-Bangladesh Treaty on Farakka Barrage and International Law Application," *Pakistan Horizon*, Vol. 56, No. 3, p. 50.
10. Ishtiyaq Hossain, op. cit. No. 8, pp. 1119-1120.
11. Rakesh Tiwari, (April 29-May 5, 2006), "Conflicts Over International Waters," *Economic and Political Weekly*, Vol. 41, No. 17, p. 1689.
12. *Ibid.*
13. Ishtiyaq Hossain, (1998), "Bangladesh-India Relations: The Ganges Water Sharing Treaty and Beyond," *Asian Affairs*, Vol. 25, No. 3, p. 139.
14. Shaista Tabasum, op.cit. No. 9, p. 57.
15. Philippe Sands, (May 1997), "Bangladesh-India: Treaty on Sharing of the Ganges Waters at Farakka," *International Legal Materials*, Vol. 36, No. 3, p. 520.
16. Treaty between Government of the Republic of India and the Government of the People's Republic of Bangladesh on Sharing of the Ganga/Ganges Waters at Farakka.
17. "India-Bangladesh Relations: Towards increased Partnership," A Report prepared by the ASPEN Institute India, p. 8.
18. *Ibid.* pp. 8-9.
19. Quoted in Mohd Aminul Karim, (November 12, 2009), "Bangladesh-India Relations: Some Recent Trends," ISAS Working Paper, No. 96.
20. *Ibid.* p. 5
21. Piyali Dutta, (September 2010), "India-Bangladesh Relations: Issues, Problems and Recent Developments," IPCS Special Report 97, p. 1.
22. "India-Bangladesh Relations". Available at: www.mea.gov.in/Portal/ForeignRelation/Bangladesh_Brief.pdf, accessed on 23/08/2014.
23. Nurul Islam, (September 4-10, 2004), "Indo-Bangladesh Economic Relations: Some Thoughts," *Economic and Political Weekly*, Vol. 39, No. 36, p. 469.
24. Quoted in Piyali Dutta, op. cit. No. 21, p. 2.
25. Joytee Bhattacharjee, (September 2012), "India-Bangladesh Relations: Finding a Way Forward," *ORF Issue Brief*, p. 4.
26. Mohd Aminul Karim, op. cit. No. 19, p. 9 .

27. Prabir De and Biswa N. Bhatacharya, (December 2007), "Deepening India-Bangladesh Economic Cooperation: Challenges and Opportunities," RIS Discussion Papers No. 30, pp. 17-18.
28. Nurul Islam, op. cit. No. 23, p. 4072.
29. Prabir De and Biswa N. Bhatacharya, op. cit. No. 27, p. 56.
30. *Ibid.*
31. Quoted in Smruti S. Pattanaik, (May 16, 2014), "Politics of Illegal Immigration and India Bangladesh Relations," *IDSA Issue Brief*, p. 4.
32. Mohd Aminul Karim, op. cit. No. 19, p. 8.
33. Namrata Goswami, "Bangladesh illegal Migration into Assam: Issues and concerns from the Field," *IDSA Issue Brief*, p. 2.
34. Chirantan Kumar, (Janyary 2009), "Migration and Refugee Issue Between India and Bangladesh," *Scholar's Voice: A New Way of Thinking*, Vol. 1, No. 1, pp. 64-65.
35. Mohd Aminul Karim, op. cit. No. 19, p. 8.
36. Namrata Goswami, op. cit. No. 33, p. 2.
37. Cited in Smruti S. Pattanaik, op.cit. No. 31. P. 4
38. Namrata Goswami, op.cit. No. 33, p. 2.
39. *Ibid.* p. 3.
40. Cited in *Ibid.* p. 4.
41. Anand Kumar, (August 8, 2014), "Competitive Politics Over Illegal Migration from Bangladesh," IDSA *Comment*. Available at: http://www.Idsa.in/idsacomments/illegalmigrationfrom Bangladesh_akumar_080814.html, accessed on 5/9/ 2014.
42. Sreeradha Datta, (October-December 2011), "Show Tangible Results Leading to Visible Benefits," in "India and Bangladesh –A New Phase in Bilateral Relations," *Indian Foreign Affairs Journal*, Vol. 6, No. 4, p. 403.
43. Smruti S. Pattanaik, (September 9, 2011), "India-Bangladesh Land Border: A Flawed Inheritance and a Problematic Future," *Strategic Analysis*, Vol. 35, No. 5, p. 749.
44. Quoted in Sumruti S. Pattanaik, op.cit. No. 31, p. 2.
45. "Unquiet Border," (April 28-May 4, 2001), *Economic and Political Weekly*, Vol. 36, No. 17, p. 1365.
46. Dipanjan Roy, (September 7, 2011), "India, Bangladesh settle Boundary Dispute". Available at: www.indiatoday.in/story/india-bangladesh-settle-boundary-dispute/1/150380.htm, accessed on 20/9/2014.
47. Pushpita Das, (December 27, 2010), "Enclaves and Adverse Possession: Time to Deliver on the Promise". Available at: www.idsa.in/idsacomments/enclavesandAdversePosessions timetodeliver onthe promise_pda_2710.htm, accessed on 7/9/2014.
48. *Ibid.*
49. Nilim Dutta, (September 24, 2011), "Finally, Mending our Fences," Tehelka Magazine, Vol. 38, Issue 24.

50. Radha Kumar, (December 2013), "Failing Bangladesh: Legislators Against National Interest," *Policy Brief*, Delhi Policy Group, p. 5.
51. Quoted in *ibid*. p. 3.
52. Begum Khaleda Zia, (September-October 2012), "Bangladesh-India Relations, Challenges and Prospects," *Strategic Analysis*, Vol. 36, No. 5, p. 722.

5

Strategic Dimensions of India's Relations with Sri Lanka: The LTTE Factor

Subhransu Sekhar Mishra

The security environment of a state is largely governed by its geographical location, which is closely linked to its domestic, regional and international setting. In this context, the internal dimension in terms of its domestic milieu has strong bearings on its foreign policy. So, in the geo-political configuration of South Asia, India's pre-eminent position has been a cause of concern and comfort for its smaller neighbours who have been overawed by India's power. So, it is pertinent to study strategic relationship of Sri Lanka with India, which occupies a significant position in the regional set-up.

Broadly, Sri Lanka assumes great importance to India in terms of its location and strategic importance. India and Sri Lanka are situated in the outer rim areas of the Indian Ocean and, thus, have tremendous potential to develop maritime trade with the Afro-Asian countries and the various other countries of the world. Located at the vital sea lines of communications, Sri Lanka has immense strategic importance in maritime security. Thus the geo-strategic dimension continues to be one of the independent variable in the context of Indo-Sri Lanka relations. Since colonial days, naval strategists have emphasised the importance of Sri Lanka in the strategic moves and defence calculations of India. For the British colonial power, Sri Lanka had been an integral part to the defence of the Indian sub-continent as it served as a vital link in their sea communications and military expansion eastwards after the Suez Canal.

Even afterits independence, India inherited the British legacy of strategic unity of India encompassing its immediate neighbours. So it continued to adhere to the principles of strategic importance of Sri Lanka on the lines of the British attachment to the crown colony. This is evident from the fact that in the early years, just after independence and even the years immediately preceding them, Indian writers, politicians and strategists had sought to emphasise the strategic unity of India and Sri Lanka and have argued for a closer union between the two countries.

(1) From India's security point of view, Sri Lanka assumes serious strategic importance in the Indian Ocean region. It becomes crystal clear from the statement of the then first Prime Minister of Ceylon, D.S. Senanayake, when he expressed, "We are in an especially dangerous position, because we are in one of the strategic highways of the world. The country, which captures Ceylon could dominate the Indian Ocean.

(2) However, India under Nehru had begun with good ties with neighbouring countries. Having attained its independence after a long colonial rule, it is repugnant for India to think of dominating her neighbours in the name of safeguarding its security.

(3) Hence, it has sought to prevent any external military presence in the Indian Ocean by promoting good neighbourliness and peaceful regional co-operation.

But, during this period, Sri Lanka entertained intermittent fear of hostile intentions from India. It was made clear by John Kotelawala when he stated in 1955, the day Ceylon dispensed with Englishman completely, the Island would go under India'.

(4) Though there was no clear-cut threat from any quarters at this stage, there were however some indirect references to India. On the contrary, under Nehru, India pursued a policy of enlightened self-interest without any antagonism towards its small neighbours. But it had its own geopolitical sensitivities' to the developments in Sri Lanka.

(5) Further, India has viewed the military presence of any major power in the South Asian region as a threat to the regional security, which in itself is the main concern of India. In this context, the view of India of substantial strategic unity encompassing its neighbours impinges upon the bilateral and regional relations in the South Asian region. Hence, geographical factor has always been

more important in determining the nature of the Indo-Lanka relationship than disparities in their size and population.

(6) In addition to this, the concept of strategic unity of South Asia by India has been emphasised with Sri Lanka as an organic part of its defence calculations. Separated from India by a narrow stretch of water, Sri Lanka 'is close enough to be influenced by India but unlike the other small states in the region which are geographically linked to India by a land mass, she is distant enough to maintain her own identity.

(7) Such a perception has resulted in an ambivalent attitude of Sri Lanka towards India resulting in a kind of love and hate relationship.

It is important to mention here that when S. W. R. D. Bandaranaike came to power in 1956, the Sri Lankan perception of Indian threat appeared to have faded away. Gradually, under Mr and Mrs Bandaranaike's rule in Sri Lanka, the Indo-Sri Lanka relations turned very friendly and cordial. During this phase, India extended her defence parameters concomitant to the growth of her military-industrial potential, especially in the 1970s, and Sri Lanka realised the Indian strategic perspective. Thus, the Bandaranaike period of 1956-65 and 1970-77 interspersed as it was between the regimes of Dudley Senanayake (1965-70) provided a striking contrast to the earlier phase of Indo-Lanka relations. This was partly because the Bandaranaikes were personally close to the Nehru family and shared the anti-colonial and non-alignment ideology of India.

Military Involvement of Extra-Regional Powers and India's Concern

As discussed earlier, in the aftermath of independence, Sri Lanka ensured its defence and security by entering into an agreement with the British government.

(8) Slowly, as a sign of mutual peace and understanding, Mr S.W. R. D. Bandaranaike demonstrated his faith in India by getting the British vacate their basis from Trincomalee and Katunayake in 1957. However, the defence agreement was not abrogated.

With the UNP coming to power under J. R. Jayewardene in 1977, there was a total shift in the foreign policy priorities of Sri Lanka. The new policy was pro-American in its stand with overtones of anti-India. Hence, in 1980s, Sri Lanka had to grant certain facilities and concessions to the United States of America (USA) in the nature of Trincomalee Tank Farm deal and the Voice of America (VOA) agreement. The Trincomalee Tank Farm deal was given to a Singapore-based USA Company after rejecting the Indian tender.

(9) Thus, India became extremely sensitive to the possibility of the USA role in the South Asian region, particularly on an overt or covert arrangement with Sri Lanka. Provision for the use by the American Navy of the strategic harbour of Trincomalee such a scenario was highly dangerous for India as it constituted a grave threat to its security.

(10) In the aftermath of July 1983 violence, the Tamil separatist guerrillas launched serious attacks on security forces, civilians and others who had opposed them. The Government of Sri Lanka lacked proper military apparatus to meet the growing insurgency in the country. Hence, President Jayewardene requested for military assistance from both Britain and the USA. The USA, which had improved relations with Sri Lanka, responded unfavourably as it disliked bypassing India. In the meantime, India became concerned with rumours that Sri Lanka had asked for military assistance from the USA, the United Kingdom (UK), Pakistan, Israel and Bangladesh in the wake of 1983 riots.

(11) In addition to this, the Israeli Interest Section was set up 'under the auspices of the USA Embassy' in Colombo on 24th May, 1984. There were conflicting reports about the number of Israeli experts but it was admitted that the Israeli military advisers were involved in the training the Sri Lankan armed forces in counter-insurgency and internal security. In this process the USA had an indirect military involvement through the Israeli presence in Sri Lanka.

Though China maintained that the ethnic conflict of Sri Lanka was an internal affair of Sri Lanka, but it has been supplying arms to Sri Lanka after 1983.

(13) Regarding the involvement of Pakistan, Sri Lanka requested Pakistan for military help after the July 1983 violence and so there have been regular exchange of officials and supply of arms by Pakistan. In 1985, Pakistan is reportedly training Sri Lankan home guards and air force and naval personnel.

(14) It was also supplying large amount of heavy and medium artillery to Sri Lanka for its fight against the Tamil separatists.

Following the July 1983 disturbance in Sri Lanka there emerged a new strategic thinking in India, which emphasised the strategic unity of South Asia and India's predominant role in it. Relating to defence and security, which took concrete shape through Mrs Indira Gandhi who enunciated the idea, is popularly known as the Indira Doctrine.

(15) This doctrine was reflected in the foreign policy-making of India, which sought for the consolidation of regional security interests. In this context, the military presence of external power in Sri Lanka had a serious impact on the Indo-Lanka relations.

LTTE Factor in Indo-Lanka Relations

In South Asia, as in other regions, internal political, economic and social processes within countries are seen to affect the nature of relationship between them at both bilateral and regional levels. Therefore, ethnic conflicts within the countries of South Asia generate internal pulls and pressures which affect inter-state relations within the region.

(16) In this context, the ethnic conflict in Sri Lanka has serious implications for India owing to the Tamil people of Tamil Nadu who sympathises with their brethren in Sri Lanka. As it is evident from the earlier discussion, the Indian perception of threat to its security in the Indian Ocean region is largely governed by political and military developments in Sri Lanka. Hence, the deteriorating ethnic conflict has been a major intriguing problem in the relations between India and Sri Lanka since 1983.

Regarding the Sri Lankan Tamils who had raised the call for a separate state, as early as 1976, the Indian government remained aloof from such political developments in Sri Lanka. Since 1983, however, India voiced its concern for the safety and security of the Tamils in Sri Lanka. Hence, when the riots broke out between the Tamil and the Sinhalese communities in July 1983, India found itself in a delicate situation. It felt that it had some moral responsibility in the safety and security of the Tamils in Sri Lanka and moreover in ensuring their safety. India had to impress upon Sri Lanka that it had no intention of interfering in the internal affairs of the island. Therefore from security point of view, the major concern of India was to prevent the crisis from escalating to a degree that might warrant the involvement of extra regional powers.'

(17) In India, the ethnic riots of Sri Lanka had its immediate impact in Tamil Nadu where the government and opposition political parties put pressure on the central government in New Delhi to intervene in Sri Lanka on behalf of the Tamils there. Hence, it is important to note the fact that the Tamil Nadu political parties have a long history of support for various causes espoused by the Tamils of Sri Lanka. In this context, they have supported the Tamil demands of language, federalism and most recently even for the establishment of a separate state of *Eelam* in the Tamil populated

northern and eastern parts of Sri Lanka, in accordance with the political demand of the Tamil United Liberation Front (TULF) in Sri Lanka since 1976.

(18) The separatist demand spawned a number of Tamil militant groups in Sri Lanka and the leaders of these groups sought sanctuary in Tamil Nadu and were even closely associated with the political leaders of the state. Moreover, the ethnic riots of July 1983, which caused death and destruction to the Tamils in Sri Lanka, brought large influx of Tamil refugees to Tamil Nadu. Hence, the Indian government was urged to take immediate steps for the solution of the Tamil problem.

(19) In the meantime, the Tamil Nadu factor considerably influenced the formulation of the Indian foreign policy towards Sri Lanka.

(20) The arrival of thousands of Tamil refugees in Tamil Nadu with their tales of atrocities by the Sri Lankan Sinhala nationalists against them aroused passions in Tamil Nadu. The two major political parties in Tamil Nadu, DMK, or Dravida Munnettra Kazhagam and AIADMK, (All India Anna Dravida Munnetra Kazhagam) further politicised the Sri Lanka issue and exerted pressures on the central government to deal with more firmly towards Sri Lanka including direct military intervention, if necessary.

Gradually, during the years of 1970s–1980s, private entities and elements in the state government of Tamil Nadu were believed to be encouraging the funding and training for the Liberation Tigers of Tamil Eelam, (LTTE) a separatist insurgent force which was at the forefront of Tamil uprising in the island. In 1987, faced with growing anger amongst its own Tamils, and a flood of refugees, India intervened directly in the conflict for the first time after the Sri Lankan government attempted to regain control of the northern Jaffna region by means of an economic blockade and military assaults. India dubbed it as a humanitarian intervention in the face of influx of refugees from Lanka and thus it supplied food and medicine by air and sea.

After subsequent negotiations, India and Sri Lanka entered into an agreement via the 13th Amendment. The peace accord assigned a certain degree of regional autonomy in the Tamil areas with Eelam People's Revolutionary Liberation Front (EPRLF) controlling the regional council and called for the Tamil militant groups to lay down their arms. Further India was to send a peacekeeping force, named the IPKF to Sri Lanka to enforce the disarmament and to watch over the regional council. Even though the accord was signed between the governments of Sri Lanka and India, with the Tamil Tigers and other Tamil militant groups not having a role in the signing of the accord, most Tamil militant groups accepted this agreement but the LTTE rejected the accord.The result was that the LTTE now found itself engaged in a military conflict with the Indian Army, and launched their first attack on an Indian army rations truck, killing five Indian para-commandos who were on board by strapping burning tires around their necks. The government of India then decided that the IPKF should disarm the LTTE by force, and the Indian Army launched number of assaults on the LTTE, including a month-long campaign dubbed Operation Pawan to win control of the Jaffna peninsula from the LTTE. Finally, the IPKF wound up its operations in March 1990 and returned home after 967 days in Sri Lanka at the cost of a reported Rs 300 crores and at a loss of 1155 lives with three times as many wounded. So the IPKF operation by India was primarily guided by its long-term military interests.

(21) Later, with President Rajpaksa's strong anti-LTTE stand and military build-up, the nearly three-decade long armed conflict between Sri Lankan forces and the LTTE came to an end in May 2009. During the course of the conflict, India supported the right of the Government of Sri Lanka to act against terrorist forces. At the same time, it conveyed at the highest levels its deep concern at the plight of the mostly Tamil civilian population, emphasising that their rights and welfare should not get enmeshed in hostilities against the LTTE. Further, the need for national reconciliation through a political settlement of the ethnic issue has been reiterated by India at the highest levels. India's consistent position is in favour of a negotiated political settlement, which is acceptable to all communities within the framework of a united Sri Lanka and which is consistent with democracy, pluralism and respect for human rights.

Commercial Relations: Recent Bilateral Visits and Agreements

India and Sri Lanka enjoy a robust trade and investment relationship. Sri Lanka is India's largest trade partner in South Asia. India in turn is Sri Lanka's largest trade partner globally. Trade between the two countries grew particularly rapidly after the entry into force of the India-Sri Lanka Free Trade Agreement in March 2000. Over the next eight years, bilateral trade multiplied nearly five-fold. According to Sri Lankan customs data, the bilateral trade amounted to $ 4.01 billion in 2012. In recent months, the two countries have continued discussion to take the economic and commercial engagement to the next level. The Indian move for accelerated economic engagement with Sri Lanka is largely influenced by the growing Chinese involvement in the island–nation.

China has doubled its trade with Sri Lanka from 5.2 per cent in 2008 to 9.6 per cent in 2012. It also provides twice the amount of loans to Sri Lanka of all Western countries. Sri Lanka has granted China $ 4 billion in current infrastructure projects, mainly with Chinese loans. A contract recently signed with a Chinese construction company will provide for a new port city in Colombo. China has already built the island nation's first four-lane expressway, as well as its second international airport and the sea port at Hambantota, which is the world's first inbuilt harbour carved out of land.

On the otherhand, Sri Lanka has long been a priority destination for direct investment from India. India is among the four largest overall investors in Sri Lanka with cumulative investments over $ 800 million. In 2012, India emerged as the fourth largest overall investor in Sri Lanka with investments of about $ 160 million (out of a total of $ 1279.15). India's main investments are in the areas of petroleum, retail, hospitals, telecom, vanaspati, copper and other metal industries, real estate, telecommunication, hospitality and tourism, banking and financial services, IT and food processing (tea and fruit juices). Indian business organisations such as IOC, Tatas, Bharti Airtel, Piramal Glass, LIC, Ashok Leyland, L&T, Dabur and Taj Hotels are present in Sri Lanka.

The last few years have also witnessed an increasing trend of Sri Lankan investments into India. Significant examples include Ceylon Biscuits (Munchee brand), Carsons Cumberbatch (Carlsberg), Brandix (about $ 1 billion to set up a garment city in Vishakapatnam), MAS holdings, John Keels, Hayleys, and Aitken Spence (Hotels), apart from other investments in the freight servicing and logistics sector. Bilateral economic and commercial ties continued to remain stable during 2013. For the period January-October 2013, bilateral trade amounted to $ 2.96 billion with Sri Lanka's import from India amounting to $ 2.51 billion.

With the shift from relief and rehabilitation to reconstruction and development, the Government of India turned its attention to the housing requirements of the IDPs. During the visit of President Mahinda Rajapaksa to India in June 2010, an announcement was made by Prime Minister Dr Manmohan Singh that India would support a programme to reconstruct 50,000 houses in Sri Lanka. The conclusion of the armed conflict saw the emergence of a major humanitarian challenge, with nearly 300,000 Tamil civilians housed in camps for Internally Displaced Persons (IDPs). The Government of India put in place a robust programme of assistance to help the IDPs return to normal life as quickly as possible as also consistently advocated the need for them to be resettled to their original habitations as early as possible. India's immediate humanitarian assistance to IDPs included supply of 250,000 family relief packs, establishment of an emergency medical unit which treated over 50,000 IDPs, supply of over one million roofing sheets, as well as 400,000 bags of cement for constructing temporary housing and provision of 95,000 starter packs of agricultural implements. India also assisted in revival of agricultural and economic activities in areas affected by the conflict.

Moreover, Sri Lanka is one of the major recipients of development credit given by the Government of India. Under a line of credit of $167.4 million, the tsunami-damaged Colombo-Matara rail link has been repaired and upgraded. Another line of credit of $800 million for track laying and supply of rolling stock to support construction of Medawachchiya to Madhu, Madhu to Talaimannar, Omanthai to Pallai, Pallai to Kankesanthurai railway lines and setting up of signaling and telecommunications systems in Northern Sri Lanka is already operational. India is also involved in projects for renovation of Palaly Airport, Kankesanthurai Harbour, construction of a Cultural Centre in Jaffna, interconnection of electricity grids between the two countries, construction of a 150-bed hospital in Dickoya and setting up a coal power plant in Sampur as a joint venture between National Thermal Power Corporation (NTPC) and Ceylon Electricity Board (CEB).

India has showed its pro-active diplomatic move by abstaining from a U.S.-sponsored resolution on human rights in Sri Lanka at the United Nations. India had supported similar resolutions in 2012 and 2013, but abstained after the new resolution appeared much tougher on Sri Lanka than prior versions, calling for an independent international investigation of alleged war crimes committed by Sri Lankan forces in their war against the Liberation Tamil Tigers of Eelam (LTTE). In explaining its reasoning for the abstention, the Ministry of External Affairs said, "It has been India's firm belief that adopting an intrusive approach that undermines national sovereignty and institutions is counterproductive ... any external investigative mechanism with an open-ended mandate to monitor national processes for protection of human rights in a country, is not reflective of the constructive approach of dialogue and cooperation envisaged by UN General Assembly resolution 60/251 that created the HRC in 2006 as well as the UNGA resolution 65/281 that reviewed the HRC in 2011." Despite India's abstention, the resolution passed with 23 in favour, 12 against and 12 abstaining.

The resolution called for an independent international investigation into alleged war crimes and human rights violations in Sri Lanka. India's opposition to the resolution sends a strong message to Colombo at a time when it was sorely needed. Relations across the Palk Strait have been strained earlier during Mahinde Rajapaksa's first tenure but bilateral talks are producing results. Provincial elections in Sri Lanka, particularly in the Tamil-dense northern areas of the island, were largely pushed for by Indian diplomats and are seen a positive development in the island nation's post-conflict transition.

Thus, New Delhi needs to pursue its diplomacy with Sri Lanka and doing so will involve carefully moderating between meeting the needs of domestic interest groups but also steadily winning geopolitical overtures with Rajapaksa's government in Sri Lanka. Against the backdrop of expanding Chinese influence in Sri Lanka, New Delhi's interest will be best served by slowly but surely pursuing diplomacy on its own terms with Rajapaksa's government. In recent years, the relationship has been marked by close contacts at the highest political level, growing trade and investment, cooperation in the fields of development, education, culture and defence, as well as a broad understanding on major issues of international interest.

Apart from the SAARC mechanism, bilateral exchanges at various levels over the past year and significant progress in implementation of developmental assistance projects for the Internally Displaced Persons (IDPs) and disadvantaged sections of the population in Sri Lanka has helped further cement the bonds of friendship between the two countries. In 2013, Prof G.L. Peiris, Minister of External Affairs of Sri Lanka visited India for the eighth meeting of the India-Sri Lanka Joint Commission which was held on 22th January, 2013. During the visit, the two sides signed two agreements on (i) Combating International Terrorism and Illicit Drug Trafficking and (ii) Revised Double Taxation Avoidance Agreement. Mr Basil Rajapaksa, Minister for Economic Development also visited India on 4-5 July 2013. From the Indian side, a delegation representing the India Foundation led by Shri. Ravishankar Prasad, Hon'ble Deputy Leader of Opposition in the Rajya Sabha visited

Sri Lanka from 04-10 June 2013. Commerce Secretary Shri. S. R. Rao visited Sri Lanka on 24-26 June 2013.

Thus, it is imperative that India adopts a pro-active policy towards Sri Lanka, to not only save the people but also for its own security reasons. However, regarding the Tamil issue, all hoped that with the military defeat of the LTTE, there would be a political settlement to the ethnic question in Sri Lanka. But, the issue is yet to be resolved in a just and peaceful manner. India has repeatedly conveyed its willingness to do whatever is required for the satisfactory resolution of the ethnic question in a manner that respects the sentiments of all the communities in Sri Lanka. New Delhi must voice its concerns without hesitation to ensure that Colombo moves forward in resolving the ethnic issue at the earliest and in all seriousness. Simultaneously, India, in the short-term, should continue to provide the resources required for the resettlement of Tamil population and invest in the economic development of the war-ravaged Northeast of Sri Lanka.

*Dr S.S. Misra is an Associate Professor in the Deptt. of Political Science at National Defence Academy, Khadakvasla, Pune.

References

1. For more details see, K.M. Panikkar (1945), India and the Indian Ocean: An Essay on the Influence of Sea Power, London: Allen and Unwin, P. R. Ramchandra Rao (1954), India and Ceylon, Bombay: Orient Longmans, K. B. Vaidya (1959), The Naval Defence of India, Bombay: Orient Longmans, and Shelton U. Kodikara (1965), Indo-Ceylon Relations since Independence, Colombo: Ceylon Institute of World Affairs, p. 33.
2. Ramesh Prasad Sinha (1992), Sri Lanka-United States Relations, New Delhi: Commonwealth Publishers, p. 02.
3. Davendra Kaushik (1987), Perspectives on security in Indian Ocean Region, New Delhi: Allied Publishers, p. 110.
4. For details see, Shelton U. Kodikara (1982), Foreign Policy of Sri Lanka: A Third World Perspective, New Delhi: Chanakya Publications, p. 21.
5 For more details see, S. D. Muni (1993), Pangs of Proximity: India and Sri Lanka's Ethnic Conflict, New Delhi: Sage Publications, pp. 13-28.
6 Ravi Kaul (1974), "The Indian Ocean: A Strategic Posture for India" in T. T. Poulose (ed.), Indian Ocean Power Rivalry, New Delhi: Young Asian Publications, p. 66.
7. Gamini Keerawella (1990), "Peace and Security Perceptions of a Small States: Sri Lankan Response to Super Power Naval Rivalry in the Indian Ocean-1970-77", in Shelton U. Kodikara (ed.), South Asian

Strategic Issues: Sri Lankan Perspectives, New Delhi: Sage Publications, p. 179.

8. W. Howard Wrigging (1960), Ceylon Dilemmas of New Nations, Princeton: Princeton University, p. 389.
9. Urmila Phadnis (1989), Ethnicity and National-Building in South Asia, New Delhi: Sage Publications, p. 223, and Institute of Defence Studies and Analysis (1985), IDSA News Review on South Asia/Indian Ocean, 18(3), pp. 203-204.
10. K. M. de Silva (1995), Regional Powers and Small State Security: India and Sri Lanka 1947-90, Baltimore: John Hopkins University Press, pp. 152-153.
11 For more details see, Edgar O Ballance (1989), The Cyanide War: Tamil Insurrection in Sri Lanka 1973-88, London: Brassey, p. 37.
13. P. Venkateshawar Rao (1989), "Foreign Involvement in Sri Lanka", Round Table, 309, p. 89.
14. John Kaniyalil (1986), "The Pak-Lanka Connection", Strategic Analysis, 09(11), p. 1076.
15. Shelton U. Kodikara (1987), "International Dimension of Ethnic Conflict in Sri Lanka: Involvement of India and Non-State Actors", Bulletin of Peace Proposals, 08(4), pp. 644-645.
16. Bentram E. S. J. Bastiampillai (1990), "Ethnic Conflict in South Asia and Inter-State Relations especially in Relation to Sri Lanka", in Shelton U. Kodikara (ed.), Op. Cit, p. 82.
17. Gauray Ghose and Patrick James (2006), "Third-Party Intervention in Ethnic Conflict: Role Theory and Major Powers in South Asia", in Santosh C. Saha (ed.), Perspectives on Contemporary Ethnic Conflict: Primal Violence or the Politics of Conviction?,Lanharm: Rowman and Lifflefield Publishers, p. 35.
18. See, S. D. Muni (1993), Op. Cit, pp. 63-67.
19. Gauray Ghose and Patrick James (2006), "Third-Party Intervention in Ethnic Conflict: Role Theory and Major Powers in South Asia", in Santosh C. Saha (ed.), Op. Cit, pp. 35-36.
20. For more details see, A. Sivarajah (1990), "Indo-Sri Lanka Relations and Sri Lanka's Ethnic Crisis: The Tamil Nadu Factor", in Shelton U. Kodikara (ed.), Op. Cit, pp. 135-159.
21. For details see, S.S. Misra (1995), Ethnic Conflict and National Security in Sri Lanka, New Delhi: Kalinga Publications, pp. 93-125.

6

India-Maldives Relations: Towards Upswing Direction

Mohammed Badrul Alam

The bilateral treaty signed on 8th August, 1949 provides the framework for India-Maldives relations and is guided by the principle of beneficial bilateralism. Implicit in this principle is mutual appreciation of concerns and interests by the two countries, and equal respect and sympathy for each other's sensitivities. The high level visits have cemented India-Maldives relations and developed mutual understanding between the leaders.

Unlike Sri Lanka, Maldives is not afflicted with the big power versus small power syndrome for the simple reason that its relationship with India is based on understanding, mutual respect and genuine desire for cooperation and promotion of goodwill that both the countries have observed in the conduct of their bilateral relations. This was evident from the amicable way in which they reached an agreement in 1976 to demarcate their maritime boundary by adopting the median line principle.

For Maldives, its geo-strategic land-locked position is a cause for its vulnerability, which became high in the wake of militarisation of the Indian Ocean and the heightening Super Power rivalry in the 1970s and the 1980s. Being a vulnerable country, Maldives considers India as an important source for its security. Its vulnerability arising out of its geo-strategic location is aggravated by the absence of a required military strength to protect its security. Over the years India has provided a variety of assistance and played a greater role in infrastructure development. In 1986, the two countries signed a five-year economic and technical co-operation agreement under which India extended a package of economic, technical and commercial assistance.

Many areas of co-operation were worked out at the first India-Maldives Joint Commission meeting held in Male in January 1990. They included assistance on arresting the green house effect and training civil servants to man the country's foreign office. India also agreed to help Maldives in maintaining its museums, increase the frequency of its flights to Male, and send experts to set up a natural disaster warning centre on the island. In the field of science and technology arrangements were worked out for Maldives' use of Indian satellite (INSAT-1D) for the reception and recording of meteorological data as well as the re-broadcasting of Indian television programmes on the local Maldivian Television network.[1]

Political Relations

Since the establishment of diplomatic relations with India on 1st November 1965, relations between India and Maldives have been marked by continued friendship, outstanding co-operation and beneficial bilateralism. Throughout the history of consistent and close co-operation between both the countries, which at any point of time was free of any bilateral irritants, the Maldives' relations with India are unmatched by any other country in the region as both the countries have remained strongly committed to an enduring friendship. Besides United Kingdom and Sri Lanka, India is the third country with which Maldives established such continues and uninterrupted relations since independence on 26th July, 1965.

The high level visits have cemented India-Maldives relations and developed mutual understanding between their leaders. There have been frequent exchanges of visits of political leaders since the establishment of the diplomatic relations. Prime Minister Indira Gandhi was the second foreign dignitary to visit Maldives in 1975 after the British Queen and India was the first country to establish a diplomatic mission in Male in1976.[2]

Despite the changes in the Government or the leadership there never occurred any shift or change in the pattern of the bilateral relations between India and Maldives. Despite the Indo-centric character of the South Asian region and the micro - archipelagic nature of the Maldives and thus the power disparity, both the countries have for long observed a principle of mutual respect, assistance and concern for each others' sensitivities. As a result, the relations between the two countries have been deeply vested in close understanding and bonded in an inherent desire for co-operation and promotion of goodwill.

Since the establishment of the bilateral relations, the Government of Maldives profoundly valued India's assurances of support and assistance in all matters. It is very important to note that India has proved to be a very close friend of the Maldives in its time of need, not just on a mere occasion but on several occasions. India's swift response during the coup incident of 3rd November, 1988 and its unconditional support and timely assistance to Maldives in the wake of the Tsunami disaster in December 2004 are two clear examples among many that stand proof of India's closeness with Maldives.[3]

Bilateral relations have been nurtured and strengthened by regular contacts at all levels. Since establishment of diplomatic relations, there were many high level visits between India and Maldives. Recently, President Abdulla Yameen visited India with a high level delegation on a State visit from January 1-4, 2014, which was his first official visit abroad.

There is a regular exchange of high level ministerial visits also in the recent past. India's Minister of External Affairs, Shri Salman Khurshid visited Maldives in February 2014. From Maldives, Ministerial level visits during 2014 were by Minister of Economic Development Mr Mohamed Saeed on January 2014, Minister of Agriculture and Fisheries Dr Mohamed Shainee in February 2014, Minister of Defence and National Security Col (retd) Mohamed Nazim in March 2014, and Minister of Islamic Affairs, Mr Mohamed Shaheem on April 2014.

High Level Visits

For over three decades, there has been an extensive amount of exchange of visits between the two countries ranging from Heads of State, Heads of Government to Ministers and other high level dignitaries. Former President His Excellency Maumoon Abdul Gayoom has visited India more than sixteen times in different capacities while just about every Prime Minister of India, starting from Prime Minister Indira Gandhi in January 1975, has undertaken Official/State Visits to the Maldives. The first State Visit abroad of the incumbent President of the Republic of Maldives, His Excellency Abdulla Yameen Abdul Gayoom was made to India. Most recent high level visit from India to Maldives was made by Minister of External Affairs His Excellency Salman Khurshid to participate at the South Asian Association of Regional Cooperation (SAARC) Inter-Summit.

Heads of State/Government Visits

The Maldives

In 1974, Prime Minister Mr Ahmed Zaki made an official visit to India.

In June 1980, His Excellency Mr Maumoon Abdul Gayoom, President of Maldives undertook his first bilateral visit to India. Since then he has undertaken four bilateral visits (February 1985, December 1988, September 1989 and March 1990), five state visits (September 1983, January 1991, March 1994 and August 2000, February 2008), and official visits from 27th March to 1st April, 2005 and 27th January, 2007 to 1st February, 2007 to attend the International Conference on "Peace, Non-Violence and Empowerment -Gandhian Philosophy in the 21st Century" convened by the Indian National Congress.

President Gayoom also visited India in March 1983 to attend the Seventh NAM Summit and in November 1986, May 1995 and April 2007, to attend the Second, the Eighth and Fourteenth SAARC Summits, respectively. In August 1991 and June/July 1998, President Gayoom visited India in his capacity as the Chairman of SAARC.

In June 1991, President Gayoom visited India to commiserate the Indian Government and the late Rajiv Gandhi's family following his assassination.

In December 2008, His Excellency Mohamed Nasheed, President of Maldives has undertaken a State Visit to India, which was his first visit abroad. President Nasheed later visited India thrice during his tenure in office. President Nasheed visited India in October 2009 to attend Delhi High Level Conference on Climate Change: Technology Development and Transfer, in October 2010 on official visit and in February 2011 on official visit.

Likewise first visit abroad by His Excellency Dr Mohamed Waheed, President of Maldives was to India, in May 2012.

The first State Visit abroad of the incumbent President of the Republic of Maldives, His Excellency Abdulla Yameen Abdul Gayoom was made to India in January 2014.

India

Prime Minister Indira Gandhi made an official visit to the Maldives in January 1975.

Successive Prime Minister's of India have undertaken official/ state visits to the Maldives since then: Prime Minister Rajiv Gandhi in February 1986, Prime Minister Vishwanath Pratap Singh in June 1990, Prime Minister Chandra Shekhar in November 1990 to attend the 5th SAARC Summit, Prime Minister P.V. Narasimha Rao in April 1995 for the formal joint opening of Indira Gandhi Memorial Hospital (IGMH), Prime Minister Inder Kumar Gujral May 1997 to attend the Ninth SAARC Summit, and Prime Minister Atal Bihari Vajpayee Maldives in September 2002. The latest being visit to Maldives by Prime Minister Dr Manmohan Singh in November 2011 to attend the Ninth SAARC Summit and on a bilateral visit.

Economic and Commercial Relations

India and Maldives signed a trade agreement in 1981, which provides for export of essential commodities. Growing from modest beginnings, India-Maldives bilateral trade now stands at Rs 700 crores. Indian exports to the Maldives include agriculture and poultry produce, sugar, fruits, vegetables, spices, rice, wheat flour (Atta), textiles, drugs and medicines, a variety of engineering and industrial products, sand and aggregate, cement for building etc. Indian imports primarily scrap metals from the Maldives. Under the bilateral agreement, India provides essential food items like rice, wheat flour, sugar, dal, onion, potato and eggs and construction material such as sand and stone aggregates to Maldives on favourable terms.

Bilateral Trade Agreements

Under the Bilateral Trade Agreement which was signed in 1981, both countries agreed to grant most favoured nation status to each other. Within the provisions of this agreement, India continues to provide certain commodities to Maldives which may even fall under

Bilateral Trade between India and Maldives

Figures (in Rupees Crores)

Year	*Total Exports to Maldives*	*Total Imports from Maldives*	*Total Trade*
2007-08	360.55	16.69	377.24
2008-09	590.28	17.93	608.21
2009-10	378.49	17.07	395.57
2010-11	455.54	145.43	600.97
2011-12	597.78	92.04	689.82
2012-13	666.21	34.22	700.43
2013-14	653.24	23.91	677.15

Source: http://www.mea.gov.in

the prohibited/restricted import categories in India. It should be taken into account that the main bulk of items such as rice, wheat flour, sugar, potatoes, onions, eggs, vegetables and other commodities such as river sand and construction materials are imported from India, increasingly making Maldives an attractive market for the growing Indian investors in this sector.

Trade with India

While the exports from Maldives to India are of not much significance, the imports from India to the Maldives are quite substantial. There has been a steady increase in the imports particularly during the last few years.

The Government of Maldives has liberalised trade and investment policies for foreign investors and there exist a favourable, investor-friendly business environment in the country. Likewise the booming Indian economy is open to investors in different sectors of development. For investment and business opportunities in Maldives and India, investors of either country could use business organisations and institutions as vehicles to promote their business entrepreneurship.

These bodies further provide a variety of business facilitation services by closely working with Government and business promotion organisations in India and the Maldives. They also play host to the high-level Government dignitaries who visit our two countries and help build close working relationships between Governments and business.

Major activities of these bodies include exchange of business delegations and joint task forces that help identify the bilateral business co-operation and its potentiality and make suitable policy recommendations to Governments. Business co-operation along with the inter-governmental undertakings is also facilitated through Government and business synergy by promoting business linkages for investment in tourism, trade and other joint ventures.

According to the latest trade data available, the value of total merchandise exports fell to $14.2 million at the end of February 2009, registering a monthly decrease of 19 per cent and a fall of 41 per cent compared to the corresponding month of 2008.

Total merchandise imports (f.o.b) totalled $59.7 million, declining by 19 per cent compared to the previous month while it fell by 56 per cent compared to the corresponding month of 2008. Thus, the trade deficit decreased to $45.6 million from $56.7 million in January 2009 and $113.1 million in February 2008.

Earnings on total merchandise exports during the first two months of 2009 stood at $31.6 million, indicating a drop of 46 per cent (or $27.5 million) compared to the same period of 2008. Similarly, the value of merchandise imports (f.o.b) for this period, which totalled $133.9 million, decreased by 45 per cent (or $108.6 million) over the corresponding period of 2008. Hence, the trade deficit stood at $102.3 million in comparison to $183.4 million in 2008.

Reflecting the slowdown in tourism activity, gross international reserves declined to $223.4 million at the end of the review month, from $224.6 million at the end of last month, although reserves in terms of import cover increased slightly to 2.1 months from 2.0 months in January 2009 due to the decline in imports. When compared with February 2008, gross international reserves showed a decline of $86.4 million while reserves in months of imports dropped by 0.9 months.[4]

Development Co-operation

State Bank of India has been playing a vital role in the economic development of the Maldives since February, 1974 by providing loan assistance for promotion of island resorts, export of marine products and business enterprises. Taj Group of India runs Taj Exotica Resort and Spa and Vivanta Coral Reef Resort.

Other commercial projects that are currently being undertaken by Indian companies in Maldives are as follows:

- Setting up of a 25 MW wind farm at an investment of $40 million in the Southern Province of Maldives by Suzlon Energy of India
- Construction of 1000 low-cost housing units in Malé by TATA Housing Development Co. Ltd (February 2010)
- Setting up for a 24-MW Solar Power Project by Bommidala Infrastructure (India) at an investment of $ 91 million (agreement signed with the Upper South Utility Limited, July 2010)
- Creation of a Unique Global Knowledge, Medical and Tourist Hub in Gan in Laamu Atoll of South Central Province by Island Development Company Pvt. Ltd. (IDC), a joint venture of Universal Empire Infrastructures Ltd., (UEIL) India, with Works Corporation of Maldives, (WCL) (June 2011)
- Handling of waste management in Malé Area ($49 million project) by Tatva Global Renewable Energy (July 2013)[5]

Assistance from the Maldives to India

Assistance from the Maldives in the recent past has been more in the nature of token gestures following natural disasters such as the earthquakes of 2001 in Gujarat, and in 2003 in Maharashtra, when the Government of Maldives provided $ 25,000 on each occasion. In addition limited training opportunities were provided to teachers from Minicoy in Dhivehi Language and vocational training and adult education for a 2-member team from India.

Assistance from India to the Maldives

Assistance from India to the Maldives has been largely through grant aid projects, human resource development through long-term scholarships and training, technical assistance and deputation of experts.

Project Assistance

Major infrastructure projects that have been implemented include, the Indira Gandhi Memorial Hospital (IGMH) Project, the Maldives Institute of Techncial Education Project, Population and Development Consolidation Programme, and the restoration of the Dharumavantha Rasgefaanu Miskiiy Project, and the faculty of Hospitality and Tourism Studies.

The most significant assistance in the recent past has been the $ 40 million line of credit for the housing sector.

The on-going projects include the Maldives Mapping and National GIS Development Project, Hulhumale' greening and Hulhumale' breakwater projects, Strengthening National Planning Capacity Project.

Wherever possible, India has been offering assistance to Maldives in its developmental process. The major projects executed by India in Maldives are as follows:

(i) Indira Gandhi Memorial Hospital (IGMH)

During former Prime Minister Shri Rajiv Gandhi's visit to Male' in 1986, it was agreed to establish a medical complex in Male' with Indian assistance. Accordingly, the 200-bed hospital was established at an estimated cost of Rs 42.5 crores and inaugurated in April 1995. IGMH, Male now serves as the most advanced tertiary care hospital in Maldives and is easily the most visible symbol of India's assistance to the Maldives. Though at present, the Government of Maldives is responsible for managing/running the hospital, Government of India continues to offer substantial assistance to the institution. During the visit of Hon'ble Prime Minister of India

Dr Manmohan Singh to Maldives in November 2011, Government of India signed an agreement to undertake major renovation of IGMH at a total cost of Rs 37.24 crores.

(ii) Faculty of Engineering Technology (FET)

Maldives Institute of Technical Education (MITE) was set up as a grant-in-aid project of Government of India in 1996. Having a capacity to train at least 200 students a year in various technical/ vocational disciplines, MITE was renamed as Faculty of Engineering Technology (FET) in order to better reflect the academic programmes conducted by it, is functioning well.

Tsunami Related Assistance

Following the tsunami waves that hit Maldives on the morning of 26th December, 2004, India was the first country to rush relief and aid to the Maldives. A Coast Guard Dornier aircraft arrived on the morning of 27th December followed by two Indian Air Force Avros carrying relief materials on the same day. All the aircraft stayed back to continue their relief operations in the Maldives. INS *Mysore* carrying relief material, facilities for a 20-bed hospital and two helicopters arrived on December 28. She was joined by INS *Udaygiri* and INS *Aditya* on December 29.

The ships operated in the most affected Southern Atolls. The ships delivered foodstuff and medicines, treated patients in a field hospital set up by their medics, undertook repair of electricity generators and communication equipments and also evacuated patients in the ship borne helicopters when required. The total cost of India's relief operations has been estimated at Rs 36.39 crores. Government of India also sanctioned a budget support aid of Rs 10 crores to Maldives in 2005 in response to President Gayoom's request for financial help in view of the serious financial difficulties Maldives was facing on account of the tsunami and related factors.

Again in 2007, following President Gayoom's appeal in the aftermath of tidal surges in Maldives, Government of India gave cash assistance of Rs 10 crores.[6]

$ 40 million Line of Credit for Housing Sector

In December 2010, Government of India announced a new Line of Credit (LOC) worth $ 40 million to the Government of Maldives for construction of 500 housing units. The LOC on a two per cent concessional interest rate with a repayment period of 20 years is to be facilitated through EXIM (Export-Import) Bank of India. An agreement on the LOC was signed between the EXIM BANK and the Government of Maldives in August 2011 and actual construction work is expected to commence shortly.

Human Resources Development

Indian assistance to the Maldives in the area of Human Resources Development is through long-term and short-term training under three main schemes - Indian Technical Education Cooperation (ITEC) Programme, Aid to Maldives Programme and Commonwealth Programme. The areas of specialisation for long-term training include, medicine, social sciences, commerce, IT and defence related studies, while short-term training include IT, computer studies and other technical and vocational training programmes.

Bilateral Agreements between India and Maldives

Agreement	*Date Signed*
Exchange of Letters on Extending the Memorandum of Understanding on Manpower Requirements of the Indira Gandhi Memorial Hospital	2 January 2014
Memorandum of Understanding on Cooperation in the field of Health	2 January 2014
Agreement on the Transfer of Sentenced Persons	12 November 2011
Memorandum of Understating on Combating International Terrorism, Illicit Drug Trafficking and Enhancing Bilateral Cooperation in Capacity Building, Disaster Management and Coastal Security	12 November 2011
Memorandum of Understating on Renovation of Indira Gandhi Memorial Hospital	12 November 2011
Programme of Cooperation for the years 2012-2015	12 November 2011
Agreement on the Standby Credit Facility	12 November 2011
Agreement on the Transfer of Sentenced Persons	12 November 2011
Agreement on co-operation in the field of Science and Technology	11 February 2008
MOU on Cooperation in Information Technology	8 September 2003
Agreement for Recognition of Certificates Under the Terms of the International Convention on Standards of Training, Certification and Watchkeeping for Seafarers 1978, as amended in 1995	March 2003

(Contd.)

(Contd. Table)

Agreement	*Date Signed*
Tripartite Agreement between the Republic of Maldives; Ministry of External Affairs, Government of India; and Educational Consultants India Limited (EDCIL), New Delhi	12 January 2000
Bilateral Agreement on Mutual Administrative Assistance for the Proper Application of Customs' Laws and for the Prevention, Investigation and Combating Customs Offences	25 March 1999
MOU Concerning Manpower Requirements of IGMH	15 April 1991
Agreement on Economic and Technical Co-operation	7 February 1986
Cultural Co-operation Agreement	7 September 1983
Trade Agreement	31 March 1981
Air Services Agreement	5 November 1979
Visa Understanding	11 March 1979
Agreement on Maritime Boundary in the Arabian Sea and Related Matters	28 December 1976

Source: Embassy of Maldives, New Delhi http://www.maldiveshighcom.in/common.php?flg=Agreements

Technology Adoption Programme in Education Sector

In January 2011, Government of India signed an agreement with the Government of Maldives for a $5.30 million project fully funded by the GoI towards Technology Adoption Programme in Education Sector in Maldives. The project, currently executed by NIIT and EEEC (India) over a 27 month period (2011-2013), has completed more than 4000 certifications benefitting around 2,300 Maldivian teachers and youth across islands in the country.

Air Connectivity

Air India operates daily flights to Malé from Thiruvananthapuram, Bangalore and Chennai. Island Aviation Service (Maldivian Aero) is operating daily flights to Thiruvananthapuram, Mumbai and Chennai. In November 2012, Spice Jet of India started daily commercial operations on the Male-Cochin sector.

The proximity of location and improvements in air connectivity in recent years has led to a very substantial increase in the number of Indians visiting Maldives for tourism (around 30,000) and business purposes. Likewise, the number of Maldivians seeking long-term visa for pursuing higher studies/medical treatment in India has also shown a sharp increase over the last two years.[7]

Cultural Relations

Both the countries share long cultural links and continuous efforts are underway to further strengthen these linkages. Three historical mosques (Friday Mosque and Dharumavantha Rasgefaanu Mosque - Male', Fenfushi Mosque - South Ari Atoll) were successfully restored by Indian experts from NRLCCP, Lucknow. Exchange of cultural troupes takes place regularly between the countries. Hindi commercial films, TV serials and music are immensely popular in Maldives.

The India Cultural Center (ICC), established in Male in July 2011, conducts regular courses in yoga, classical music and dance. ICC programmes have become immensely popular among Maldivians of all ages.

Tourism

The Number of Indian Tourists visiting the Maldives remained at an average of 11,000 per year since 2002. There has not been any increase primarily due to lack of direct air connections to the Maldives from India other than from Trivandrum. Also traditionally the tourism sector in the Maldives has focussed on the European and the Japanese market and therefore no adequate promotions or marketing carried out in India. However, following the tsunami of 2004 and the subsequent slump in the tourist arrivals, greater efforts are being made to attract Indian tourists to the Maldives.

Indian investments in the tourism sector in the Maldives is significant. State Bank of India has been playing a vital role in the economic development of the Maldives since February 1974, by providing loan assistance for promotion of tourism industry. While the Taj Group operates two resorts Taj Exotica & Spa and Vivanta Corel Reef Resort in the Maldives, there are other individuals and companies from India who have also invested in the tourism sector in the Maldives.

Defence Cooperation

Both countries certainly have a long and proud record of strengthening their defence ties through a wide range of activities. The Maldives and India have been conducting a series of Coast Guard maritime joint training exercises codenamed "DOSTI" since 1991 in addition to other joint defence interactions. These bi-annual Maldives – India DOSTI exercises were initiated with the objective of strengthening cooperation between the Coast Guards of both countries, with a view to enhance mutual capabilities for search and rescue operations, combating piracy and armed robbery, damage control and casual evacuation at sea for safer seas. The joint training exercise expanded to include Sri Lanka which resulted in having bi-annual "Trilateral Joint Coast Guard Exercises". In addition, a joint army training exercise to enhance the close military ties codenamed "Ekuverin" exists between the Maldives and India. A large number of defence services personnel from the Maldives are trained in various defence establishments in India every year. Consequently, Indian armed forces have played an instrumental role and have closely worked with the Maldivian counterparts to enhance the overall defence and security capability of the Maldives.[8]

Collaboration in Science and Technology

Another important emerging area highlighting the relations between the two countries is the collaboration and assistance in the field of Science and Technology. Efforts are being made in the Maldives to keep pace with the advances in the area of science and technology and to make the most out of the growing potential to the benefit of our citizens in all walks of life. The tremendous achievements made by India in this field would be a source of immense benefit to the Maldives in its efforts to develop this important area.

Tension Areas between India and Maldives

The Maldives has shared the views of India and endeavoured to support India on various regional and international issues. To mention a few, in the late 1980s, unlike its some other members, Maldives held the viewpoint and shared India's apprehension pertinent to opposing changes to the Charter of South Asian Association for Regional Cooperation (SAARC) relating to bilateral issues. Moreover, the Maldives also shares common views on a range of international issues of mutual interest such as environmental protection, international peace, fight against terrorism and UN reform. Most recently, the Maldives has assured to India that it would extend its "full support" to India's entry into the United Nation's Security Council as a permanent member.

Conclusion

In spite of Maldives and India facing some common issues such as maritime security, terrorism, and enhanced defense and economic co-operation, both the countries have rather managed well to take the relationship to a higher benchmark. It is expected that, in the intermediate to long-term, the relationship will witness further upward swing for a more durable and win-win proposition.

References

1. International politics, Rumki Basu.
2. India's relations with her neighbours, Ramesh Trivedi, Gyan Publishing House, 2008.
3. http://www.maldiveshighcom.in/common.php?flg=relation
4. http://www.maldiveshighcom.in/common.php?flg=Trade
5. http://www.mea.gov.in/Portal/ForeignRelation/India-Maldives_Relations.pdf
6. http://mea.gov.in/Portal/ForeignRelation/Maldives-January-2012.pdf
7. http://www.mea.gov.in/Portal/ForeignRelation/India-Maldives_Relations.pdf
8. http://www.maldiveshighcom.in/common.php?flg=relation

7

India-Pakistan Relations: A Conundrum

Veena Ravikumar

In the international relations of South Asia, India and Pakistan form unhappy components of the large, almost continental, mass. The history of both impinge on each other so much that they impact the rest of the nations in this region. The complexity of the relationship is so much that hardened analysts have give up the hope of any solution, while cynics say this will just go on and there is no end to the skirmishing over small issues and of course, big ones.

History

The main problem is based on history. History has interceded and interfered with the growth of both these nations. United precariously, while a segment spoke tenuously about the two-nations theory, its advantages and disadvantages, both India and Pakistan were at a disadvantage. More so, Pakistan. Pakistan, since its inception, began searching for its national identity. There seemed to be an inordinate overlapping of regional and religious identity articulated most clearly by the Pashtun nationalist Wali Khan nearly two decades ago when he declared that he had been a Pashtun for 4000 years, a Muslim for 1400 years and a Pakistani for 40 years.[1]

Six decades later, the question remains whether Pakistan is a land for Muslims or a nation of Muslims moving towards its destiny as an Islamic state? The notion of language and religion became a Pandora's box of conflicting identities. Unfortunately, the problem still persists.

State Structure - Authoritarian Rule - Islam

Another problem is that the centrist state structures reinforce imposition from above of Pakistani nationalism and 'Punjabisation' of the state. This is a common allegation pointed at the state. Bouts of authoritarian rule have reinforced centrifugal ethnic, linguistic and regional forces. This was seen in the Bangladesh crisis, 1971. After this, in a bid to consolidate themselves, both Zulfikar Ali Bhutto and Zia-ul-Haq turned to populism through Islam. This was also to strengthen their sense of national identity. Populism raised even higher expectations which could not be adequately met by an increasingly authoritarian regime; Islam turned out to be far more complex and brought about more religious divisions.

General Ayub Khan, before relinquishing power also explored the religious option but his successors did more than that. General Yahya Khan imposed martial rule and made sure that the army would never ever play second fiddle to a civil dispensation. The Proclamation of Legal Framework Order, 1970, also emphasised the higher role of the Pakistani army. When Zulfikar Ali Bhutto ignored Mujib-ur-Rehman's majority of the Awami League, which won 160 seats and 39.2 per cent of the votes, the role of the army became important. The crucial point being that powerful role of the military has always been a painful chapter in the peace-making between India and Pakistan. The idea of one state, India, being democratic in nature with an electorate, participative majority and a Pakistan with high degree of Islamisation, not a bad thing in itself, but manipulating the concept of Islam makes a case for a skewed power situation. This asymmetry is not conducive towards a healthy relationship between India and Pakistan.

The idea of a new state being created, that is, Bangladesh in 1971, brought out all Pakistani's anger and ire. The idea that the Indian army had trained the East Pakistan army, the Mukti Bahini, was intolerable. It was not recognised that the East Pakistani rebellion was a popular movement against West Pakistan and what it stood for: a different language— Punjabi and Urdu in West Pakistan while in East Pakistan Bengali was the dominant language; perception of West Pakistan which entailed looking down upon East Pakistanis as puny, un-handsome while they thought of themselves as tall and strapping. Culturally, West Pakistan was far more connected to the Middle East while East Pakistan to West Bengal in India, so much so that on Eid, there would be decorations with Rangoli (a very Indian tradition) and Rabindra Sangeet. This definitely brought about a chasm. When the West Pakistani army assaulted the East Pakistani students and intellectuals at the outset and massacred them, the Indian army under the leadership of General Sam Manekshaw, stepped in and helped quell West Pakistan atrocities. It was not an overly long campaign in East Pakistan: General Niazi surrendered to General Jagjit Singh Aurora and General J F R Jacob at Ramna Race Course in Dacca on December 16, 1971. The surrender was accepted, with dignity. But the disfiguring of the Pakistani state, the division between the two made for bitterness on the part of Pakistan towards India. This is probably the second most earth-shaking event in the history of Pakistan after the traumatic events of the Partition. Even the 1965 war did not evoke this kind of anger towards India because the Pakistan military thought of itself as having won the war.

Lack of Democratic Culture

Lack of democratic culture is the real reason for the army gaining inordinate power in Pakistan. Further, at the time of partition, the class interest of those who came to power militated against the establishment of a truly democratic state. Their motive was not to establish good self-government, but to escape majority rule (the Hindus) in undivided India. Pakistani politics had no mass base; leadership was scattered and weak. Therefore, everything pointed to a strong centre. Lack of electoral politics inhibited growth of political parties.

Even though Zulfikar Ali Bhutto's creation, the Pakistan People's Party, was a symbol of democracy yet eventually it was not so effective. In fact, he almost became feudal in rule and centrist. He also used the 'K' word, the Kashmir word to rouse hatred against India. After the 1965 India-Pakistan war, the notion of hate India syndrome was very much in Bhutto's vocabulary. This was in cognisance of the aggressive posture of the Pakistan army.

Lieutenant General Assad Durrani, the former director of ISI, did reveal that money was passed on for distribution amongst politicians to ensure defeat of Benazir Bhutto (about Rs 60 million). General Hamid Gul created the Islamic Jamhoori Iltehad (IJI) to oppose PPP. With all this activity, the role of the Pakistani army only increased. So much so that they lost the main picture and probably did more harm to their own nation.

Omar Norman, a political analyst, talks about political processes in Pakistan being shaped by four factors. First, failure of the Muslim League to transform itself in to a national party (such as the Congress Party did in India for quite a few years); second, a highly centralised form of government (which India cannot do in all fairness); three, Punjabi and Muhajir elite virtually monopolised decision-making in Pakistan (impossible in India with different castes, affiliations and alliances) and finally, growth of regional tensions as the primary source of political conflict (admittedly, India as a neighbour has created regional rivalry and conflict in South Asia.[2]

Moreover, Pakistan took seven years to frame a constitution and automatically brought about a pre-eminence of the executive. This is what they called 'controlled democracy'. In this atmosphere, within 1953-58, Pakistan had six Prime Ministers and all were removed through intrigues. The 1956 Constitution was abrogated on September 7, 1958. Any kind of going back to political cohesiveness was marked by petty intrigues and squabbles. Justifying military intervention, General Ayub Khan said, 'the army alone could act as a coercive force and restore normalcy'. This became the cornerstone of Pakistan's army policy.

Militarisation of Pakistan Army

Militarisation of Pakistan not only hurt India-Pakistan relations, but also the Pakistani state itself. The Pakistani army, with its own sense of 'machismo', dealt with its internal affairs with as heavy a hand as it did with external policy. Nonetheless, it did cultivate good relations with United States, so much so that the phrase 'Army, Allah, America!' became synonymous with decision-making in Pakistan.

1989-99 was the period of 'guided democracy'. The military in Pakistan was behind the scenes in decision-making in foreign policy and defence affairs. Benazir Bhutto, too, had to give in. This is implicit in her book, *'Daughter of the East'*. The President was sometimes powerful and sometimes not, in collaboration with the army or manipulated. The press was mostly muzzled.

Islam became a force in building the nation and ideology of Pakistan. Religion was to be a unifier, an integral part of the theocratic state that Pakistan wanted to build. With mass mobilisation of a large number of illiterate electorate, it became a matter of primordial identity. Moreover, it became an instrument of political legitimacy.

How can a nation with the absolutist form of a particular religion befriend a neighbour with a very different religion? This is a fundamentally an esoteric question, one of both metaphysics and politics. Both nations will have to rise above it but that is easier said than done.

During the Soviet invasion of Afghanistan, religion in Pakistan became a weapon to oppose communist ideology. At the same time, Talibanisation of Afghanistan fiercely resisted the then Soviets in their soil and it spread to Pakistan too. After the Soviet withdrawal, the Taliban became an important force and managed to have an impact on Pakistan's politics and society.

But also, religion, as said earlier, was coinage to legitimise political power. In fact, in 1965, Ayub Khan had allegedly taken the help of religious groups to issue a 'fatwa' or dicta to delegitimise Fatima Jinnah's coming to power. He was convinced that women cannot become the head of an Islamic state. He cultivated the Pirs to seek political legitimacy. In a different scenario under Yahya Khan's rule in 1971, he called upon the Ulema's support the government for army action in East Pakistan. Pakistan got close to the Middle East in the 'Islamic Socialism' aspect. Again, the point here is Pakistan wanting to prove its religious identity with the Middle East, getting funds from them for its nuclear projects and wary of being a part of the South Asian fraternity. Maybe that insecurity can be understood because of the dominance of India in South Asia.

Even the 1970 elections were fought mainly on the premise of anti-Indianism. Islamic revivalism took a radical turn in the 1970s because of the revolution in Iran, the Arab-Israel war and the Soviet interventions in Afghanistan and the growth of Madrassas. In April 1977, Z.A. Bhutto announced the Shariat laws banning horse racing and alcohol, declaring Friday as the official holiday in keeping with Islamic ideology (July 1, 1977). Was Islamisation of Z.A. Bhutto a matter of regime survival? Probably, yes.

During Zia-ul-Haq's period, Islam was aggressively used to consolidate his power, legitimise his rule and exclude any threat to his government. Zia's reign was a mix of the military and religion. In 1979, he banned all forms of political activities. He tried to consolidate his rule with the help of fundamentalist groups. In December 1, 1984, Zia announced elections. The main issue was Islamisation for Pakistan and support of the Islamic ideology, which would usher rule of Islamic values. All laws passed by the Majlis-i-Shoora, would be reviewed by the Federal Shariat court, to see if they were not repugnant to Islam. In keeping with Zia-ul-Haq's religious and military philosophy, his attitude towards India was essentially hostile. He regarded India as a Hindu state and an adversary. Intolerance and violence received encouragement during his regime, which was also rooted, at least partly, in the frustrations arising from the poor electoral performance of the religious parties.[3]

One of the most controversial among Zia-ul-Haq's Islamisation programmes was the introduction of the Hudood ordinances imposing Islamic penalties for certain offences. Here, the Pakistani Sunnis' and Shias' differences came up. The Blasphemy Law was the terrible confinement of religious freedom and ending culture of tolerance and freedom of expression, 'deliberate and malicious acts intended to outrage religious feelings of any class by insulting its religious beliefs'. Sayid Farooq, who actually knew the Koran by rote and was a religious person, was stoned to death by a mob who claimed he had burnt the Koran.[4] Considering this, the Indian reaction was extreme, too, for fear of an advance to stabilizing relations. How could it not be?

Of course, the same holds good where Pakistan is considered after the 2002 Godhra riots. The aftermath brought about a bloodbath in Gujarat and fingers pointing to the state government rule under Narendra Modi and the sharp resentment and division between the Hindus and Muslims and the impact on Indian foreign policy was seen. With religious intolerance seen on both sides, it is a zero sum game most of the time. Nevertheless, in the history of nations, neighbours have to make efforts to repair relations despite obstacles to their doing so.

Kashmir

Yet, there is no getting away from the fact that Kashmir has been the largest thorn in India-Pakistan relations. Disputed territory from the onset of Partition, it would take several books to lay out this problem in all its complexity. But it might do to observe it as a huge problem not conducive to the betterment of relations between India and Pakistan. In fact, it has provoked wars in 1948, 1965, threatened war in1987 and led to sporadic fighting from 1984 onwards on the Siachen glacier and in Kargil 1999, till today a site of dispute. The 1974 Indian nuclear implosion brought more insecurities to Pakistan; it increased regional rivalry and upped the arms trade. The danger of nuclear conflict persisted in the 1990s, even when both India and Pakistan attained nuclear status in May of 1998. Though the confrontation in Kargil in 1999 could have brought in high rancour to the nuclear locking point, it did not. Both the nations displayed maturity, especially India, since it did not make air forays into Pakistan territory.

This distrust and actual skirmish which was seen in the Kargil conflict, the architect of which was General Parvez Musharraf, created again, more distrust in Indians as the lines to Lahore from

New Delhi had taken place and the famous embrace between Mr Vajpayee and Mr Nawaz Sharif had taken place at the Nazar-e-Sharif. This was taken by India as a huge betrayal.

Kashmir has and always will remain the 'hot' point between India and Pakistan. This is why the escalation of hostilities in the 1990s, with the result that development of South Asia as a region is not possible, for the most part investment in defence gets high as compared to infrastructure and resource projects (India's is $ 47.4 billion and Pakistan's is $ 5.7 billion).[5] In the 21st century as well, tempers and motivations are as high as before with a resurgence of the debate as to whether the Instrument of Accession had been signed before Indian troops were sent to Jammu and Kashmir.

Unfortunately, the identity of both India and Pakistan got linked with Kashmir. Sir Radcliffe did a disservice to both India and Pakistan and then to Israel and Palestine, drawing false, whimsical boundaries and making them huge problems of self-determination. This kind of origin of a leftover of the British paramountcy reduced India's chances of friendship.

Maybe a kind of frigidity also came about between 1971 (Bangladesh crisis) and 1991 (foreign secretary level talks) more for a number of historical reasons but definitely the rancour over Kashmir, both emotive and real existed. The existence of India-Pakistan peace process is evidenced by several factors. First, both countries have regularly engaged in bilateral talks to resolve differences on a wide range of issues: border demarcation, boundary adjustment, water distribution, trade and commerce issues, protection of minorities, Kashmir, conventional and nuclear confidence building measures (CBMs). Since 1977, all these issues have been discussed as a part of composite dialogue invoking eight issues: peace and security including CBMs, Jammu and Kashmir, Siachen, Sir Creek, Tulbul, Wullar, Baghlihar and Kishenganga water projects; terrorism and drug trafficking, economic and commercial promotion of friendly exchanges in various forms. Both India and Pakistan do have a fairly compliance oriented record.[5]

Besides the near nuclear crisis between India and Pakistan, 1986-87 Brasstacks, 1990 Kashmir crisis, 1999 Kargil War and 2002 eyeball-to-eyeball confrontation, there have been border skirmishes and conflicts of a lesser nature.

According to Howard Wriggins, this has to do with Pakistan's insecurity vis-a-vis India's size, political and economic predominance in the region. "However unjustified Indian leaders may have thought it, Pakistan's overriding concern vis-a-vis India is the fear of India's size, the size of its army... and fear compounded out of not infrequent public statements by prominent Indians regarding the tragedy of partition and reiterating the inherent unity of the subcontinent."[6]

Above all, it is the unresolved issue of Kashmir that is the most important one hanging over any kind of confrontation or peace-making aspects in India-Pakistan relations. Territorially, Kashmir cannot be touched. Each political party in India or Pakistan will lose its constituency of perceived to be giving away any part of territory. Soft borders have been agreed upon and complied with mostly. The Line of Control came into usage, reluctantly complied with by the former foreign secretary and diplomat Mr J.N. Dixit.[7] It meant a small concession, but a concession nevertheless. More steps were in the pipeline but for the fall of the Musharaff regime in 2008.

The most number of CBMs took place in 1990s, one of which was a flag meeting of military commanders at the LoC (1999) and another was the exchange of lists of nuclear facilities (1992); both were important steps in peace negotiations.[8]

In spite of these measures in place, intermittent firing takes place as a matter of course, soldiers on both sides die, as a matter of course. And the 'K' word never recedes from the frame. On September 20, 2014, Bilawal Bhutto made his speech at a Sind function where he said that he would wrest back the whole of Kashmir since it belonged to Pakistan. It may have been an election gimmick, but he invoked the soul of his dead, martyred mother Benazir Bhutto and went into full force against India.[9] "I will take back Kashmir, all of it, and I will not leave behind a single inch of it because, like the other provinces, it belongs to Pakistan", said Bilawal Bhutto addressing PPP workers. Former Prime Ministers, Yousaf Raza Gilani and Raja Pervaiz Asharaf flanked him at the event. India, of course, reacted to this saying that Bilawal's remarks were "far from reality which takes us back into the past century", said Syed Akbaruddin, External Affairs Ministry spokesperson. In the same vein, BJP spokesperson Shahnawaz Hussain said, "Kashmir is very much a part of India and will remain so. Any discussion on it is not acceptable to us. Kashmir resides in the hearts of Indians."[10]

There is an almost unreal scenario that exists with the problem of Kashmir on both sides of the border. On the Indian side, some Kashmiris who want to break away from the Indian state see inaction and malfeasance in every action of the Indian government. Article 370, which gave J and K special status has aroused jealousy and ire in the rest of India, making it out as if Kashmir is special and is being granted these special rights. But in actual fact, Kashmir is special. It is a frontline state with the problems of one. Having mentioned plebiscite once at the United Nations and withdrawn it, Jawaharlal Nehru was thought to be emotional and at fault. Today, the contemporary situation is such that Kashmiris want 'Azadi'. There are various autonomy packages that have been presented, but without success. Every situation gets politicised, so much so that even the Indian Army and Air Force disaster relief efforts became suspect and while being helped, some threw stones at these soldiers. There were heart-rending scenes of water rising to third floor, carcasses floating, men, women and actually no children, lost their lives and yet resentment prevailed. It is understandable to a certain extent as the Kashmiri countryside is blotted with the army (around 3,37,000).[14] Human rights violations were many by the army. No doubt appropriate action was taken but it had left scars with the local population, almost as a conquering army does. When at the core of contestation lies the militarisation of Kashmir, it is natural that the relationship between India and Pakistan is bedevilled by many further layers of resentment and anxiety.

Stephen Cohen cites an observation by G. Parthasarathy, a former Indian High Commissioner to Pakistan that an India-Pakistan reconciliation is like trying to treat two patients whose only disease is an allergy to each other.[11]

Jihad and Kashmir

Kashmir is the reason for some of the Pakistanis to think of Jihad. Ayesha Jalal in her book '*Partisans of Allah- Jehad in South Asia*' begins with lack of elementary spirituality in the different calls to prayers.[12] Once a simple, beautiful and melodious invocation of the divine, the 'Azan' (call) according to her, is in danger of becoming nothing but a shrill and strident display of human arrogance. She underlines the distinction between religion as faith and religion as a demarcation of difference and in this treatise is trying to gain a deeper understanding of religion as faith, wherein she discovers the intrinsic connection between the concept of Jihad as endeavour and the Muslim faith.[18] In the Unitarian Islamic view, faith in one God is balanced by an ethical conception of life. The Quranic emphasis on egalitarianism promotes a God-centric humanism, as distinct from the anthropocentric standard of the secular West.[13] She debates and agonises over the concept of jihad as the "holy war" against infidels, as it is in contemporary connotation.

Jihad in Kashmir ostensibly is waging war to liberate the fellow co-religionists. Even the Lashkar-e-Taiba, now a banned organisation, arose for this purpose. *Jihad* today is a pliable instrument in the hands of a few who are more politically motivated than ethically grounded.[14] Of course, Jalal wants to tease out the shifting interpretations of *Jihad* in different historical phases to restore its essential meaning as an ethical struggle to be human and not as a disequilibrium force to plague the contemporary world.[15]

Her analysis, no doubt deep, is truly academic and agonised, but the call for *Jihad* in Kashmir emanated from both a deep hatred of the 'other', the Hindus in Kashmir, and a deeper sense of entitlement to the territory in Kashmir. Lashkar-e-Taiba played on this particular aspect, brought out in its own publication '*Jehad in the Present Times*'. It targets the English speaking and makes for a substantial case of *jihad* in Kashmir replete with references to history of the *jihad* in Kashmir and suitable quotations from the Hadith, the Quran and Sayyid Ahmad's and Shah Ismail's writings.[16] There is, moreover, a dogged insistence on *jihad* in Kashmir. While admitting that the international situation is not conducive to *jihad*, Vazirabadi's appeal for Jihad is endorsed by Hafiz Saeed and incidentally ISI (Inter-Services Intelligence), that Pakistan can become the strongest force in the subcontinent by helping the Kashmiris.[23] Saeed categorically asserts that freeing Kashmir from India will result in the success of other Muslim dissidence movements in the world.[17] Restoring Kashmir as 'Dar-ul-Islam' and merging it with Pakistan would secure both of them, as well as Afghanistan from the threat posed by Hinduism. The legitimacy of Pakistan to plot the demise of India was full blown and therefore, also, the legitimacy of *jihad*.

Further, the idea of Islam as a dominant faith and a way of life gave the forces of jihad complete rights in Kashmir. The jihadists of Kashmir were also inducted through the Hizbul Mujahideen in Afghanistan. They too, had the major aim of resting Kashmir. The fact they were jihadists trained by the Al Qaeda made them more determined and dangerous. The aim of bringing in the argument of the jihadist movement is to project the danger that is Lashkar-e-Taiba, a banned organisation spreading militancy in the Kashmir Valley. With this hardened stance and factor and insidious role of the ISI, is it not somewhat impossible to keep aside these very factors, keeping in mind India-Pakistan relations? It is but as a neighbour, and as a part of the enhanced notion of South Asia, it is imperative to bury the hatchet. India offered assistance to Pakistan for the floods in August 2014. Kashmir too was devastated by floods, even so rumours were rife about the commendable role by the Indian Armed Forces. They were suspect even while they rehabilitated the populace. On the other hand, Kashmiri Hindus and rest of India heard rumours of militants not allowing food and medicines to reach the distressed.

Kargil in 1999 made all this suspicious. Having quietly gathered equipment in terms of military hardware, winter gear, eight helipads and on a surprise on India left India feeling. It was definitely an obstacle in bettering India-Pakistan relations. The nuclearisation of both India and Pakistan in May 1998 added fuel to the fire. If the *jihad* in Kashmir is any indication of the complex, intricate and incomplete, problematique, nuclearisation is even more so. In Robert Jervis' theoretical mode, the arms race as a spiral dilemma encouraged Pakistan to develop nuclear weapons as a so-called response to India's nuclear explosion, first in 1974 and then in 1998.[18] It was truly a security dilemma for Pakistan and it needed to have this gap bridged.

It was truly a security dilemma for Pakistan and it needed to have this gap bridged. The advent of nuclear weapons dramatically altered the India-Pakistan relationship, generating a surge of hostility between them. Yet, the trends of globalisation made economic cooperation and change possible. However, it did not push aside terrorism. Even though both states were nuclear and the Kargil war had taken place where Pakistan still claimed that the intruders were 'freedom fighters' did not hack up its troops when theprey were forced to retreat. Both India and Pakistan did not want to escalate the situation with nuclear power ascribed to them. Nevertheless, in December 2001, another crisis broke out when terrorists attacked India's Parliament and India angrily threatened to retaliate.[10]

Both sides mobilised fully along the entire border and this happened again in 2004 and again in late 2008 when a small group of Pakistan-based terrorists held hostages in Mumbai city and also killed 170 people with small arms. This created an immeasurable amount of tension between India and Pakistan and practically all talks broke down. Ostensibly, the blame of the terrorists was laid down at the feet of the ISI, an arm of the Pakistan Army. Government of India sent over a dossier and the Government of Pakistan questioned the finer points. Again, a near breakdown of the India-Pakistan relationship took place.

Coming back to the nuclear question, from 1947 to about 1977, only a few nuclear scientists and bureaucrats urged Pakistan to producc nuclear weapons. But after India's nuclear test in 1974, there was an urgency to acquire it. And under General Zia-ul-Haq it became imperative. After this, every senior Pakistani civilian and military official internalised the criticality of the acquisition of nuclear power.

The United States turned a blind eye to Pakistan's nuclearisation, mainly, as a balance to Soviet Union. The U.S. was guarding its interests in Afghanistan and looking for a 'balancer' in South Asia. Considering the interests of both powers like the U.S. and Soviet Union in South Asia, both India and Pakistan felt insecure and one can atleast certainly try to understand the security-insecurity paradox. This could have brought India and Pakistan closer but it did not.

Pakistan's policy, of course, was accelerated with India's 1974 nuclear implosion and covertly, under Dr A.Q. Khan's supervision Pakistan built its nuclear weapons. Yet, despite its all the troubles and hardships that Pakistan obtained, they ironically did not play a major role in the country's security calculus beyond enhancing a vague notion of deterrence during deep crisis with India in the 1980s and 1990s. Military thinking remained focused on conventional weapons fighting. Even with the possession of existential nuclear deterrent capability, defence planners preferred to reply on asymmetric strategies that were deemed to be cheaper options in Kashmir and Afghanistan via the Taliban. Pakistan players failed to understand the implications of pursuing a proxy war strategy in their own neighbourhood. Supporting these insurgencies under the nuclear shadow as a regional policy had the risk of blowback. This strategy was dangerous given the fact that the possession of nuclear capabilities was itself isolating Pakistan and evoking sanctions.[20]

Pakistan, pursuing its acquisition had an unprecedented consequence for nuclear proliferation. Pakistani policy-makers did not expect their lax nuclear oversight would create the permissive environment, which enabled A.Q. Khan and his colleagues to establish his far-reaching nuclear supply network.[21] But it did and even today Pakistan is paying the price.

Musharaff's takeover as Army Chief in 1998 was under tense regional and domestic atmosphere. As mentioned earlier, the Kargil conflict, a high intensity one took place in 1999. Musharaff took power on October 12, 1999. Nuclear weapons played an important part in his policy orientation.[22]

The economic revival of Pakistan became his focus since Pakistan was almost mentioned as a 'failed state'. But after September 11, 2001, the attacks on the twin towers in New York, and the attack on the Pentagon, Pakistan became an ally of the U.S. in the war on terror. This saved Pakistan from failing and it made an economic turn around by courtesy of the U.S. bases being established in Pakistan. Immediately after 9/11, when confronted with the choice of reversing course on Afghanistan and abandoning the Taliban, preserving Pakistan's strategic assets was a key factor in his decision to join the U.S. led coalition.

There were many challenges Musharaff had to deal with the U.S. as an ally; India had to be somewhat mollified after Kargil; Afghanistan's Taliban had to be constrained and most of all, needed to direct an overtly nuclearised Pakistan. The trajectory, nuclear and otherwise had to be firmly in place, no mean task. The Indian nuclear tests of May 11 and 13, 1998 and the reply-back of Pakistan on May 28 and 30, 1998 at Chagai, no doubt was satisfying and vested parity and yet insecurity, from the situation, but the 9/11 was curiously a stabiliser in the relations between India and Pakistan as both were drawn into the war on terrorism.

President Musharraf, ironically did both things— dialoguing and following aggressive policies. For example, the Agra summit (after Kargil), the Confidence Building Measures 2006 (post a vicious stand-off in 2004 at the border).

The most insidious attack was, of course, as mentioned earlier in Mumbai 2008 when it traumatised India. Pakistan, India felt was not taking the grievance seriously. The point being that peace processes laid down along the targeted attacks do not make for a better India-Pakistan relations. The meeting at Sharm-el-Shaikh, did not resolve many issues after the freezing over the psot-Mumbai attacks. President Musharaff's statement on launching attacks on terrorism itself, no doubt, well meant was no perceived as sincere. Moreover, there was a crisis of legitimacy of Musharraf's government itself. There was also a decline in civil-military relations. There, then, became a matter of stability within Pakistan; with the assassination of Benazir Bhutto, the fall of Musharraf and the coming to power again of Nawaz Sharif (2013 General elections).

India-Pakistan Relations: Post Indian Elections 2014

The amazing unwarranted sweep Narendra Modi and the BJP made in the most recent elections in 2014 has made a sea change in Indian politics.

The monolithic Congress Party of the pre-independence era ruled from 1947 to 1977 and built themselves as a monolithic formidable single party. It was only after Mrs Indira Gandhi had declared emergency that the opposition came together and became stronger. She came back to rule once again till her death. The role of the veterans grew in the Congress Party and the vital issues of both foreign and economic policies were laid out by them. Somehow, ennui and a deep dynastic tendency set in without much room for change.

The stated foreign policy, no doubt, took into consideration Nehruvian ideals of good relations with neighbours, the concept of non alignment which made India stay equi-distant from both the US and Russia; and in general, working for economic development and good relations. Indian leadership definitely perceived themselves as leaders of non-aligned movement and especially of the developing nations.

With the stupendous unbloc majority the BJP party gained, Mr Modi, as PM can write in his own agenda and push for whatever he and the party wants. He has made a dramatic and yet needed gesture by inviting the heads of states of SAARC by calling them for his swearing in ceremony. Everyone from neighbouring states, most of all, Mr Nawaz Sharif, PM of Pakistan, Hamid Karzai of Afghanistan, Mr Rajapakse of Sri Lanka, Speaker of Bangladesh Assembly, Prime Minister Koirala of Nepal were all present.

It was both a gesture to initiate foreign policy on a warm, personalised basis and also to celebrate Mr Modi's coming into power. A lot of political analysts wondered if all this would make for only rhetoric or translate into solid policy.

The fact of the matter is Mr. Nawaz Sharif did arrive for the swearing in on May 26, accompanied by his Advisor on National Security and Foreign Affairs Sartaj Aziz, Special Assistant Aizaz Chaudhry among others.[23]

In this congratulatory vein, and in a positive gesture, Islamabad conveyed to New Delhi that about 150 Indian prisoners lodged in Pakistan's jails would be freed.

One must further understand that this decision to come to India came after two days deliberation within Pakistan's establishment – political, military and bureaucracy. Significantly, Nawaz Sharif's brother and Punjab Chief Minister Shahbaz Sharif met for Pakistan's Army Chief General Raheel Sharif for about half an hour and conveyed to him the importance of the visit to India (PML-N sources told PTI in Islamabad). The diplomatic advice rendered to Mr Nawaz

Sharif was also to undertake the visit for the state of improving bilateral ties.

Meanwhile, senior BJP leader and now Finance Minister Arun Jaitley signalled that the gathering of these foreign leaders should not be seen through the "prism of bilateral issues. The invitation to all leaders of SAARC nations to be present at the ceremony is to showcase Indian democracy, and its strengths to our neighbours and world at large. It is a democracy event. It should not be viewed through the prism of bilateral issues between countries. While celebrating the success of India's democracy, the fact that our neighbours, through their leaders, will be represented re-affirms India's faith in both democracy and greater integration of the region", he said.[30]

Nevertheless, as political analysts and author Sanjay Baru mentioned on TV, all the neighbours who had gathered were all Heads elected by their people, essentially a show of democracy in South Asia.

But where Pakistan, and Nawaz Sharif is concerned, the imperative to realise that he will be coming to India soon after the terror attack against Herat (Afghanistan) and Lashkar boss Hafiz Saeed's warning against coming to Delhi, set the stage for an unprecedented visit and escalates the inaugural ceremony into a star-studded International show of strength for Modi even before his formal takeover.[31]

Pakistan, though it may not come out in the Press, was to ask for a resumption of composite dialogue disrupted after 26/11.

What is also observed by the rest of political analysts is that the bar is getting setting higher from the word 'go' by the very fact that a sworn hardliner, like Modi coming into the Prime Minister's office resorts to a sleight of hand coup calling his neighbours, a very astute and diplomatic move.

Both Kashmir separatists and Kashmiri politicians seem to approve of Nawaz Sharif coming in to the swearing-in ceremony. Moderate Hurriyat Conference leader Mirwaiz Omar Farooq hoped Nawaz Sharif's visit would help in creating a conducive atmosphere between the two countries.

"It is a positive decision and will help in harmonizing relations". He hoped the visit would pave the way for the resolution of the Kashmir dispute. Hardline Hurriyat leader Syed Ali Geelani echoed this, calling Sharif's move "a good decision".[31]

Chief Minister Omar Abdullah expressed happiness over Sharif's visit, "very glad to hear Pakistan PM has accepted the invite, shows that he can prevail over forces inimical to good relations with India. I hope this will mark a new beginning in the ties between our two countries. The people of J and K will be watching closely".

Opposition PDP Chief Mehbooba Mufti said the occasion would introduce a lot of "positivity" she referred to Atal Bihari Vajpayee's aims of bringing about resolution to the Kashmir problem.

Deconstructing these quotes, they are filled with an array of unnatural expectations. Not only that, it is as if it were one visit that will take care of, if not, pave the way for a happy resolutions of a six decade problem or problems.

One merely wants to caution. Positive feelings and benevolent wishes are one thing, but on the ground reality with its myriads of problems quite another. As a gesture of reaching out, one of acceptance is a graceful and diplomatic one on both sides. To expect far more on a journey that has just begun, from a party that has, no doubt, done much for India-Pakistan relations, but yet remains one based on a conservative ideology. It is expecting way too much.

As said earlier, one of the more crisp, positive and real gestures was the release of 151 Indian fishermen from Pakistan's jails. Not merely a gesture, but a positive reinforcement of a positive spirit while entering into celebrations with a new government.

Also getting curiouser and curiouser as Alice would say in Alice in Wonderland...that BJP's allies would really not appreciate this friendship in any manner whatsoever and to share the space with the Pakistan PM (we are talking about the Shiv Sena, RSS, VHP functionaries) is again a cause for wonderment.

If the theoretical construct were to be gone into, the level of analysis in this situation would refer to the overriding concept of 'realpolitik'. Once a party in opposition earlier has won, it also feels the sense of responsibility in governance and foreign policy. Prior to having won the elections with such a huge majority, it was easier to be antagonistic to UPA's foreign policy, calling it a 'soft stand' towards Pakistan, Bangladesh, Sri Lanka and other nations. It is a very different approach that the new PM has already adopted. Calling the neighbouring nations to his swear-in was not just a matter of reaching out metaphorically but really.

The new government, looking to solve problems could not have possibly withdrawn from an outward looking, solution oriented policy, and foreign policy if one may say so.

It is to Mr Modi's credit of being a realist that he stretched out his hand in friendship and equally, it is to the credit of the neighbour nations that they shook it with an equal amount of vigour.

Nevertheless, hopeful and optimistic as all this sounds and looks, one will still have to see how the ground reality is taken into account and the actuals taken care of.

Kashmir, or the 'K' word, the most important component in India-Pakistan relations was not taken up in the Nawaz Sharif-Modi meeting. The slightly relatively softer issues of Sir Creek, Wullar barrage, water sharing. What is encouraging though that during talks between Mr Modi and Mr Nawaz Sharif the two substantive topics discussed were trade and cross-border terrorism. It is not very clear that resumption of what was called the composite dialogue would happen soon.

The intriguing point is that two PM's, one with a monolithic Muslim agenda and backing and the other from a majority party new in power after a decade, with a Hindutva agenda are able to meet and talk. Political structures and paradigms are very different in both nations. Pakistan has a democratic political structure struggling to stay that way with a strong military structure alongside it, which it has to be wary of and carry along in its policy formulations. Whether it was the Zulfikar Bhutto government, the Benazir Bhutto government or Nawaz Sharif in his earlier tenure as PM needed the validation of the army in some form. The Pakistan army is spread both extensively and intensively, as brought by a venerable defence and South Asian analyst as Stephen Cohen in various publications of his.

Considering this, in the future, too points of convergence will be difficult to negotiate.

What one has not yet seen but is below the surface is the VHP, the RSS role and to what extent and degree it will make its points and come to matter. But as a party, the BJP with its decisive majority in parliament with 282 seats, plus another 50 held by its allies, the BJP has the mandate that Modi needs to pursue a bold creative foreign policy agenda. He can use his political capital especially in this initial period to advance India's interest.

This is a case not just for India's national interest but more so, for national integration. Regional integration, always on the South Asian table can rarely be realised. The BJP now has the opportunity to make real progress. Improving relationships with neighbours (especially Pakistan), particularly in terms of trade and infrastructure connectivity could be BJP's accomplishment towards integrating South Asia.[24]

It is to be realised and celebrated that the leaders of South Asian nations picked up on the invitation by Modi and probably wanted to give a positive response in order to keep the collective together and functioning.

What is most important, as mentioned earlier, is that Nawaz Sharif in the face of army reluctance also managed to arrive for the ceremony.

Even more intriguing is the fact of the openness and bonhomie that prevailed over the meetings.

If Nawaz Sharif had not attended the Modi swearing-in ceremony, there would have been a host of complicated signals between the two nations and a major set back in the relations especially between India and Pakistan.

As the talks were on in New Delhi, firing was reported on the India-Pakistan border. Luckily, it was not given the importance it normally does or again, it could have become a major bone of contention, adding negativity to the meeting between the two Prime Ministers, of India and Pakistan.

On the ground reality of India-Pakistan relations after the 2014 elections is that there needs to be substantive discussion and implementation on two major points, as always.

Firstly, cross-border terrorism and; secondly, trade along with most favoured nation or something to that effect status. Cross-border terrorism affects both nations as an aspect of terror-inducing and terror-increasing mechanism. It is dangerous and harmful to economic and friendly relations. Money laundering, drugs across borders and people-militant interface bring about highly incendiary situations. Therefore, cross-border terrorism simply has to stop. Both nations blame each other, rightly so. Nevertheless, this is not a tool of foreign policy; it destroys rather than creating any atmosphere of peace.

Where trade is concerned, it is understood that both India and Pakistan are losing out in this area. The middle class businessman and the trading class person want to just make heir finances viable. The economies of across the border will turn out much cheaper, and be more beneficial.

There is a component earlier mentioned but needs to be expanded some more- the question of Pakistan army and politics.

As perceived, Pakistan is a prisoner of its geography and history. Its strategic location at the cusp of the Middle East, and South Asia and at the one end of Central Asia and China gives it significance on the regional and global scene. The Pakistan perception of fear of proximity of a large, dominant neighbour India, shapes Pakistan's foreign and defence policies on the one hand, and informs its domestic debates on the other.[33]

Of course, the volatility of South Asia lies in the fact that both India and Pakistan have nuclear weapons.

Pakistan's wars and history with India have made both nations wary of each other. It has also thrust Pakistani military into the centre of decision-making on issues related to its foreign policy, especially policy toward India (Kashmir specifically) and Afghanistan, as well as nuclear matters.

It must be realised that Pakistan army has held the reins effectively for more than thirty eight years since its independence. Pakistan is wracked by internal divisions between provinces; and between the forces of modernism and militant and radical Islam.

There is a subterranean arms race between India and Pakistan that is dangerous for the region. Former Pakistani Army Chief Kayani promised to put the army back in the barracks but this is not possible. The slow destruction of institutions: the judiciary, constitution, the bureaucracy and the legislature has been evident and this has increased the role of the army.

General Zia-ul-Haq began the systematic process of Islamisation of the Army with a monolithic, nuclear power oriented fronting of the army.

This changed to the notion of the Pakistan Army as a corporate entity as put down in Ayesha Siddiqa's book *Military Inc.* She attempts to quantify the extent of the military's business interests in Pakistan and comes up with a figure of $10 billion. Whether the figure is correct or not, it underlines the extent to state resources available to the army, and such items like health and education not given much berth.

Both the size and nature of the Pakistan army have a huge impact on Pakistan's economy and society. Pakistan today has an army of 80,000 including 550,000 regular army and the rest as paramilitary.

According to World Bank data, in 2005, defence spending as a percentage of Gross Domestic Product in Pakistan was around 3.4 per cent compared to with India's 2.3 per cent, amongst the highest burdens of military spending in the world. The rationale was Pakistan needed it for its own security.

India holds the counterpoint that in the light of this, India needs to pull up its own military arsenal. These kinds of justifications are bound to take both nations in a collision path.

In Pakistan's case, this aspect of military domination impacts the economy of the nation as one has seen it.

Just after independence, respect was shown to the Pakistan army for it was a structured institution and the constitution was not in place. Gradually, corruption set in and the role of Islamisation further eroded its values (not that that was imperative but it brought in the negative aspect). Further, the intelligence wing gained precedence in the context of both internal (secessionism, Baluchistan, Swat) and external (India). With these as ongoing perceived threats the Pakistan army, on the one hand, represented strength and structure and on the other allowed regressive forces to permeate it. The Afghan problem, no doubt, increased the complexity with Talibanisation and across the border fleeing of immigrants. 9/11 jolted this systemic change further. Making way for the United States in this part of the world, Pakistan's so called ally injected Pakistan's economy but put it in a 'hard place'.

It would take a thesis to analyse Islamisation and the impact of the army, the increasing role of the Pakistani army and then the challenges to it in Swat, Baluchistan etc. that has brought down its credibility as ISI has divided the army.

All this is merely to enumerate the complexities and difficulties in carrying out the environment for a futuristic well placed India-Pakistan relations: to show the military component as very high and most times untenable, and that more recently, there has been dilution of the credibility of the Pakistan army, most of all since the present Pakistan government seems to portray stability, there seems to be less of a role for the army. This seems no longer to be the case as, Nawaz Sharif has been challenged by Tehreek-e-Insaf's Imran Khan and cleric Tahirul Qadri creating a destabilising polity making spaces for the army to step in.

There is an inordinate fear in the West and where India is concerned about a nuclearised Pakistan. As to the exact location of power whose hand is on the nuclear button and whether so called radical elements will be able to get their hands on them.

Keeping this in mind, it is even more imperative that there be dialogue and softening of relations between India and Pakistan.

In the light of all this, it will be quite difficult for India-Pakistan to take up very different kind of relationship even if the regime in New Delhi is different, as is in Pakistan, a civil regime.

After the elections in India, the bar of expectations has risen higher on both sides. It is to be expected but what needs to be done very quickly is to act on potential possibilities and the actual do-ables and on the side keep negotiating the tougher aspects of India-Pakistan relations.

There will, in all probability, be a different kind of dynamism with the change in government. And as always, both nations will be inclined to have bilateral talks to resolve differences as they have even earlier. Bilateral talks engagement can be on a wide range of issues: border demarcation, boundary adjustment, water distribution, trade and commerce issues, protection of minorities, Kashmir, conventional and nuclear confidence building measures. All these have been discussed since 1990s and later as part of the composite dialogue. These discussions will have to go on.

The change post-2014 elections is that with the invitation to the SAARC members, the framework has got expanded and there is genuine desire to be inclusive and not let the India-Pakistan bilateral issues subsume the SAARC agenda. Considering the history, this is truly a change in foreign policy.

Not that many drastic changes in policy towards neighbours such as Pakistan can be made. And, not that the former PM Mr Manmohan Singh did not try. India and Pakistan were on a dialogue course and progressing on several issues as Siachen, Sir Creek, water sharing etc. but several events overtook the possibility of a true dialogue – some of these were: 28/11 horrendous aggressive attacks in Mumbai (2008); Mr Manmohan Singh having coalition partners who at times did not agree on the methodology of peace talks with Pakistan and such like obstacles.

Considering all this, one hopes that post-2014 elections, there will be substantive dialogue between the two neighbouring nations, India and Pakistan especially on urgently promised issues such as cross-border terrorism and invigorating the economy between the two nations.

India-Pakistan relations is a truly hyphenated relationship, a veritable merry-go-round or a graph that goes up and down in an irrational manner. Nothing is impossible. Both nations have to get over the trust deficit (a cliché but true nevertheless). Just as India has taken some small steps towards China, keeping the border issues aside, India-Pakistan can take the same route and keep Kashmir on the back burner, for a while and do a lot more for the economic engagement on both states- lower tariffs, increase trade, invest in both nations (joint ventures), resume the gas pipeline. Also, cricket has been a major glue to the befriending of nations; Bollywood movies, heroes and heroines are very much liked in Pakistan; Pakistani serials are popular in India. An increase in these may raise the voice of discourse as people to people contact surely will.

These are not cosmetic or trite suppositions but ones, which will lead to better relations.

There are problems that will persist in the relationship: the instability in Pakistan even now, the remarks made by Nawaz Sharif as regards dialogue in Kashmir issue (September 26, 2014) and Prime Minister Modi's rejoinder that it can only take place without shadow of terrorism. For there to be the ongoing trajectory of peace, there has to be a re-imagined Pakistan according to Husain Haqqani, former Ambassador of Pakistan to United States.[25] According to him, there is an alternative vision of Pakistan of Pakistan as a pluralist, multi-ethnic, modern democratic Muslim state functioning under rule of law for the material well-being of its citizens.[26] Again he says that the first step in re-imagining Pakistan would be to abandon the narrow ideological paradigm of Pakistani nationalism. This would also make it easier for Pakistan to tackle *jihadi* terrorism, which must be eliminated for its own sake. Only by reimagining itself can Pakistan find peace with itself and its neighbours and stop being viewed by the rest of the world as a failing state, a troubled state or a crisis state.[27]

On the part of India, some suspicions and misperceptions need to be kept aside. There has to be a serious dialogue aspect by treating the Muslims as part of the Indian nation and finally be as fair and connected to Kashmir problems and aim to resolve it.

8

India, Pakistan and Imperatives for Sustaining Peace

Dr Mohammed Badrul Alam

Peace process in the shape of confidence-building measures (CBMs) are recognisable as "arrangements designed to enhance...assurance of mind and belief in the trust-worthiness of states...confidence is the product of much broader patterns of relations than those which relate to military strategy. In fact the latter have to be woven into a complex texture of economic, cultural, technical and social relationships."[1] This suggests military and non-military initiatives undertaken by antagonistic states to reduce tensions and enhance mutual confidence. This chapter will examine and evaluate various confidence-building measures, military as well as non-military that were initiated between India and Pakistan. The chapter will also address and delineate definition and conceptual notion as well as some of the pertinent aspects of ongoing peace process including Track-II diplomacy and nuclear risk reduction measures being undertaken by India and Pakistan.

CBMs are designed essentially to increase understanding by reducing suspicions. They are separable into military and non-military CBMs and into those having a unilateral, bilateral or international content. Military CBMs are also classifiable into transparency, communications and constraint measures to perform the related functions of information, notification, observation and stabilisation. [2] CBMs can further be catalogued into provisions enabling information exchange, mutual access to observation or arrangements to handle incidents and crises. (UN 1982)

A counsel of perfection suggests their pursuit in all these separate directions. But, negotiating and implementing "CBMs requires political will, but only modest amounts of capital need be expended to begin the process... [CBMs] have met the minimal requirements of not worsening any state's security and not increasing existing levels of hostility."[3]

Challenges to CBMs in South Asia

Synthesising "security consensus" in South Asia has proved difficult since four seminal factors lie at the roots of insecurities in the region.[4]

They are:

Firstly, the bitter hostilities and tensions distinguishing Indo-Pak relations that have resulted in several conflicts, overt and covert in the past, which casts a pall over the region. These enmities are deeply inter-twined with their domestic politics and have now acquired a serious nuclear dimension.

Secondly, the preponderance of India in the South Asian polity is unique; its Indo-centricity erects a psychological barrier that accentuates the insecurities of its small neighbours since marked differences in politico-military weight between states is hardly conducive to building confidence between them.

Thirdly, the civil society is replete with socio-economic and ethno-political strife manifested by caste, class and sectarian conflicts, communal violence and armed struggles against central authority. Inter- and intra-state insecurities are linked and spill across national borders; they have often been fomented by the regional countries against their neighbours.

Fourthly, the newer security threats and threat perceptions in South Asia "largely arise from non-military causes like cross-border movements of population; ethno-political, socio-economic, and communal-religious politics; terrorism, with its seminal linkages to money-laundering operations, and drugs/arms smuggling; environmental degradation, spawning its related problems of deforestation and desertification; internal migration; chaotic urbanisation, and so on".[5] But regional elites are focused on traditional/military sources of insecurity.

Nature of CBMs in South Asia:

Military CBMs

Between India and Pakistan, at the military level, several CBMs have been initiated with varying scopes and limitations. Here are some of these military CBMs.

Communication Measures: Military Hotlines

Following the 1971 war between India and Pakistan, a secured communication link, or "hotline," between the Pakistani and Indian Directors General of Military Operations (DGMOs) was established. In December 1990, India and Pakistan agreed to re-establish the DGMO hotline and to use it on a weekly basis, if only to exchange routine information. At the February 1999 Lahore Summit, India and Pakistan agreed to review all existing communication links with a view to upgrade and approve the DGMO and other hotlines.

Hotline between Prime Ministers

The first hotline was installed in 1989 by Prime Ministers Benazir Bhutto and Rajiv Gandhi of Pakistan and India respectively. In November 1990, Indian Prime Minister Chandra Shekhar and Pakistani Prime Minister Nawaz Sharif re-established the hotline to facilitate direct communication. In May 1997, Indian Prime Minister I.K. Gujral and Pakistan's Prime Minister Nawaz Sharif pledged to reinstate the hotline.

Declarations on Non-Use of Force, Bilateral Resolution of Differences

The 1966 Tashkent Declaration facilitated by the Soviet Union, formally concluded the 1965 Indo-Pak war. It stipulated that relations between India and Pakistan shall be based on the principle of non-interference in the internal affairs of the other. The 1972 Simla Accord followed the 1971 Indo-Pak war which obliges both countries to renounce the use of force as a means of settling outstanding disputes between the two countries. In addition, both sides agreed to resolve their disputes in bilateral forum only.

Notification Measures: Military Exercises

An Agreement of Prior Notification of Military Exercises was completed in April 1991. Notification is required for exercises comprising two or more divisions in specified locations. Near the Line of Control, notification is required for any exercises involving division level or above. Troop maneuvers directed towards the international border are proscribed. Exercises at the corps level must be held forty-five kilometers away from the border. At the division level, exercises must be held twenty-five kilometers away from the border. No military activity is permitted within five kilometers of the border.

Non-intrusion of Air Space

An Agreement on the Prevention of the Violation of the Air Space was signed in April 1991, and entered into force in August

1992. It stipulates that combat fixed-wing aircraft are not to fly within ten kilometers of foreign airspace. Unarmed transport and logistics aircraft are permitted up to 1,000 meters from the border; flights within this range for supply or rescue missions are permitted if advance notice is given.

Transparency Measures

Pakistan invited observers to watch major military exercises (Zarb-e-Momin) in 1989 while India in 1990 in order to diffuse tension arising from a major 1990 military exercise, invited US observers to monitor troop and equipment deployment as an assurance of non-hostile intent.

Constraint Measures: Non-Attack of Nuclear Facilities

An Agreement on the Non-Attack of Nuclear Facilities was signed by Indian Prime Minister Rajiv Gandhi and Pakistani Prime Minister Benazir Bhutto in December 1988. It was ratified by both countries and implemented in January 1992. The agreement requires an annual exchange of lists detailing the location of all nuclear-related facilities in each country. The measure further pledges both sides not to attack listed facilities.

Bilateral Accord on Chemical Weapons

A Joint Declaration on the Prohibition of Chemical Weapons was concluded in August 1992. Both countries agreed not to develop, produce, acquire, or use chemical weapons.

Non-Harassment of Diplomatic Personnel

In November 1990 the Indian and Pakistani Foreign Secretaries worked out a code of conduct to protect diplomatic personnel, guaranteeing them freedom from harassment.

Additional Highlights of the February 1999 Lahore Summit

Both India and Pakistan agreed to provide each other with advance notification in respect of their ballistic missile flight tests. India and Pakistan also agreed to maintain the respective unilateral moratorium on conducting further nuclear test explosions unless either side, in excess of it national sovereignty decided that extraordinary events had jeopardized its supreme national interests. Furthermore, the Memorandum of Understanding (MoU) sought a review of the existing communication links between Directors General Military Operations (DGMOs) with a view to upgrading and improving these links, and to provide for fail-safe and secure communications.

Other Suggestions on Military CBMs

On October 18, 2001, Pakistan's Ambassador to the UN, Mr Munir Akram, while addressing the UN General Assembly's debate on international peace and security, said that to promote nuclear restraint and prevent the use of nuclear weapons, Pakistan and India could agree to:[6]

1. formalise their respective unilateral nuclear test moratorium, perhaps through a bilateral treaty;
2. not operationally weaponise nuclear capable missile systems;
3. not operationally deploy nuclear-capable ballistic missiles, and to keep them on de-alert;
4. formalise the previous understanding to provide prior and adequate notification of flight tests of missiles;
5. observe a moratorium on the acquisition, deployment or development of anti-ballistic systems;
6. implement further confidence-building and transparency measures to reduce the risk of the use of nuclear weapons by miscalculation or accident;
7. open discussions on the nuclear security doctrines of the two countries with a view to forestalling an all out nuclear arms race and an agreement on non-use of force, including the non-use of nuclear weapons.

Non-Military CBMs

As in the case of military CBMs, non-military CBMs are also germane in diffusing tension between the two adversaries, India and Pakistan.

Non-military CBMs cover areas such as the following. [7]

- Collaboration in science and technology
- Dialogue on art and culture
- Free movement of People and ideas (easing of visa restrictions for the nationals of adversarial countries)
- Exchange of information, views and analyses, i.e., newspapers, books, magazines
- Commerce and trade
- Strengthening democracy
- Goodwill Measures

Although termed as short-term by analysts and observers, both India and Pakistan since their independence in 1947, have embarked on number of peace making steps as good will measures.[8] These measures adopted by the two countries exist in the form of:

- Transfer of official assets (1948)

- Prevention of an even larger exodus of refugees (1948)
- Protection of rights of minorities (1950)
- Maintenance of places of worship (1953,1955)
- Resolution of some lingering territories claim (1958,1959, 1960, and 1963)
- Indus Water Treaty (1960)
- Tashkent Agreement (1966)
- Agreement relating to the Rann of Kutch dispute (1968)
- Some provisions in the Simla Agreement (1972)
- Joint Commission agreement signed in March 1983 to cooperate in areas other than military and political matters.

Some of the more contemporary CBMs initiated and undertaken by India and Pakistan in the non-military arena are the following. [9]

1. Various military goodwill measures (1993).
   (i) Participation of senior military and civilian officials in various seminars in each other's country (1993).
   (ii) Inviting Guest Speakers at each other's national defence colleges.
   (iii) Participation and visits of various sports teams particularly Cricket and Hockey (which received a set back when BJP, the ruling government in New Delhi decided to disallow sporting contact but it has now been allowed in 2003).
2. Visits of Parliamentarians.
3. Visits of businessmen.
4. In May 1984 and followed by another meeting of Indo-Pakistan Joint Commission held in July 1989, decisions were made to promote tourism, easing visa difficulties.
5. Opening of the regular bus service between Indian-administered Srinagar and Pakistan-administered Muzaffarabad in April 2005 and between Poonch and Rawalakote in June 2006.
6. Resumption of Amritsar (India)-Lahore (Pakistan) bus service.
7. Khokrapar-Munabao rail link is at an advance state of completion.
8. Family re-union and meetings planned along the Line of Control in Mendhar, Poonch, Suchetgarh, Uri, Tangdhar.
9. Trade and commerce across Jammu-Sialkot line.
10. Promotion of Pilgrimage centers and Open Visa systems on both sides.

The Kashmir Issue

Kashmir has been a bone issue of contention between India and Pakistan ever since both countries achieved independence in 1947 from the British colonial rule. While India considers Jammu and

Kashmir to be an integral part of it union, Pakistan advocates in favour of self-determination to be given to the people of Kashmir valley for determining their future as well the state's status. Pakistan also considers Indian accession of Kashmir as a legal ploy devoid of any popular support.

Kashmir, both India and Pakistan have realised an urgent need in developing a structured dialogue.[10] This may include the following in terms of ushering CBMs:

- Formalising structure of dialogue, in terms of mechanisms and issues involved in the dispute.
- Formal recognition by the two sides that there is no military solution to the Kashmir dispute.
- In determining the wishes of the Kashmir's population, representatives of all different constituents and faiths of J and K need to be effectively involved in the dialogue process.
- Encouraging and initiating intra-Kashmir dialogue on both sides of the LoC on the final status of Kashmir.
- Involving people of Kashmir ("Kashmiriyat") in the bilateral dialogue process of Kashmir.
- Setting a timeframe for structured dialogue on Kashmir.
- The resolution of the Kashmir conflict and restoration and development of mutual trust should be treated as interdependent processes.
- Kashmir solution must be based on the principle of mutual respect of India and Pakistan have for each other and dignity and justice for the people of Kashmir.
- The pursuit of solution around zero-sum game needs to be avoided.
- The process of de-escalation of hostilities needs to be initiated and efforts should be made to de-link Kashmir from point-scoring domestic agendas.
- The hostile domestic propaganda around Kashmir in both electronic and print media needs to be stopped.
- Unofficial dialogue through Track-II should be encouraged by the two governments to assist official-level talks between India and Pakistan.
- The heads of governments of both sides should meet twice a year to assess the progress of the dialogue and sort out the deadlocks around various points.

On the more immediate issue of de-escalation along the Line of Control in Kashmir, some of the CBMs suggested along these lines can also be pursued.[11]

- Relocation of heavy weapons which are considered a major cause of tension-escalation across the LoC.
- Exercises along the LoC and working boundary may not exceed one division involving 12,500-15,000 troops, and the number of combat vehicles must not exceed 100 combat vehicles and 50 artillery pieces.
- Continuous scheduled and unscheduled visits to forward areas by journalists, representatives of various national and international human rights organisations, diplomats, defence and UN military observers.
- Commitment not to violate airspace across the LoC/Working Boundary.
- Military commanders of India and Pakistan should meet and explore the reduction of troops in both Indian and Pakistan administered Kashmir.
- On Siachen and Sir Creek: avoid lateral movement of troops on the glacier, total commitment against using artillery fire and no violation of air space in the region.

Track-II Diplomacy and CBMs

Track-II diplomacy is a process of active interaction between individuals in countries in dispute who in their private capacities exchange innovative ideas and various plausible options with or without the prior knowledge of the authorities and governments of their respective countries. However, these types of interactions and exchanges are not officially authorised or mandated from either of the governments. Government officials at the very least, under Track-II diplomacy, have the benefit of valuable feedback and input that could possibly be expanded in Track-I dialogue with some modifications or alterations.

Definition and Characteristics

Track-II diplomacy is often defined as a process of unofficial dialogue among non-official representatives of the parties locked in a dispute.[12] Influential persons or opinion-makers, who have the ability to influence both the government and the public, undertake the Track-II process. Track-II diplomacy may involve a neutral third party either for observation purposes or for the initial push. This is particularly relevant when there is a backlog of suspicion and animosities along with institutionalised intolerance, hatred and distrust. In such situations the participation of government officials is prone to a wide range of misinterpretations and misperceptions, which policy and decision-makers can hardly afford. Thus, influential, non-governmental individuals on both sides, who are seen to be relatively balanced in their approach are brought together to discuss the issues. The basic objective of Track-II is to prevent conflict and to facilitate the process of conflict resolution. Being influential persons most of the members of the Track-II concept have either direct access to their governments or are in a position to effectively influence the public opinion in their respective countries. The governments are informed either directly or by suggestions floated through the media.

A scrutiny of the groups engaged in Track-II diplomacy reveals two dominant characteristics; (a) all members of these groups are often fully cognizant of the need to resolve the disputes as speedily as possible, (b) and all have the ability to make constructive contributions towards the desired resolution of ongoing conflicts in one form or the other. Many of these individuals are already involved in their individual capacities, to improve conflicting regional situations either through their writings (both general and research) or through teaching, seminars, conferences, travel etc.

A Track-II group is often formed in two ways. First, it might be the product of a macro level initiative of an individual or an institution like a university or research institute or a newspaper group etc. Second, it might be formed by the encouragement and efforts of interested outsiders. However, it needs to be clarified that groups formed because of the efforts of outsiders invariably emphasise a scrupulous avoidance of external interference. It is indeed up to the participants to jointly agree to have an outsider as their chairperson who is known for his expertise and knowledge of the area and whose balanced and impartial treatment of the issues has already earned him the respect of many insiders.

Objectives

The major objectives of the Track-II diplomacy are threefold; (a) to make attempts to resolve ongoing disputes; (b) to discourage and prevent the emergence of new disputes; and (c) to make efforts with a view to bringing the two estranged countries and societies closer by introducing innovative and workable confidence building measures (CBMs). Indeed, it is the most difficult objective to attain, especially if the dispute has lasted for more than a decade.

Nuclear Risk Reduction Measures

Another of the CBMs that have been discussed in scholarly writings pertain to initiating nuclear risk reduction measures between India and Pakistan after the two countries went for overt nuclearisation in the summer of 1998. Broadly stated, nuclear risk reduction measures in South Asia context may envisage the following.[13]

- To serve as a central clearinghouse for data exchanges and notifications of existing agreements and to formalise the provision of information in a transparent manner.
- To help institutionalise and foster proper implementation of unilateral, bilateral or multilateral measures for nuclear risk reduction, arms control, and/or force reduction in the region.
- To build trust and confidence by providing data that could assist monitoring and compliance - as well as to nullify misperceptions.

Even a preliminary investigative study and analysis of basic nuclear risk reduction measures (NRRM) in the four key areas of potential risks such as miscalculation, unauthorised use, accidents and panic behaviour as proposed by members of an influential peace group, MIND (Movement in India for Nuclear Disarmament), are yet to be initiated by either India or Pakistan at the present time. According to Praful Bidwai and Achin Vanaik, "the role of NRRM should not be exaggerated. NRRMs can make South Asia less unsafe in nuclear terms. But they can not make it nuclear safe. NRRMs or kindred confidence-building measures have another limitation. They become most effective when located in a cooperative context. But that is no excuse for not beginning a process to negotiate NRRMs for the safety and security of South Asian peoples."[14]

Nuclear Risk Reduction Centres

In line with nuclear risk reduction measures, scholars have also voiced support of having nuclear risk reduction centres in both India and Pakistan. Michael Kreppon has argued in favour of 'ten commandments' of nuclear risk reduction that had evolved to help keep the Cold War from becoming white hot. [15]

These commandments were:

- Don't change the territorial status quo in sensitive areas by use of force.
- Avoid nuclear brinkmanship.
- Avoid dangerous military practices.
- Put in place special reassurances measures for ballistic missiles and other nuclear forces.
- Implement properly treaty obligations, risk reductions, and confidence-building measures.
- Agree on Verification arrangements, including intrusive monitoring.

- Establish reliable lines of communication, between political leaders and between military leaders.
- Establish redundant and reliable command and control arrangements a well as intelligence-gathering capabilities to know what the other side is up to, especially in a crisis.
- Keep working hard on these arrangements. Improve them. Don't take anything for granted.
- Hope for plain dumb luck or divine intervention.

Paused Deployment Posture

Another major step which can take India and Pakistan towards nuclear risk reduction and confidence building would be a bilateral agreement what can be termed as a posture of "paused deployment".[16] By a Paused Deployment Posture (PDP), it may mean deliberate, mutually verifiable built-in-delay of about a day in the arming of delivery vehicles with nuclear weapons, agreed upon by both countries. Sometimes, called 'de-alert', delay could be by a full day or more or just few hours and by precluding instant deployment, it will greatly diminish the probability of hasty, emotionally driven or accidental use of nuclear arms and hence provide much needed breathing space to respective decision-makers on both sides for finding ways and means at diffusing an impending crisis.

Paradoxes in Pursuing the CBM Modality

Proceeding further, three unresolved paradoxes can be identified in South Asian region concerning the applicability and viability of CBMs. These steps have relevance for other conflict-prone regions in other parts of the world as well.

First, CBMs admittedly " provide the atmospherics for improving inter-State relations, and providing the instrumentality to proceed further with an arms control and disarmament process."[17] They can establish trust between adversarial states; but the paradox remains that trust is required before CBMs can be negotiated. The need for some limited confidence between adversarial states is therefore essential before CBMs can be negotiated.

Second, CBMs are difficult to establish, but easy to disrupt and abandon. Continued adherence to them requires adversarial states to perceive the balance of advantage to lie in not abrogating them, particularly during periods of deep crises. Experience reveals, on the contrary, that the hotline established between the Directors General of Military Operations became non-functional during the Indo-Pak war of 1971 due to telephones being either left unattended or manned by junior officers with no real authority. In addition, during the Brasstacks crisis (1987), "...information shared through the hotline was deemed unreliable because of mutual suspicions; hence, information supplied on Pakistani request was only minimally complied with".[18] Obviously, hotlines can only be relevant in crises if trust is evident on both sides. They are known to work satisfactorily in times of peace. Hence the paradox that states may abide by CBMs in normal times, but ignore them in emergency situations.

Third, public declarations can serve as useful CBMs to alleviate tensions and promote stability; they "can take the form of joint summit statements, negotiated agreements of a declaratory nature—such as non-attack pledges—and/or unilateral statements".[19] The historical record shows that national leaders in India and Pakistan routinely make conciliatory statements, but they are meant either for domestic consumption or to impress international audiences or lower the other's guard. The paradox then emerges: "Rather than promote security and confidence building, such declarations have often exacerbated existing regional tensions."[20]

The Sum of All Parts

In spite of the seemingly difficult terrain in generating and implementing confidence-building measures in South Asia, all are not doom and gloom as this chapter suggests. It is thus plausible to make the following conclusions based on existing regional and sub-regional arrangements in South Asia.

1. India and Pakistan, as the two new nuclear weapon states in the nuclear club, have embarked upon nuclear risk reduction measures through a series of bilateral agreements.
2. In South Asia, both India and Pakistan have initiated a series of meaningful Track-II dialogues and discussions at the people to people basis outside of the regular governmental to governmental channels. Ideas of having a nuclear risk reduction centre in both the countries have received favourable reactions both inside and outside of South Asia including the skeptics who felt such a proposal to be too ambitious and hence unrealistic and unworkable.
3. In South Asia, through SAARC (South Asian Association for Regional Cooperation) both India and Pakistan have tried to address various bilateral issues; including trade, commerce, and cultural contacts within the regional framework.
4. At the highest level of government, both India and Pakistan have tried to evolve composite dialogue (including on the vexed

issue of Kashmir). In particular, between 1999-2008, President Pervez Musharraf of Pakistan and Prime Ministers of India during that phase, Atal Behari Vajpayee and Dr Manmohan Singh, have met several times one on one and have agreed on the basic modalities of confidence-building measures. The very fact that the current Government of India led by Shri Narendra Modi from the BJP who won a massive majority in the 2014 Lok Sabha election has committed itself to pursue and continue the path of dialogue since 2004 is a welcome sign. It is extremely imperative that even after the heinous terrorist attack in Mumbai on 26 November, 2008 and repeated terrorist attacks in Pakistani cities, both sides agree that the peace process must continue unabated.

5. Although the hardliners in India and Pakistan still profess to have nuclear superiority over their respective rivals, yet the pro-engagement wing seems to have the upper hand at the present time.
6. By branding President Pervez Musharraf who was in power, 1999-2008 and other leaders including the present Prime Minister Nawaz Shariff, of Pakistan as irrational minds have only raised the spectre of nuclear threat in South Asia. The key to stability lies in dealing with whoever is in de facto charge in Islamabad.
7. Confidence-building measures such as the establishment of secured Hot Lines between New Delhi and Islamabad provides a mechanism for the reduction of tension and in diffusing any imminent security issue that may snowball in to a potential grave crisis. However, the key lies in building and expanding beyond these CBMs which are/were already agreed upon among the known (India/Pakistan) adversaries.

Six elements are critical to sustain this process of dialogue.[21]

- One, preservation of agreements and CBMs (military and non-military) instituted so far between India and Pakistan.
- Two, promoting resolution of disputes so that peace process gains momentum into a conflict resolution mode.
- Three, a problem-solving proactive approach applied by both sides.
- Four, principle of reciprocity and goodwill guiding the dialogue process.
- Five, political contacts sufficiently at high level to the highest level are needed to discuss issues critically and keep the engagement process moving.
- Six, evolving a convergent vision for a future of peace and cooperation in the entire South Asian region.

In this regard, a high-level Track-II meeting in 2009 between India and Pakistan has suggested several concrete ways to take forward the bilateral relationship.[22]

1. Peace between and stability in India-Pakistan relations is vital for the well being of South Asia. After nearly 67 years of hostility between India and Pakistan, it is critical that all stakeholders work for sustainable peace between the two countries. Civil societies in India and Pakistan, by and large, support the goal of peace and reconciliation; peace constituencies in both countries must, therefore, be further strengthened by providing them greater space, depth and support. It is essential that the trust deficit and the burden of history not be allowed to impact on the task of moving relations forward.
2. Trust can be best built through multiple uninterruptible dialogues, positive incremental steps, Confidence and Trust-building Measures, and most critically through acts of bold statesmanship and farsightedness by the leaders of the two countries.
3. A grand reconciliation can only be ensured, in the long-term, through engagement at every level: civil society meetings, official dialogues, proactive engagement of political leaders, cooperation between business and corporate leaders, visits of artists, sportsmen, media, talks between the armed forces, Track-II dialogues, etc.
4. Temporary and occasional setback in inter-governmental relations should not be allowed to impinge on people-to-people cooperation. Attempts should be made to facilitate a visa-free regime for important stakeholders: including academics, journalists, businessmen, students, artists and former senior officials.
5. Progress made in previous rounds of talks should be carried forward in the official dialogue so that there is an element of continuity.
6. Terrorism is of deep concern to India and Pakistan. The memory of the 26/11 Mumbai attacks is still alive and continues to inform public opinion in India. Today, terrorism and extremism pose an existential threat to Pakistan. Indian concerns about terrorism and the terrorist threats to India are as much of a serious concern for Pakistan. Terrorism and extremism need to be addressed upfront and comprehensively and permanently defeated.
7. India and Pakistan should seriously consider initiating an institutionalised, regular but discreet dialogue between the

intelligence chiefs and units (the heads of R&AW, IB and ISI and IB Pakistan) of both countries.

8. The back channel talks on Jammu and Kashmir must be resumed at an early date keeping in view the fact that all stake-holders, particularly the people of J and K, will have to be consulted at some stage. If Jammu and Kashmir is considered as a piece of real estate there is little hope of a way ahead. Therefore, the overall welfare of the people of Jammu and Kashmir must be considered to be of paramount concern. In this context, all agreed CBMs must be more robustly and honestly implemented.
9. The media are playing a critical role in shaping popular perceptions. They have thus a great responsibility to help strengthen the constituency for peace. A continuing dialogue between journalists, editors and proprietors of media houses is needed in ushering a climate of trust.
10. A sustained dialogue on ensuring strategic stability in South Asia must be an essential part of the bilateral dialogue. There is also need for discussion amongst experts on critical doctrinal issues and the need to work towards creating a Nuclear Safety, Assistance and Collaboration Regime in the region within the framework of minimum deterrence. In this context, a trilateral nuclear dialogue which includes China must also be pursued.
11. The issue of water is becoming a matter of great concern and there is a need to address misperceptions in this regard. The Indus Water Treaty has withstood the test of time and has a well-established dispute-settlement mechanism. Any concern about hydro-resources of the Indus river system should be taken up through the Permanent Indus Water Commission. Within the framework of the treaty, the two countries must also share best practices on water management with each other. Environmental and other experts with domain knowledge, from both countries, must be encouraged to provide concrete recommendations for better and optimal management of hydro resources given the huge challenge that the scarcity of water will pose for the region in the future in terms of human security.
12. A stable, prosperous, sovereign and independent Afghanistan is in the interest of India and Pakistan and both countries must work assiduously for this goal and hold regular talks to allay each other's apprehensions.
13. Track-II dialogues are designed to move beyond officially stated positions, find a way forward, and can provide alternative approaches to the governments of Pakistan and India as well as

other important stakeholders. It is vital that Track-II dialogues be encouraged by both New Delhi and Islamabad.

What is more important in the context of bringing about peace between India and Pakistan is the perception of risk which appear to be only limited regional perceptions of the shared bilateral risks of nuclear war and avoidance of possible catastrophe. In the short to intermediate term, viable solutions must be evolved for solving the various, bilateral intractable issues so as to have saleability and acceptability by all stakeholders. There is also a compelling need to recalibrate other national strategic priorities - national defence, Kashmir, viable civil society, convert 'trust deficit' into 'trust surplus', etc. The issue is complicated further by the profound asymmetry between Pakistan's obsession with India in its security thinking and India's substantial strategic space and its focus on a range of security imperatives of which Pakistan is but one.

Annex

Source: The Henry L. Stimson Center, Washington, DC

URL: http://www.stimson.org/data-sets/south-asia-confidence-building-measures-cbm-timeline/

South Asia Confidence Building Measures (CBM) Timeline

2014 – Present

2014

January 1, India and Pakistan exchanged lists of their nuclear installations, as part of an agreement banning the countries from attacking each other's nuclear facilities. The exchange has occured on the first day of each year since 1992.

January 17, The Military officials from Pakistan and India agreed to further strengthen the ceasefire along the Line of Control (LoC) during a brigadier-level flag meeting held at the Rawalakot-Poonch crossing point at the LoC.

January 18, Commerce Ministers agreed to establish reciprocal Non-Discriminatory Market Access (NDMA).The ministers also agreed to open the Wagah-Attari border for trade at all times of the year.

February 12, Trade across the Line of Control (LoC) in Kashmir resumes after being suspended for a month.

References

1. Hoist Johan Jorgen. 1983. "Confidence Building Measures: A Conceptual Framework", *Survival*, Vol. 25, No.1, January/February, pp. 2 and 4. *Indian Express*, New Delhi, December 19, 2003.

2. Hoist, *Ibid*, No.1.
3. Kreppon, Michael.1998. "Conflict Avoidance, Confidence-Building, and Peacemaking", in Michael Krepon, Khurshid Khoja, Michael Newbill, Jenny S. Drezin Eds. *A Handbook of Confidence Building Measures for Regional Security*, 3rd Edition, The Henry L. Stimson Center, Handbook No.1, March , p. 4.
4. Dhanpala, Jayanta. 1993. "Conclusion", in Jayanta Dhanapala; *Regional Approaches to Disarmament: Security and Stability*. Cambridge; Cambridge University Press, p. 271.
5. Chari, P.R. 1988. *Newer Sources of Insecurity: The Crisis of Governance in India*. RCSS Policy Study, Colombo: Regional Center for Strategic Studies, p. 2.
6. Ahmar, Moonis(ed.). 2003. *Paradigms of Conflict Resolution in South Asia*. Dhaka: Bangladesh, The University Press Limited, pp. 49-50.
7. Chari, *Ibid*, No. 5.
8. Ahmar, *Ibid*, No. 6.
9. Cheema Pervaiz Iqbal. 2004. "Assessing the Role of Confidence-Building Measures in the India, Pakistan Tangle", Islamabad; Pakistan, Islamabad Policy Research Institute(IPRI), Winter , p. 22; also, see, *The Hindu*, Chennai, April 15, 2005; also, see, *The Hindustan Times*, Delhi, April 18, 2005; also, see, "Another Indo-Pak Road to Peace", *The Hindustan Times*, Delhi, June 2, 2006, see, Annex, for full details
10. Ahmar, *Ibid*, No. 6.
11. Cloughley, Brian. 1998. "Nuclear Risk Reduction Measures in Kashmir", *Nuclear Risk Reduction Measures in South Asia*. Washington, D.C. The Henry L. Stimson Center, Report Number 26, p.70; see, *The Indian Express*, New Delhi, May 25, 2005; also, see, *The Times of India*, New Delhi, May 24, 2006.
12. Cloughley, *Ibid*, No.11.
13. Khan Rafi Uz Zaman. 2003. "Nuclear Risk Reduction Centers", Washington, D.C, The Henry L. Stimson Center, October.
14. Bidwai, Praful. 2002. "From the Worlds' Most Dangerous Place", June 3, available at www.antiwar.com/bidwai/particleid=607.
15. Kreppon Michael and Jerry S. Drezin.1999. " Introduction", in Michael Kreppon, Jerry S. Drezin, Michael Newbill, eds; *Declaratory Diplomacy: Rhetorical Initiatives and Confidence-Building*, Report No. 27, April, p. 11.
16. Rajaraman, R. 1999. "Delayed Deployment: Towards Nuclear Risk Reduction", *The Times of India*, October 1.
17. Bajpai, Kanti; P.R. Chari, Pervaiz Iqbal Cheema, Stephen P. Cohen, Sumit Ganguly. 1995. *Brasstacks and Beyond: Perception and Management of Crisis in South Asia*. New Delhi: Manohar, p. 41.

18. Bajpai, *Ibid*, No.17.
19. Kreppon and Drezin, *Ibid*, No. 19.
20. Chari, *Ibid*, No. 5.
21. See, Maleeha Lodhi. 2006. "Nuclear Cloud over South Asia", *The Times of India*, New Delhi, May 1, Also, See, Shaun Gregory, "A Formidable Challenge: Nuclear Command and Control in South Asia", Disarmament Diplomacy, The Acronym Institute, Issue No. 54, February 2001, see, "An Empty Threat", *The Times of India*, January 22, 2009.
22. "Building Stability in India-Pakistan Relations", *The Hindu*, Chennai, February 15, 2010.

9

India-Pakistan Peace Process under the UPA Government and Beyond

Amulya K Tripathy and Roshni Kujur

Introduction

India-Pakistan relations have never been cordial since Independence of both. So, even after the change of both the government the situation remains almost same. This Chapter basically deals with India's relations with Pakistan during UPA government. As at present NDA, under the Prime Ministership Narendra Modi has assumed power in India and started it's Foreign Policy from the Ceremony of Oath taking itself, by inviting Heads of all South Asian Countries. So, basic observance on UPA's policy towards Pakistan has taken place in this study.

The United Progressive Alliance (UPA) came into being in May 2004 to translate the mandate of the people of India expressed through the General Elections of 2004 into a new agenda of governance aimed at providing a responsible, responsive, caring and inclusive Government. The UPA, and its supporters, pledged themselves to preserve, protect and promote social harmony and to enforce the law without fear or favour to deal with all obscurantist and fundamentalist elements who seek to disturb social amity and peace.

An informal alliance had existed prior to the elections as several of the current constituent parties had developed seat-sharing agreements in many states. However, it was only after the election that the results of negotiations between parties were announced. The UPA government's policies were initially guided by a common minimum programme that the alliance hammered out with fruitful consultations with Jyoti Basu and Harkishan Singh Surjeet of the 59-member Left Front. Hence, government policies were generally perceived as centre-left, reflecting the centrist policies of the INC. The congress party is today more closely aligned with the neo-liberalism, strongly advocates social democracy and social liberalism. During the tenure of Jharkhand CM Madhu Koda, the constituents of the UPA were, by mutual consent, supporting his government. At present the UPA is no longer supported by the Left parties. It survived a vote of confidence in the Parliament on 22 July, 2008.

The UPA was formed soon after the 2004 general elections after it became clear that the previous ruling coalition, the National Democratic Alliance (NDA) had been defeated. The NDA has won only 169 MPs in the 543 member 14th Lok Sabha, as opposed the UPA tally of 222 seats. The Left Front with 59 MPs (excluding the speaker), the Samajwadi Party with 39 MPs and the Bahujan Samaj Party with 19 MPs were other significant blocks that opted to support UPA at various phases of its rule. The UPA did not enjoy a simple majority on its own in the Parliament, rather it has relied on the external support to ensure that it enjoys the confidence of the Indian Parliament similar to the formula adopted by the previous minority governments of the United Front, the NDA, the Congress government of Narasimha Rao, and earlier governments of V.P. Singh and Chandrashekhar.

Manmohan Singh's Government has continued the foreign policy that was started by P.V. Narasimha Rao and continued by Vajpayee led NDA's foreign policy. The Prime Minister has continued the peace process with Pakistan initiated by his predecessor, Atal Bihari Vajpayee. Exchange of high-level visits by top leaders from both countries have highlighted his tenure, as has reduced terrorism and increased prosperity in the state of Kashmir.

Prime Minister Manmohan Singh immediately after his election vowed that he would place top priority on carrying forward a nascent peace process with Pakistan and hold talks with all Kashmiri groups to resolve the vexed dispute. But New Delhi would not sacrifice its "national security imperatives" said Manmohan Singh, which is seen as an indication that there would be no let up in the assault on militancy in Kashmir.

"We seek the most friendly relations with our neighbours, more so with Pakistan than with any other country," Singh said, days before the rivals are due to hold talks on nuclear confidence-building measures as part of a peace roadmap agreed by the outgoing Government of Prime Minister Atal Behari Vajpayee. "We must find ways and means to resolve all outstanding problems that have been a source of friction and the unfortunate history of our relations with Pakistan," said Manmohan Singh.

"As far as the Jammu and Kashmir policy is concerned, our party has always been in favour of discussion with all interested groups," said the Prime Minister. We will explore all possible opportunities to bring peace and progress to this vital state that is Jammu and Kashmir."

The Congress party of Manmohan Singh, which swept Vajpayee's BJP-led coalition out of power in polls, had backed the peace process and Congress leaders have reiterated that they would persist with the rapprochement. Pakistan has said that it welcomes the "good vibes" coming from Congress and reaffirmed its commitment to the peace talks.

Indian and Pakistani officials agreed in February, 2002 on a basic roadmap to resolve a wide range of problems that plague relations between the neighbours, including Kashmir, cause of two of three wars fought between the two countries since independence in 1947.[1]

The Congress has been consistent, on the issue of dialogue with Pakistan on all issues including Jammu and Kashmir. It has always advocated formal and informal talks on the basis of the historic Shimla Agreement of 1972. At the same time, the Congress is firm in its view that Pakistan's sponsorship of cross-border terrorism must end completely once and for all. If it continues the Indian state has the responsibility to protect its citizens.[2]

Indian and Pakistani officials agreed in February 2002 on a basic roadmap to resolve a wide range of problems that plague relations between the neighbours, including Kashmir, cause of two of three wars fought between the two countries since independence in 1947.[3]

The Congress has been consistent, on the issue of dialogue with Pakistan on all issues including Jammu and Kashmir. It has always advocated formal and informal talks on the basis of the historic Shimla Agreement of 1972. At the same time, the Congress is firm in its view that Pakistan's sponsorship of cross-border terrorism must end completely once and for all. It is continuous the India has the responsibility to protect its citizens.[4] With this end in view, soon after assuming government the UPA Government resumed talks between India and Pakistan.

Joint Statement – June 2004

As a start of the new dispensation both India and Pakistan appeared seeking ways of achieving and finding the ways to patch up the ties with each other. Pakistan too was eager to normalise the relations, or even that such sentiments weigh with Pakistan's rulers or that they now saw danger to their power from the fanatics they had thought they could use against New Delhi.[5] After a month of government formation on June 2004, the foreign secretaries of India and Pakistan met in New Delhi and issued a joint statement to mark the resumption of the dialogue. It recalled the reassurance contained in the joint press statement of January 6, 2004 and they exchanged views on carrying the process forward in an atmosphere free from terrorism and violence.

India and Pakistan resumed the composite dialogue process that covered eight issues agreed upon in 1997 between Prime Minister Inder Kumar Gujral and Nawaz Sharif. The eight issues are Jammu and Kashmir; Siachen; Wullar Barrage/Tulbul Navigation Project; Sir Creek; Terrorism and Drug Trafficking; Economic and Commercial Cooperation; Peace and Security; and Promotion of Friendly Exchanges in various fields. The last round of talks was held in October 1998 in Islamabad, on Peace and Security, CBMs and Jammu and Kashmir. These were followed by talks during November 5-13 in New Delhi on the remaining baskets. Until 1998, eight rounds of talks on Siachen, six rounds on Sir Creek and nine rounds on Tulbul/Wular project have been completed.

The 1998 New Delhi talks generated some optimism and prompted Prime Minister Atal Bihari Vajpayee to undertake the historic bus trip to Lahore, which culminated in the Lahore Declaration of February 21, 1999. However, the peace overtures proved short-lived as India and Pakistan were locked in a war in the Kargil region of Jammu and Kashmir after armed Pakistan intruders occupied several peaks on the Indian side across the Line of Control (LoC). In October 1999, Nawaz Sharif was overthrown and the Lahore Agreement became another signed document in the history of India-Pakistan relations.

A shift occurred when Vajpayee made the peace offer in Srinagar on April 18, 2003. Snapped air, rail and diplomatic links were restored as Confidence Building Measures as spadework for bilateral engagements. India made a 12-point peace. The meeting of the two foreign ministers resulted in an agreement on Nuclear Confidence Building Measures (NCBMs).[6]

Nuclear Confidence Building Measures (June 19- 20, 2004)

India and Pakistan committed themselves to hold discussions and work towards implementation of the Lahore Memorandum of Understanding (MoU) of 1999. This is a significant development because the military regime in Pakistan has now chosen to recognise the Lahore Declaration after four years. However, it is desirable to note here that that when Atal Bihari Vajpayee and Nawaz Sharif were signing the Lahore Declaration, the Pakistan military under General Musharraf was finalising an operation for intrusion into the Kargil region of Jammu and Kashmir. The Jammat-e-Islami (JI) activists had also staged demonstrations in Lahore against Vajpayee's visit and criticised a rapprochement between India and Pakistan.[7]

The Lahore Declaration was followed by a Memorandum of Understanding (MoU) signed by the two Foreign Secretaries (K. Raghunath and Shamshad Ahmed). It reiterates the determination of both the countries in implementing the Shimla Agreement in letter and spirit. It encompasses all those issues which call upon the two sides to undertake "bilateral consultations on security concepts and nuclear doctrines, with a view to developing measures for confidence building in the nuclear and conventional fields, aimed at avoidance of conflict". It also calls for the two sides to "provide each other with advance notification in respect of ballistic missile flight tests"; "undertake national measures to reduce the risks of accidental or unauthorised use of nuclear weapons"; "abide by the respective unilateral moratorium on further nuclear tests"; and "periodically review the implementation of existing CBMs", including links between the respective Director General's, Military Operations.

On the nuclear issue, the two sides have reaffirmed their 'unilateral moratorium' on conducting further nuclear tests until 'extraordinary events jeopardise their supreme interests'. Interestingly, there are no scoring points over the nuclear flashpoint hypothesis. Further, both have called for "regular working level meetings to be held among all the nuclear powers to discuss issues of common concern". It suggests a welcome understanding between India and Pakistan to take the nuclear debate from the regional to the global level.

The CBMs agreed upon at the Foreign Secretary level included immediate restoration of the strengths of their respective High Commissions from 75 to 110; reopening of the consulates in Mumbai and Karachi; and immediate release of all fishermen detained by both sides. Riaz Khokhar termed the talks as 'useful' and a 'good first step'. Natwar Singh called the talks 'positive and concrete'.[8]

At the talks a decision was taken to discuss the bus links between Srinagar and Muzaffarabad, and Munabao and Khokrapar, along with the other six issues at a later date in July-August 2004. India has also proposed a new bus service between Sialkot (Pakistan) and Suchetgarh (Jammu and Kashmir). Initially, when India had proposed a bus service between Srinagar and Muzaffarabad, Pakistan was fairly apprehensive in accepting it. Pakistan felt that the passengers in the bus should travel with UN documents which was clearly unacceptable to India. The idea to bring the people of the two Kashmirs closer through bus services seems to have impressed Pakistan lately. A section of political parties in Pakistan, including the hardliners, have been critical of the above proposal. According to them a bus service between the two Kashmirs unless done with UN documents, would affect the 'Kashmir cause' and strengthen India's 'forced grabbing' of Kashmir. These and similar proposals have good potential to improve Indo-Pak bilateral relations. However, the fact that mere fencing along the LoC is perceived by Pakistan as legitimising the LoC, has caused serious concern in Islamabad.[9]

New York Meeting-September 2004

Next step in the process is the meeting in New York. Indian Prime Minister Manmohan Singh and Pakistani General Parvez Musharraf met in New York on September 2004 and agreed to explore options. This is a quest that goes beyond a Kashmir solution. It concerns the future of Indo-Pak relations.

Manmohan Singh expressed his views in a newspaper interview saying, 'Short of secession, short of re-drawing boundaries, the Indian establishment can live with anything. Meanwhile, we need soft borders -then borders are not so important.'[10]

At New York itself, Musharraf made it abundantly clear that he was engaged in something of a cat and mouse game. "You can talk about terrorism," he said, "We can say it is freedom movement. You can say we have terrorist camps in Pakistan. We can say India is violating human rights in Kashmir."[11] He made it clear, moreover, that he believed that he was negotiating from a position of relative strength, and unambiguously rejected any proposal to convert the LoC into an international border: "My mind is closed to this proposal. The LoC cannot be the solution to the Kashmir dispute. The Line of Control has been the dispute we have fought wars for. What are you suggesting is that a conflict should be the solution. Isn't it unnatural?"[12] He added further, that he was "giving bilateralism a final chance."[13]

2005 talks

President Gen Musharraf visited New Delhi in April to watch the cricket match between the teams of India and Pakistan. The visit was utilised by the leaders to discuss bilateral issues. The Prime Minister and the President met again later in September in New York on the sidelines of the UN General Assembly session. Signing of the agreement on Pre-notification of Flights, Testing of Ballistic Missiles and MoU for the establishment of communication links between the maritime security agencies of the two countries during the visit of External Affairs Minister to Islamabad in October was among the many of the confidence building measures agreed upon between the two countries during the year.

Introduction of additional transport links between the two countries particularly the Srinagar-Muzaffrabad route helped to enhance people-to-people contacts. The lethal earthquake in October affected the people on both sides of the Line of Control in Kashmir. It created a sense of shared grief between them. Despite its own people being affected cruelly by the earthquake, India offered substantial assistance to the people on the other side. As of November 17 India had made available 1300 tonnes of relief supplies by air, road and rail. This assistance was in addition to the relief material sent by private entities, which the Government of India facilitated in terms of transport etc. New Delhi also committed $ 25 millions as funding for the long-term task of rehabilitation and reconstruction efforts in the earthquake affected areas of the Pakistan-occupied Kashmir.

The Havana Meeting 2006

Prime Minister Manmohan Singh met the Pakistani President Pervez Musharraf on the sidelines of the Non-aligned summit. There was an hour-long meeting at Havana on 17 September, 2006. In this meeting Prime Minister Manmohan Singh and Pakistani President Pervez Musharraf decided to put in place an institutional mechanism to counter terrorism.

At the end of the one-on-one talks which they described as “cordial, frank and detailed,” the two leaders agreed to an India-Pakistan anti-terrorism institutional mechanism to identify and implement counter-terrorism initiatives and investigations. A joint statement was read out by Manmohan Singh at a media appearance along with General Musharraf.

The statement went on to say that the two leaders met in the aftermath of the Mumbai blasts and “strongly condemned all acts of terrorism and agreed that terrorism is a scourge that needs to be effectively dealt with."

They also agreed to the resumption of the composite dialogue between the Foreign Secretaries "at the earliest," noting that the peace process must be maintained and its success was important for both countries and the future of the entire region.

On Jammu and Kashmir, they decided to continue the "joint search for mutually acceptable options for a peaceful negotiated settlement of all issues between India and Pakistan, including the issue of Jammu and Kashmir, in a sincere and purposeful manner." Referring to the 'useful discussions' on Jammu and Kashmir, the joint statement went on to say "there is a need to build on convergences and narrow down divergences."

The two leaders agreed that experts would work out the modalities of a joint survey of Sir Creek "without prejudice to each other's positions on the issue." The two leaders also decided to move ahead with the implementation of the agreements already reached on the confidence building measures along the Line of Control in Jammu and Kashmir, including bus services, crossing points and truck services.

Neither of the two leaders would go beyond the carefully formulated joint statement that was worked out after hours of discussions among the members of the delegation, including the National Security Adviser M.K. Narayanan and the Foreign Secretary-designate Shivshankar Menon on the Indian side and Pakistan's Secretary of the National Security Council Tariq Aziz, Foreign Minister Kasuri and Foreign Secretary Riaz Khan.

Asked by the Indian media as he was passing through the hotel lobby if the new agreement represented a breakthrough, Gen. Musharraf said, "Yes, it is very good." He pronounced himself happy over the outcome. He would not be drawn into a detailed discussion, pointing out that he had committed himself to not saying anything more than what the statement said, lest it should hamper the dialogue process.

Before the meeting of the two leaders, they were accompanied by their delegations for a brief interaction. The Indian delegation included Mr Narayanan, Minister of State for External Affairs Anand Sharma, Mr Shivshankar Menon and Media Adviser to the Prime Minister Sanjaya Baru. The Pakistani side included Mr Kasuri, Mr Riaz Khan, and Minister of State Sumaira Malik.

Indian officials later expressed satisfaction over the outcome of the meeting, noting that major issues, including the formulation on terrorism were being negotiated till the very last. The reference to terrorism and the constitution of a joint mechanism to counter it were in tune with the Prime Minister's stand that he can carry Indian public opinion with him only if there were credible assurances on terrorism. At the same time, the resumption of the Foreign Secretary-level dialogue, addressing the issues of Jammu and Kashmir, Siachen and Sir Creek satisfied the Pakistani side.

In his address to the NAM summit on Friday night, Gen. Musharraf said, "A historic opportunity exists that must be seized by the leadership of the two countries to bring to a close the chapter of tensions and conflict in our region."

"It is of paramount importance that we devote all energies to address the major challenges of our region by ensuring poverty alleviation, universal education, better health and higher standards of living for our people," he said.

Gen. Musharraf said the three years of peace process between India and Pakistan had led to confidence building and improved environment in bilateral relations.

"Pakistan is making sincere efforts to promote peace and cooperation in South Asia. Three years of peace process with India have led to confidence building and improved environment. We are determined to pursue the peace process to resolve all outstanding issues with India, including the Jammu and Kashmir dispute."

He also called upon NAM members to focus on just and equitable solutions to international conflicts and disputes by establishing a mechanism for the purpose.

He urged NAM to promote a comprehensive strategy to combat terrorism. "NAM should promote a comprehensive strategy to combat and eliminate terrorism in all its forms and manifestations. It should require a two-pronged approach: first combating terrorist sanctuaries, including through active international cooperation, [and] secondly addressing the underlined cause of terrorism and extremism, which includes political disputes and conflicts, economic and social injustices."[14]

Mumbai 26/11 Attacks: 2008

The world saw a day of infamy on November 26, 2008. Around 8.30 p.m., a group of ten Pakistani terrorists belonging to the Lashkar-e Toiba (LeT) an ally of Al Queda and a strategic asset of Pakistan's Inter Services Intelligence (ISI), secretly landed in the seafront of Mumbai, the jewel of India and the business and financial capital of a newly-emerging economic power, dividing themselves into four groups and went around spreading death and destruction over a wide area in the seafront.

The following facts available give us an idea of the magnitude of the terrorist strikes, the like of which the world had not seen before:

- There were 13 incidents of intense firing with assault rifles at different places, including the Chhatrapati Shivaji Train (CST) terminus, the Metro Cinema junction, the Cama and Albless hospital, outside the Olympia restaurant in Colaba, the lobbies of the Taj Mahal and Oberoi/Trident hotels, and the Leopald Care behind the Taj Mahal Hotel.
- Near the Metro Cinema junction some terrorists hijacked a police vehicle and went around spraying bullets on passer-by.
- There were seven incidents involving explosive devices – outside the Taj Mahal Hotel, in the BPT Colony at Mazgaon, three near the Oberoi/Trident Hotels, the Colaba market and inside a taxi.
- There were some incidents of throwing hand-grenades – two of them at the Cama hospital and on Free Press Road.
- There were three incidents of Fidayeen style infiltration into buildings followed by a prolonged confrontation with the security forces before being killed. These took place in the Taj Mahal and the Oberoi/Trident hotels and in the Narriman House in Colaba, where a Jewish religious-cum-cultural centre is located, headed by a Jewish Rabbi. Jewish people of different nationalities often congregate there. The centre also has cheap accommodation for Jewish visitors from abroad.
- According to the local authorities, most of the hotel guests who were subsequently rescued by the National Security Guards (NSG) had run into their room and locked themselves up when the terrorist forced their way into the lobbies and restaurants and started opening fire. They were not hostages.
- However, the terrorists took six Jewish people hostages in Narriman House. They were found dead when the NSG made their entry and killed the terrorists. It was not known how they died – though there were bullet wounds or beheading as the *jihadis* normally do.
- Almost all the terrorist strikes took place against targets near the sea. The terrorists did not venture out into the interior.[15]

The use of boats and dinghies for the clandestine transport of men and material for terrorist strikes on land is an old modus operandi used in the past against Israel. The anti-India *jihadis* emulated their West Asian counterparts. The success of the terrorists in evading detection by our Coast Guard and the police revealed a serious gap in our maritime counter-terrorism architecture.

The Mumbai attacks proved to be as direct stabbing on the Indo-Pak peace dialogues. The incident acted as the deadly end and key point of distrust among both states. It indulged the subcontinent in the wave of terrorism and defamed Pakistan as the global nursery of terrorism. The Mumbai attacks gained limitless support from the international community due to the direct assault on the foreigners. Indians claimed Mumbai terror the 26/11 as the 9/11 of India and urged for unjustified pressure on Pakistan to stop terrorism, ignoring their own fascists group terrorism.

Indian Prime Minister Manmohan Singh and Pakistani Prime Minister Yousuf Raza Gilani decided to resume peace negotiations disrupted by the November terrorist attacks in Mumbai, but the Indian leader called on Pakistan to eliminate its "infrastructure of terrorism" as a precondition to future talks.[16]

In a joint statement issued by the leaders after their meeting on 16 July, 2009 in Egypt, Asif Ali Zardari President of Pakistan made an optimistic remark that peace process with India halted after the November 2008 Mumbai terrorist attack could resume again.[17]

After the Mumbai attack, the Ministry undertook several steps both bilaterally with Pakistan and internationally to obtain Pakistan's cooperation in bringing the Pakistan-based perpetrators to justice and to ensure that such acts do not recur. As a result, the United Nations Al-Qaeda and Taliban Sanctions Committee listed individual entities based in Pakistan including leaders of the Lashkar-e-Taiba under Security Council Resolution 1267. The Jamat-ud-Daawa was also listed as an alias of the Lashkar-e-Taiba. On 12 February, 2009, Indian High Commissioner in Islamabad was formally informed of Pakistan's response to the dossier that India had made available on 5 January linking the terrorist attacks on Mumbai to perpetrators in Pakistan. In their response, Pakistani authorities admitted that elements in Pakistan were involved in the terrorist attacks on Mumbai. Pakistan also sought further information and material relating to the investigation. The then EAM Shri Pranab Mukherjee termed this a positive development in a suo moto statement on 13 February in Parliament. On 13 March, 2009, the Government of India provided detailed responses and material to the Pakistan High Commissioner in New Delhi to all 30 questions raised by Pakistan which in turn was acknowledged by Pakistan Ministry of Foreign Affairs.

Despite the above developments and despite high-level statements from Pakistan promising cooperation regarding the Mumbai attack, in terms of actual action taken the response has been disappointing. As a result, there has been a sharp deterioration in bilateral relations.

Responding to the announcement of the new US strategy for Afghanistan and Pakistan, MEA spokesperson on 30 March, 2009 welcomed the very "clear expression of will to carry through the struggle against extremism in Afghanistan and its roots in Pakistan" and expressed India's "readiness to play a constructive role as a responsible power in defeating extremism of all kinds."

Confidence Building Measures- 2004-2008

Around 15 rounds of negotiations were carried by initially National Security Adviser J.N. Dixit on the one side and President Musharraf's aide Tariq Aziz on the other. Following Mr Dixit's demise in 2005 his position was taken over by Special Envoy Satinder Lambah. These negotiations which were carried between 2005 and 2007 evidently flowed from proposals articulated by President Musharraf and Prime Minister Manmohan Singh. President Musharraf proposed that:

1. J and K should be divided into seven regions.
2. There should be a process of "demilitarisation" in identified regions. He subsequently asked for the withdrawal of Indian forces from three urban centres-Srinagar, Kupwara and Baramulla.
3. There should be "self-governance" in Jammu and Kashmir. He did not indicate whether this would be equally applicable to Pakistan Occupied Kashmir and the Northern Areas of J and K, under Pakistan's control.
4. India and Pakistan should agree to "Joint Management" of the State. He did not specify whether "Joint Management" would equally apply to POK and the Northern Areas.

Prime Minister Manmohan Singh, in turn, outlined his vision on how to move forward in resolving the issue of Jammu and Kashmir on March 24, 2006, highlighting the following points.

1. Borders cannot be redrawn but we can move towards making them irrelevant-towards making them "just lines on a map".
2. People on both sides of the Line of Control (LoC) should be able to move freely and trade with each other.
3. A situation can be envisaged where the two parts of Jammu and Kashmir can, with active encouragement from the

Governments of India and Pakistan, work out cooperative and consultative mechanisms, so as to maximise the gains of cooperation in solving problems of social and economic development of the region.

Responding to General Musharraf's proposal for "demilitarisation," India had indicated its readiness to reduce and redeploy forces in Jammu and Kashmir on a reciprocal basis, once it is reassured that there is an irrevocable end to infiltration across the Line of Control. There also appears to have been understanding on the need for mechanisms and institutions to promote cooperation in areas like trade, travel, tourism, education, health, environment and water resources.

There have been a series of measures to promote travel, trade and dialogue across the LoC after the Pugwash Meeting of 2004. For the first time after five decades, people in Jammu and Kashmir are being given facilities to travel across the LoC to meet friends and relatives. In the Kashmir valley, a bus service has been instituted between Srinagar and Muzaffarabad and in the Jammu Region, between Poonch and Rawalkot. Five crossing points have, in addition, been opened to enable people to meet friends and relatives across the LoC. Trade across the LoC has been permitted for the first time, with goods carried by trucks on the Srinagar-Muzaffarabad road. There are also proposals under discussion to establish bus links between Jammu and Sialkot in the Jammu Region and between Kargil and Skardu linking the valley of Kashmir with the Northern Areas, under Pakistan's control. While the goods presently traded are restricted to locally produced products, this trade can be vastly expanded as India and Pakistan move towards their stated goal of establishing a South Asian Economic Union. There are, however, still misgivings and grievances that despite the new openings for trade and travel, the procedures for such cross LoC links have been made so cumbersome and restrictive that there are numerous complaints from people, who find permission to travel either delayed, or effectively denied. Many of these confidence building measures figured in recommendations made during the Pugwash meeting in Kathmandu and several other Track-II meetings held between 2004 and 2007.

During subsequent meeting organised by the Pugwash International in Islamabad in March 2006 in which participants from India included not only separatist leaders but also representatives from mainstream Parties. There was recognition that considerable ground needed to be covered on more clearly outlining the parameters of what precisely would emerge from the principles like self-governance, demilitarisation and an irrevocable end to terrorism. Interestingly, President Musharraf referred to his proposals for demilitarisation and self-governance. He told participants that "an ultimate solution on these lines would make the LoC irrelevant," thereby signalling his move away from Pakistan's traditional position of demanding a plebiscite in accordance with UN Resolutions and endorsing Prime Minister Manmohan Singh's belief that while borders could not be changed, they could be made "irrelevant".[18]

While the Pakistan Government has taken the position that Confidence Building Measures are no substitute for a "result oriented" dialogue on Jammu and Kashmir, the Pakistani participants agreed that India and Pakistan should "implement in letter and spirit, the series of existing Confidence Building Measures, particularly those relating to easing travel and trade across the Line of Control. The security establishments in both India and Pakistan have been averse to seeing these CBMs implemented in letter and spirit.

The following is a list of the agreements reached as a part of confidence building measures between the two countries.

- Joint Economic Commissions and Joint Business Councils were reactivated in 2004;
- The first bus service between Srinagar and Muzaffarabad was started in 2005;
- Bus services from Lahore to Amritsar, Amritsar to Nankana Sahib and train links between Munabao in Rajasthan and Khokhrapar in Sindh were started in 2006;
- The Samjhauta Express, which runs between Delhi and Lahore, resumed service in 2005, and despite the 2007 blasts, has continued to run since;
- The first overland truck route between the two countries was opened at the Wagah border crossing in 2007;
- Air links were increased from 12 to 28 flights weekly, triple-entry permit for cross-LoC travel introduced and the frequency of the Srinagar-Muzaffarabad bus service increased from fortnightly to weekly, in 2008;
- Agreement on Advance Notification of Ballistic Missile Tests - brought into effect in 2005 and required both parties to inform the other 72 hours in advance before testing any ballistic missiles within a 40 km radius of the International Border and the Line of Control;

- Establishment of a Communication Link between Pakistan Maritime Security Agency and Indian Coast Guard-brought into effect in 2005, primarily to facilitate early exchange of information regarding fishermen apprehended for straying into each other's waters;
- Humanitarian aid in terms of food, medicine and etc., was extended by India and accepted by Pakistan, in the aftermath of the earthquake in Pakistan Administered Kashmir in 2005;[19]
- A Joint Anti-Terrorism Institutional Mechanism to identify and implement counter-terrorism initiatives and investigations in both the countries was brought into effect in 2006;
- An agreement facilitating regular contact between state-run think tanks, *Institute of Defence Studies and Analyses* (New Delhi), and *Institute of Strategic Studies* (Islamabad) was brought into being in 2008. This agreement is meant to contribute to building channels of communication at the level of scholars;
- The first meeting of a Joint Judicial Committee of judges belonging to both countries was conducted in 2008. This committee is meant to look into the welfare and release of prisoners jailed in both countries. More than 500 prisoners have been released by both sides in repeated instances in 2003, 2004, 2005, 2007, 2008 and 2009;
- Foreign Ministers of both countries agreed to a series of Kashmir-specific CBMs to facilitate crossing the LoC in 2008. A new dimension was added to Indo-Pak trade relationship with the revival of cross- LoC trade in October 2008;
- Both countries agreed to host festivals displaying each other's movies in 2006. The Pakistani Government allowed for the legal release of Indian films in Pakistan in 2008.[20]

UPA Government- 2nd Term-2009

In the Indian General Election in 2009, the UPA won a convincing 262 seats with the Indian National Congress alone winning 206 seats. The UPA has formed a stable majority government. All inclusive and populist policies along with a younger leadership have been credited for this. UPA won the general elections with the Congress winning 206 seats, 61 seats more than the 2004 election tally. The pre-poll coalition of UPA, which did not include Lalu Yadav's RJD, Ram Vilas Paswan's LJP and Mulayam Singh Yadav's SP, won 262 seats, and needed the support of 10 MPs to get a simple majority in the Lok Sabha. Manmohan Singh continued to be the

Prime Minister and in doing so became only the second Prime Minister of India after Jawahar Lal Nehru to return to power after a full five year term in office. RJD, SP, BSP, JD (S) and other smaller parties and independents provide external support to the government.

On the sidelines of Nuclear Security meeting in April 2010, there were no meetings between the two countries, but India made it clear that it will only resume talks if Pakistan takes actions against Lashkar-e-Taiba (LeT) and perpetrators of 26/11 terror attacks.

On the completion of one year of the second term of the UPA government on May 25, 2010, while producing the 'report card' of the government's performance in a press meet, Manmohan Singh stated that Indo-Pak relation was suffering from 'trust-deficit' and reducing this 'trust-deficit' was essential to improve their relations.

On 24th June, 2010 another round of talks was planned which was thought to be aiming at reducing this 'trust-deficit' and as advocated by India, to find "creative Solutions" on Jammu and Kashmir and other issues to build on the progress made earlier through the Composite Dialogue and back channel diplomacy.

But before the June 2010 Indo-Pak talks, both countries got engaged in another major dispute. Both got set to fight a legal battle over Kishenganga power project under construction in Jammu and Kashmir in an international court of arbitration. Pakistan is objecting to construction of 330 MW hydropower plant on Kishenganga, a tributary of the Jhelum under the 1960 Indus Water Treaty.

Uneasiness arose just before June 24, 2010 when Pakistani troops fired on Indian positions on the Line of Control in Jammu and Kashmir killing two civilians and injuring two jawans. However, India made it clear that it will focus on cross-border terrorism and would adopt "an exploratory approach" to work out steps to reduce post-Mumbai attack trust deficit between the two countries.

The June 24, 2010, talks of Islamabad were positive. Though there was no breakthrough, a positive step towards bridging the trust deficit between the two countries was made. During the talks, India raised the 'core concern of terrorism' including the activities of the Lashkar-e-Taiba (LeT) and Jamaat-ud-Dawah (JuD) and Hafiz Muhammad Saeed. The other issue discussed was Pakistan's concern about Indian presence in Afghanistan, and the Indian stand was clarified by making it related to the developmental works in Afghanistan. India, however, made it clear that attacks on Indian assets could not be allowed to continue as it affected relations between New Delhi and Islamabad. The Islamabad talks, though not very substantial but not merely "exploratory" as both sides tried to "understand each others' position".

A meeting between Indian Home Minister Mr P. Chidambaram and his Pakistani counterpart Mr Rahman Malik took place on June 25, 2010 SAARC Home Ministers' Meet, Islamabad. Mr P. Chidambaram was the first Indian Minister to visit Pakistan in three decades where he was accorded a red carpet welcome and a ceremonial Guard of Honour. He pressed for action against JuD Chief Hafiz Saeed and the handlers of the 26/11 terrorists including those who are believed to be in the Pak army. Chidambaram is believed to have sought voice samples of the Pak handlers and raised issues such as infiltration in Jammu and Kashmir also.[21]

During the Foreign Ministers' Meet which took place on 16th July, 2010, the Indian Foreign Minister S.M. Krishna and his Pakistani counterpart Shah Qureshi got caught in a diplomatic entanglement when Pak refused to engage in any substantial manner with the critical areas of 26/11, cross-border terrorism and infiltration by arguing that it could not speed up the judicial process. Further, a diplomatic quarrel broke off during the joint press conference on Baluchistan and infiltration in Jammu and Kashmir. The diplomatic discussions ended on differences and ruined the bilateral negotiations.[22]

On the occasion of the 16th SAARC Summit at Thimpu on April 29, 2012, Prime Minister Manmohan Singh and Pakistan's Prime Minister Yousuf Raza Gilani met and agreed that foreign secretaries of both countries should meet again and Indo-Pak dialogue should resume as without dialogue there was no other means addressing the bilateral issues. [23]

In the meeting India made it clear that while it wants good relations with Pakistan, it was unwilling to be tied down by any pre-conditions set by Islamabad. The Indian side appeared cautious and did not want to raise expectations of any breakthrough.

External Affairs Minister S. M. Krishna said, "we want to have good relations with Pakistan" but declined to comment on the statement made by Pakistan Foreign Office spokesman Abdul Basit that the Sharm-el Sheikh joint statement should be the basis for the meeting of the two Prime Ministers.

The joint statement in Egypt in July the previous year had triggered a controversy as it mentioned delinking of composite dialogue with the issue of terrorism and made a reference to Baluchistan where Pakistan accuses India of fomenting unrest, a charge flatly dismissed by New Delhi. Indian officials maintained that while dialogue was the only way forward, for it to be meaningful, Pakistan has to take credible action to punish the perpetrators of the Mumbai attacks and end cross-border terrorism. Pakistan has been insisting that in line with the Sharm-el Sheikh statement, the dialogue process must be delinked from the issue of terrorism. Pakistan has arrested seven of those accused in the Mumbai terror strikes. But New Delhi feels that Islamabad needs to do more on the front. It has contended that 26/11 mastermind and Jamaat-ud-Dawa (JuD) chief Hafiz Saeed was roaming about freely in that country and brazenly continuing with his anti-India rhetoric.

Pakistan has argued that the dossiers handed over by India during the Foreign Secretary-level talks in New Delhi on February 25 did not contain any evidence to nail Saeed.[24] UPA II, with 2013 witnessed the worst in the Indo-Pak peace process. The year began with Pakistan's beheading of an Indian soldier, which ended the composite dialogue process".[25]

NDA Government Policy under Modi

PM Narendra Modi began his tenure with a diplomatic coup of sort; securing attendance of all SAARC heads of states and Mauritius at his swearing-in ceremony. That did include a very visibly optimistic Pakistani PM Nawaz Sharif. The military's hardening of its position on Kashmir did not prevent Nawaz Sharif from attending Modi's swearing in, but the predictable absence of tangible results on the Kashmir issue after Sharif's trip to New Delhi was used by the military and its allies to attack the prime minister on his return to Pakistan. It was meant to be a chance to re-set ties. However, if one fast forwards three months then there was a definite freeze in the Indo-Pak relationship.

The Prime Minister and his team have made it clear that they consider foreign policy priorities to be in the neighbour. Modi's decision to invite his Pakistani counterpart, Nawaz Sharif, to his swearing-in ceremony together with all the other heads of state or government from the South Asian Association for Regional Cooperation, was considered a positive gesture on both sides of the border. The meeting between the two prime ministers was cordial and frank but—to no one's surprise—not ground breaking.

While Pakistani leaders are unanimous and sincere in welcoming warmer relations with India, civilians and military officials have opposing long-term objectives. It is doubtful that the Pakistani military supports such a change for any reasons beyond the narrowly tactical, and in fact will fight fiercely against such a change affecting its territorial claims. Sharif is pursuing an opposite strategy—trying to turn a tactical rapprochement into a more permanent arrangement.

Concluding Observation

Although India and Pakistan officially claim their goodwill towards one another, none of the conditions for a real rapprochement are met.

Despite Pakistan's assurances that it is ready to seek an agreement with Modi, as it did under the last BJP government, the consensus between civilian and military is only superficial. It would, however, be a mistake to assume that the military is resolutely opposed to all kinds of rapprochement with India. The military still needs the civilian government to break the vicious cycle of economic regression and international isolation in which successive governments (including military regimes) and adventurist policies of the security establishment have locked up the country. It, therefore, wants the Prime Minister to improve relations with New Delhi in service of that goal, but to do so without creating the kind of organic links that would emerge from the development of a strong economic relationship. Moreover, peace with India would challenge the narrative that the military's outsized role in Pakistani government and society is essential to the country's security, and would, therefore, seriously challenge its influence on Pakistani politics.

The peace-process is complicated and determined by the terrorist activities of Muslim separatist groups working in Jammu and Kashmir. As long as this terrorism is not removed totally peace between the two countries is a distant dream. There is no doubt that India is optimistic of the better relations between India and Pakistan in the coming years. It is obvious that any government which come to power give top priority to Indo-Pak peace process. The continuous and cautious efforts of the heads of the nation are necessary for bringing peace into the sub-continent which is necessary for the betterment of both the nations.

References

1. *"Peace with Pakistan a Priority: Manmohan Singh,"* Express India May 20, 2004, www.indianexpress.com.
2. K Bhushan and G. Katyal, *Manmohan Singh: Visionary to Certainty*, APH Publishing, 2004, p.113.
3. *"Peace with Pakistan a Priority: Manmohan Singh,"* Express India, May 20, 2004, indianexpress.com.

4. K Bhushan and G. Katyal, *Manmohan Singh: Visionary to Certainty*, op. cit., 2004, p.113.
5. K. Shankar Bajpai, "Three in This Marriage", March 15, 2005.
6. Asutosh Mishra, "Indo Pakistan Talks-2004: Nuclear Confidence Building Measures (NCBMs) and Kashmir", *Strategic Analysis,* Vol. 28, No. 2, Apr-Jun 2004, p.1.
7. *Ibid.*,p. 2.
8. *Ibid.*,p. 3.
9. *Ibid.*,p. 4.
10. Manmohan Singh to Jonathan Power, *Statesman*; May 20, 2004.
11. Musharraf's address to the UNGA, *Statesman*, September 22, 2004.
12. Musharraf's news conference at the United Nations, New York, September 23, 2004.
13. *Ibid.*
14. The Hindu, Sept. 17, 2006.
15. B.Raman, *Mumbai 26/11: A Day of Infamy*, Lancer Publishers and Distributors, New Delhi, 2013.
16. Washington Times July 14.
17. V. Krishna Iyer, "Statesmanship, the need of the Hour", The Hindu, editorial, May 2009.
18. G. Parthasarathy, "Track 2 and Back Channel Diplomacy in India-Pakistan Relations", December 24, 2010, http://indian diplomacy. blogspot.in.
19. The agreement to open five points on the Line of Control (LOC) in order to provide relief and medical assistance to quake victims was widely acclaimed in J&K as a genuine humanitarian gesture by the two countries. "It is a good step" said Hurriyat leader Mirwaiz Umar Farooq. Ms. Mehbooba Mufti, Chairperson of the then ruling People's Democratic Party (PDP) said such steps were imperative for taking the process of restoration of peace and reconciliation forward. "I am very happy that it is happening. It was very much needed," she said adding "this is the beginning. We'll have to go a long way before the dream of oneness, harmony and affinity is translated into reality." On November 5, 2005 the Spokesperson Navtej Sarna (Govt. of India) told a media briefing that the necessary work to operationalise the five points was under way. He said that the crossing point at Chakan da Bagh (Poonch) would be operationalised on November 7, at Kaman (Uri) on November 9 and Tithwal (Tangdhar) on November 10, 2005. He clarified that due to non-availability or damage to infrastructure at the above crossing points, crossing would be permitted on foot.
20. Samarjit Ghosh, "Two Decades of Indo-Pak CBMs: A Critique from India", Institute of Peace and Conflict Studies, New Delhi, Issue Brief 132, September 2009.
21. Peu Ghosh, "International Relations", op. cit., p. 386.

22. Peu Ghosh, "International Relations", PHI Learning Pvt. Ltd. Haryana, 2013. op.cit., p. 387.
23. *Ibid.*
24. "P.M. Gilani to Meet Prime Minister Manmohan Singh on sidelines of SAARC Summit in Thimpu", *The Economic Times*, http://articles.economictimes. indiatimes.com.
25. "UPA's long run ends as a flop on foreign affairs front" January1, 2014 http://www.dnaindia.com.

10

India-Pakistan Relations: Retrospect and Prospects

Veena Kukreja

India and Pakistan have developed adversarial relations with each other since the partition of the sub-continent. Both countries share bitter memories of three full-fledged wars and a limited war in Kargil, three decades of ongoing proxy war, and the baggage of a painful co-existence. Indo-Pakistan relations have been nurtured on institutionalised hate and mistrust. Indo-Pakistan relations have been riddled with conflicts–over a wide range of issues ranging from religion to water to territorial dispute in Kashmir – have serious ramifications for national security of both the countries.

Pakistan came into being as an insecure state. Thomas Perry Thornton points out Pakistan's paranoia: 'from its very inception Pakistan was an 'insecurity state' that perceived itself not only as small and disadvantaged but as on the defensive against a real and present threat, with its survival at stake' (Thornton, 1999: 171). According to Racine, the 'India Syndrome' of Pakistan stems from an obvious asymmetry between both countries (Racine 2002: 197). This imbalance of strength nurtures feeling of insecurity. Kashmir is the symbol of Indo-Pakistan conflict and fuels anti-Indian feelings.

Kashmir is not the cause but only a symptom of the much more deeply seated conflict. The cause is the colonial 'two-nation' theory that divided the indivisible and caused the largest forced mass migration in history in the midst of bloody communal riots raging all over the northern part of the Indian subcontinent. Kashmir is looked upon by Pakistan as the unfinished agenda of partition.

Moreover, Kashmir is strategically important to Pakistan as it controls the water heads of all the important rivers flowing into the country, which are vital for its survival. It has also become a fuel to the fury of Islamic fundamentalism that the ruling elites use as a tool for authoritarian legitimising formula that serves to stem the tide of democratisation at home. Whereas, India views Kashmir as a symbol of its secularism and composite nationhood. This basic difference in perception is one of the important factors in the whole tangle.[1] Pakistan has fought three full-scale wars with India, and a limited war in Kargil in 1999, over Kashmir which have only widened and deepened the charm, the intervals between the wars have also been full of alarms and tensions. With the overt nuclearisation of India and Pakistan in1998, Kashmir has been depicted by the Western countries as a nuclear flash-point.

Sixty Seven Years of Mutual Suspicion and Discord

During the last six and a half decades, India-Pakistan relations have not gone beyond the framework of mutual suspicion and discord. This perception goes as an input into the decision-making apparatus and policy formulations and further strengthens the same 'national psyche'. This process is a vicious circle. This has also promoted an enemy image of each other, which in turn has created a mindset of hostility and antagonism at the elite level. Besides, in Pakistan army has vested interest in propagating the territorial conflict with India. There is 'an atavistic compulsion in Pakistan's power structure's mindset which believes that its survival and security could only be secured by the fragmentation of India' (Dixit 1995: 244).

The Pakistani establishment is obsessed with Kashmir, which has, strategically, been made a national obsession for political gains. A shrill anti-India refrain overwhelms the national security discourse. The myth that has been carefully built up is that the nation has to be protected, within and without, from India's danger in the form of venal elected politicians, which only the generals can do so by occupying the political space. It justifies maintaining a large army. Every establishment and government in Pakistan has used the Kashmir dispute for its own advantage rather than for the Kashmiris. It comes in handy when attention must be diverted from domestic failures and is useful in stifling people's voices whenever necessary. Besides, as Ganguly points out, Islam could not be the main driving force behind Pakistani nationalism and after the emergence of Bangladesh Pakistan had to find something to substitute for Islam to hold the country together. It, therefore, sought to hold on to Kashmir 'from the imperatives of statecraft and little else' (Ganguly 2002: 182).

The urge to avenge Pakistan's humiliating defeat in the 1971 Indo-Pakistani war and India's role in the liberation of East Pakistan produced two responses.[2] First, it led Pakistan to embark upon the path of acquiring a nuclear arsenal to neutralise India's superiority in conventional warfare. Second, Pakistan adopted the strategy of dismembering India by fomenting and assisting secessionist movements in various parts of India.

It was only under General Zia-ul-Haq's regime that Kashmir acquired the position of being the 'core issue'. Zia initiated the systematically – designed proxy wars in Punjab (1984) and Kashmir (1989). General Zia conceived the 'operation topac' in April 1988 and outlined the likely course of Pakistan's action in Kashmir. The Pakistan Inter-Service Intelligence (ISI), enjoying autonomous power in orienting foreign and defence policies of Pakistan took over the Kashmir issue after the successful Afghan adventure.

Pakistan's proxy war and its unstinted efforts are targeted at weakening India's internal cohesion and territorial unity through what has been termed as 'death by a thousand cuts'. Pakistan has been determinedly exporting, promoting and supporting cross-border terrorism into Kashmir and (even elsewhere in India) by proclaiming that *jihadis* are not terrorists (as India calls them). They are 'freedom fighters', according to Pakistan.

In the post Zia period, with the restoration of democracy in 1988, one does not find any change in Pakistan's Kashmir policy (Kukreja 1998: 407-24). Following the February 1997 elections, Nawaz Sharif's offer of the resumption of bilateral talks was welcomed. However, in reality nothing changed (Kukreja 1998: 407-24). After Atal Bihari Vajpayee's high-profile bus journey to Lahore in February 1999, the Kargil aggression in the summer 1999 seriously dented Pakistani trustworthiness in any dialogue with India, and engendered stronger anti-Pakistani sentiment than in the past.[3]

Rajen Harshe focuses on the negative implications of cross-border terrorism to the peace initiative and maintains that the cross-border terrorism sponsored by Pakistan has to be situated in the broader context of burgeoning terrorism that has plagued contemporary Pakistan. The links between top army personnel, bureaucrats and political leaders on the one hand, and terrorists and drug barons, on the other have acquired a measure of legitimacy under the banner of Islam and *jihad* (Harshe 2005: 246-257).

The relations between India and Pakistan have entered a new phase in the post-11 September, 2011 world. General Musharraf joined the world coalition against terrorism reluctantly, under pressure and threat from Washington. The terrorist attack on Indian Parliament on December 13, 2001, which prompted New Delhi to undertake operation Parakram, pushing its troops into the forward areas in full mobilisation, all pushed Indo-Pakistan relations to the edge of another war. For the first time, India decided that it was not possible to continue the policy of trying to engage Pakistan even whilst it was a target of the latter's covert war. Diplomatic interactions were reduced to a minimum, sporting ties were frozen, cross-border transport and over flights were restricted and dialogues were put on hold.

Following the terrorist attack on the Indian Parliament on December 13, 2001 General Musharraf came under pressure from the US and had agreed publically in his January 12, 2002 speech to wage war against terrorism domestically and to renounce terrorism in Jammu and Kashmir. However, the actions Pakistan has taken against various terrorist outfits so far were superficial. Pakistan continues to support cross-border terrorism politically, diplomatically, morally and financially. Musharraf talks of Kahsmir as being part of every Pakistani's blood. The US Alliance's operation Enduring Freedom in Afghanistan has had little effect in curbing cross-border terrorism in Jammu and Kashmir.

However, in reality one finds that the evidence of close ties Islamabad has had with Taliban, Bin Laden and Al-Qaida, and these three had with terrorist militias like the Lashkar-e-Toiba (LeT), Jaish-e-Mohmmad (JeM) and Harkat-ul-Mujahiddin (HuM) directly and through Pakistan's Inter-Service Intelligence, have destroyed its credibility with the US and other countries. Recent developments reveal that Pakistan is replicating its 'bleed the neighbour' policy, used first in Afghanistan, then in India. Egged on by Islamist clerics and ably aided by Pakistan, the Taliban has made inroads in the country. The various operations by Pakistan army in the South Waziristan in March 2004 ostensibly to hunt down the Al-Qaida and Taliban elements proved to be visible failure.

Peace Process between India and Pakistan (2004-2008)

Notwithstanding this long history of antagonism the Indian Prime Minister Atal Bihari Vajpayee made three attempts to initiate the peace process in February 1999, July 2001 and April/October 2003 respectively. The 2004-2008 peace process has travelled through the Lahore, Agra and Islamabad summits. This development is attributable to the American shift post-9/11, conflict fatigue on both sides, and three assassination attempt on Musharraf's life by *jihadis* and the continuous public desire and support for peace in India, Pakistan, Jammu and Kashmir. After the zigzags of Vajpayee's bus diplomacy to Lahore, Pakistan's stab in India's back in Kargil, the fiasco of the Agra Summit, the Eid ceasefire, the 12th SAARC Summit, Musharraf's continued double speak on Kashmir, and with India's consistent commitment to the peace process without being bullied into surrendering its existence as a composite secular and federal nation, the prospect of peace between the countries appeared more probable than ever in the Post-Cold War era.[4]

The 12th SAARC Summit Conference held in Islamabad on January 6, 2004, was significant, especially in the context of Pakistan's tacit admission on terrorism. It provided India a written commitment from Musharraf that he will not permit any territory under Pakistan's control to be used to support terrorism. Besides, India retained its stand for the need to discuss all issues instead of just focusing on Kashmir as Pakistan's core demand.

After six years, in June 2004 India and Pakistan resumed the composite dialogue process that covers eight baskets of issues agreed upon in Male in 1997 between the former Indian Prime Minister I.K. Gujral and the former Pakistan Prime Minister Nawaz Sharif.[5]

Four rounds of dialogues were completed between January 2004 and November 2008 with two short interruptions. This contributed to improving relations between India and Pakistan. Significant progress was made in Nuclear Confidence Building Measures, and starting of a new rail service between Khokhrapar (Pakistan) and Munnabao (India). People-to-People contacts between the two countries increased because the visa rules were somewhat relaxed. Important progress was made on the contentions issues like the Siachan Glacier and Sir Greek boundary. Bus service and trade across the LOC in Kashmir was initiated in 2005 and 2008 respectively. This period witnessed growth in bilateral trade by 550 per cent between year 2003-04 and 2007-08 from $ 344.59 million to $ 2.23 billion, (Kukreja 2005: 271-278).

26/11 Terrorists Attacks and Suspension of Peace Process

The ominous shadow of terrorism manifested in 26/11 bloody terrorist attack in Mumbai brought the composite dialogue to an abrupt end. Though earlier terrorist attacks were equally brazen, this one had surpassed them all in its impurity, (Bahadur 2011: 355).

India maintained that it would not resume the dialogue with Pakistan until Pakistan does its best to pursue and prosecute those complicit in the crime. In response to Indian demand, Pakistan arrested seven LeT and Jamaat-ul-Dawa leaders in December 2008. One of them the most notorious – Hafiz Muhammad Saeed, was released by the court. The case against the others is proceeding at very slow pace becausc the evidence provided by India is considered very weak and insufficient by Pakistan courts.

Resumption of Peace Process (March 2011) and its Dynamics

India and Pakistan formally announced on February 2011 structured revival of the dialogue process which had been suspended since November 2008 following the 26/11 terror attacks.

Though trade and economic relations dominated the reopened dialogue process, there were several diplomatic visits that facilitated trade talks and the two sides also agreed to make efforts to create an enabling environment for trade on both sides. They also decided to set up a number of working groups/sub-groups to explore mutual cooperation. In early November 2011, the Pakistan's Federal Cabinet took a decision to grant the status of the MFN to India. India had already granted MFN status to Pakistan in 1996 but Islamabad linked the improvement of the trade ties to resolution of Kashmir issue. India welcomed Pakistan's decision. However, a day later the spokesman of Pakistan Foreign Office somewhat back-tracked by suggesting that the Federal Cabinet had agreed 'in principle' to designate India as MFN as part of the process to normalise relations with India. It will be finally given, once consultations within different departments of Pakistan government are complete and the matters involved in this status are settled with India.

Despite these positive developments, no contentions issue between India and Pakistan has moved towards solution. The Siachen Glacier and Sir Creek have not moved beyond the position in 2007-2008.

Water issue between India and Pakistan acquired prominence during 2012, *jihadi* militant outfit namely, LeT threatened to blow up India's dams. Pakistan accuses India of water hegemony. The Baglihar project continues to be a bone of contention. The latest controversy was over the Kishanganga river, called Neelum in Pakistan.

Trans-border terrorism remains India's core concern in the relationship with Pakistan and has been repeatedly raised with Pakistan, including highest level, whereby India has consistently urged Pakistan to fulfill its repeated assurance given to us not to allow the territory under its control to be used for supporting terrorism against India or for any other anti-India activity. There is no evidence that government of Pakistan is taking credible actions to control and penalise the various *jihadi* outfits avowedly working against India.

Besides, when it came to the issue of cooperation in the fight against terrorism, India has found itself cheated. Pakistan refused to allow Indian investigators to question LeT commander, Zaki-ur-Rahman Lakhvi, the mastermind behind the 26/11 attacks, (Kumar 2013:78). Moreover, Pakistan's policy of export of terrorism to India continues (Kukreja 2014: 266-267). It can be exemplified by the fact that Tahawwar Hussain Rana, the Pakistani-Canadian accused in the 12/11 Mumbai terror attack case and David Coleman Headley, co-accused in 26/11 attacks, both confessed before Chicago court that Pakistan's intelligence agency ISI played key role in organising the LeT's 26/11 attacks. Similar nexus between the LeT was also highlighted the slain Pakistani journalist Saleem Shazad in his book *Beyond Bin Laden* and *9 / 11: Insight into Taliban and Al Qaida.*

With the swearing-in as Prime Minister Nawaz Sharif for the third time on June 5, 2013, Pakistan has completed its first successful democratic transition from one civilian government to another. It is interesting to note in the run up to the 2013 election, Nawaz Sharif made encouraging gestures signaling willingness to normalise relation with India, ever before assuming formal change. However, Pakistan's army Chief General Ashfaq Kayani urged the Prime Minister designated to adopt cautious approach towards relation of India (*Times of India*, 21 May, 2013: 22).

Democracy may be resurgent in Pakistan but one of the biggest challenges in Pakistan is getting the relationship with the country's powerful military right. Although the army under Kayani has been supportive of Pakistan's democratic transition, it continues to retain pivotal role in the power structure of Pakistan. Since 1988 in the post-Zia Pakistan, army has developed a new pattern of 'non takeover' intervention in which emphasis shifted from assuming power directly, to playing move subtle, but still ubiquitous role from the sidelines. The military continues to have had an important influence over foreign and security policies and key domestic issues (Kukreja 2003: 67).

Indo-Pakistan Relations under Narendra Modi's Government

Indian Prime Minister Narendra Modi took unprecedented step to inviting neighbouring heads of states to his swearing- in ceremony.

Modi has shown penchant for unconventional diplomacy as well as desire to build better relations with all neighbours.[6] Despite the reservations expressed by the Pakistan army, Sharif accepted Modi's invite to attend his swearing-in on May 26, 2014. Herat strike on Indian consulate in Afghanistan just three days before Modi's swearing-in ceremony by LeT was timed to scuttle Sharif trip and Modi's move to improve relations.

In the first bilateral meeting with Pakistan Prime Minister Nawaz Sharif, the new Indian Prime Minister Narendra Modi focused on Pakistan's delivery on three issues – 26/11 trial, terror, and trade as major markers for improvement in relations.

It was conveyed that Pakistan must abide by its commitments to prevent territory under its control for being used for terrorism against India. Modi also told Sharif that Islamabad must take steps for speedy progress of the trial of 26/11 accused to prove it was serious. Modi also told Sharif that the two countries could move towards normalisation of trade on the basis of September 2012 roadmap on political and economic relations.

Sharif stressed that Modi and he had 'common agenda of development and economic revival' which was not possible without peace and stability in the region. Sharif told Modi he wanted to revisit the Lahore Declaration and pick up the threads from where things had to be abandoned in October 1999.

Despite the criticism Pakistani Prime Minister Nawaz Sharif has received at home for not meeting the Hurriyat leaders and for not focusing on the Kashmir issue during his meeting with his Indian counterpart Narendra Modi, Islamabad described the meeting as 'better than expected'. However, later *Dawn* reported quoting a senior PML (N) member that Sharif felt belittled in India when there was no joint conference after the one-on-one meeting between the two Prime Ministers.

India on August 18, 2014 called off the foreign secretary level talks with Pakistan scheduled for August 25, objecting to its envoy meeting Kashmir separatists on the eve of the dialogue. With the unprecedented response by calling off the talks, the Modi government demonstrated its tough side, signaling it would not – unlike previous government – wink at talks between separatists and Pakistan. There appear to be two other unstated reasons for the Modi government's decision, i.e., coming up election in Jammu and Kashmir by October-November and spate of ceasefire violations by Pakistanis troops in recent days as well as an uptick in terror attacks in the valley.

Prospects of resumption of India-Pakistan talks any time soon slide drastically on August 19 with Pakistan High Commission Abdul Basit disregarding India's red line and going ahead with his scheduled meetings with Hurriyat leader namely, Syed Ali Shah Geelani, Yasin Malik and Mirwaz Umar Farooq.

Senior Journalist Prem Shankar Jha believes that Modi government has committed big mistake by cancelling talks and cutting Hurriyat out. It has severely hurt India's long-term interests (Jha 2014: 20). This had led to the perception that the government had only isolated itself by calling off talks over what Pakistan thought was a 'routine' meeting with the separatists and in the process, set the bar too high for dialogue to resume.

According to Siddharth Varadarajan a smarter approach would have been to give Islamabad enough time to realise the depth of the new governments' concerns and to slowly but quietly escalate the India position all the way to Prime Minister Nawaz Sharif, if a favourable response was not forthcoming. A quiet resolution could have allowed Sharif to accommodate India's concerns without losing face at time when rightist political rivals (and the military establishment) are trying to weaken him (Varadarajan 2014: 12).

The first causality of the cancellation of the foreign secretary – level dialogue between India and Pakistan is likely to be bilateral trade. The least that was expected from the dialogue was that it would have the way for resumption of talks between the commerce ministries of the two countries.

Prospects

While there is absolutely, no reason to doubt Sharif's commitment to peace with India – he actually made this a plank in his election campaign and won handsomely last year – question arise about his ability to deliver. After all, regardless of democratic elections, the India policy mandate in Pakistan has remained with the army and intelligence agencies.

In the wake of current turmoil in Pakistan, while the neutering of Sharif is bad news for Pakistani democracy, it clarifies matters as far as New Delhi is concerned. India-Pakistan relations have fallen victim to the structural bipolarity of Pakistan politics. Like Sharif the previous PPP government in Islamabad too had wanted peace with India, only to be detailed by the 26/11 attacks orchestrated by Pakistan's deep state. On the other hand, General Pervez Musharraf's regime had largely enforced the ceasefire at the border and almost delivered a deal on Kashmir. New Delhi needs to be ready to respond especially if positive signals emanate from Islamabad. It's vital to keep some lines of communication open.

Any Indian policy of dealing with Pakistan has to have a short-term component built into a long-term strategy. The short-term elements that are needed for continuing engagement one more people-to-people relations; enhanced trade and economic ties, which help in building a bigger constituency for peace in both nations; and enough of a deterrent capacity for India's armed forces. In the long term, there can only be one strategy – the strengthening of democratic forces in Pakistan coupled with an army's legitimate pressure group role in its polity (Joshi 2004).

In sum, the long-term prospects for peace are contingent on the democratisation of the militarist – neo-feudal Pakistani state and the common pursuit of immense economic fallouts from the thaw in Indo-Pakistan relations. The current reigning ideology of capitalist globalisation and democratisation is likely to reinforce the peace offensive. However, given the fact that neither military's principalship nor fundamentalism is yet a spent force, we must keep our fingers crossed. In the ultimate analysis, a durable peace would remain a delusion without a full fledged and stable democratic regime in Pakistan.

Notes

1. For an analysis of the Indian, Pakistani and Kashmiri perspective on Kashmir problem refer Thomas (1992).
2. The officers of the Pakistani army while taking the oath of loyalty when passing out from military academy take two pledges – to uphold the ideology of Pakistan and avenge the military defeat of 1971. Consult Dixit 2002: 361.
3. Pakistan's confidence in dealing with India has received a shot in the arm following the emergence as a nuclear power in 1998. Another dimension of the nuclear power status is that despite the apparent failure of the Kargil adventure in 1999, Pakistani strategic thinking opens up possibilities of such adventures in future also.
4. For details refer Kukreja 2002.
5. The eight baskets are Jammu and Kashmir, Siachen, Wullar Barrage/Tulbul Navigator Project, Sir Creek, Terrorism and Drug Trafficking, Economic and Commercial Cooperation, Peace and Security and Promotion of Friendly Exchanges in various fields.

6. According to Sherry Rehman (former Minister of Information and Pakistan's Ambassador in the US in the PPP Government) considers it nothing short of a diplomatic coup.

References

Bahadur, Kalim, 2011, 'Pakistan' India's Neighbour: So Near, But So Far', *World Focus*, 378 (June).

Dixit, J.N. 1995, *Anatomy of Flawed Inheritance: Indo Pakistan Relation 1970-1994*, New Delhi, Konark.

Dixit, J.N. 2002, *India-Pakistan in War and Peace*, Delhi: Books Today.

Ganguly, Summit, 2002, 'The Islamic Dimension of the Kashmir Insurgency', in Christophe Jaffrelot (ed.), *Pakistan: Nationalism with a Nation?,* New Delhi : Manohar.

Harshe, Rajen, 2005, 'Cross-Border Terrorism: Roadblock to Peace Initiative', in Veena Kukreja and M.P. Singh (eds.), *Pakistan: Democracy, Development and Security Issues*, New Delhi: Sage Publications, 246-257.

Jha, Prem Shankar 2014, 'An Inept Pakistan Policy', *Times of India*, New Delhi, August 21, p. 20.

Joshi, Manoj 2004, 'Talking Terms: Engage with Pakistan Civil Society', *The Times of India*, New Delhi, 12 December.

Kukreja, Veena 1998, 'India and Pakistan: A New Peace Paradigm', in Subrata Mukherjee and Sushila Ramaswamy (eds), *Political Science Annual 1997*, New Delhi: Deep and Deep.

Kukreja, Veena 2002, 'Agra Summit: The Indian Perspective', *Punjab Journal of Politics*, 26(1).

Kukreja, Veena 2003, *Contemporary Pakistan: Political Processes, Conflicts and Crises*, New Delhi: Sage Publications.

Kukreja, Veena 2004, 'Pakistan-Taliban-Al Qaida Nexus', *World Focus*, 25(2).

Kukreja, Veena 2014, 'India-Pakistan Relations: The Contemporary Phase' in Mohammed Badrul Alam (ed.), *Contours of India's Foreign Policy: Changes and Challenges*, New Delhi, Reference Press.

Kumar, Satish (ed.) 2013, *India's National Security Annual Review 2012*, London, New York and Delhi: Routledge.

Racine, Jean-Lue, 2002, 'Pakistan and the India Syndrome: Between Kashmir and Nuclear Predicament in Christophe Jeffrelot (ed.), *Pakistan: Nationalism without a Nation*?, New Delhi : Manohar.

Rahman, Sherry, 'The Audacity of Hope', *Times of India*, New Delhi, May 27, 2014, p. 22.

Singh MP, and Kukreja Veena 2005, 'Peace Process between India and Pakistan' in Veena Kukreja and M.P. Singh (eds.), *Pakistan: Democracy: Development and Security Issues*, New Delhi: Sage Publications.

Singh, Jasjit (ed.) 1999, *Kargil 1999: Pakistan's Fourth War for Kashmir*, New Delhi : Knowledge World.

Thomas Raju G.C. (ed.), 1992, *Perspectives on Kashmir: The Roots of Conflict in South Asia*, Boulder: Westview Press.

Thornton, Thomas Perry, 1999, 'Pakistan : Fifty Years of Insecurity', in Selig Harrison, Paul Kreisberg and Dennis Kux (eds), *India and Pakistan : The First Fifty Years*, Cambridge, Woodrow Wilson Centre Press and Cambridge University Press.

Varadarajan, Siddharth 2014, 'The Indo-Pak Talks Mystery and a Possible Happy Ending', *Sunday, Times of India*, New Delhi, August 24, p. 12.

11

China Factor in India-Pakistan Relationship

Sajad Hussain Wani

The post-independence history of India and Pakistan has largely been a history of conflict rather than cooperation. Despite several efforts at reconciliation, the two sides remain locked in an embrace of seemingly unending conflict.[1] The history of Indo-Pak engagement is a detailed story of frequent failures with rare instances of success. Unlike so many other regions of the world, diplomatic exchanges and dialogues have failed to resolve the enormously complex disputes between the two rivals.

Pakistan's perceived perennial fear of Indian threat to its existence made its foreign policy significantly India-centric. Its fear of Indian hegemony in South Asia persuaded it to seek close and harmonious cooperation with China in the same way as the fear prompted it to join the Western sponsored alliances during the Cold War. Therefore, security against India significantly determined Pakistan's pursuance of any relationship. The Sino-Indian rivalry made China a natural ally for Pakistan. Chinese policy-makers saw Pakistan not only a bridge to the Muslim world but also believed that a friendly Muslim neighbour can be diplomatically and strategically important because it would discourage aid or assistance for any insurgency in Chinese Xinjiang province where Muslim separatists are fighting for independence from China. S.M. Burke has aptly argued that the policy-makers of China had serenely calculated from the very beginning that in the long run it would be with India that their national interests will clash and that forbearance with Pakistan in the meantime will ultimately pay a useful dividend.[2] Although the entire American led military alliances which Pakistan joined in the 1950's were aimed at containing communism.China adopted a conciliatory approach towards Pakistan.[3] While Pakistan turned to China to lessen India's threat and to achieve parity vis-à-vis India, China found in Pakistan a willing partner and a feasible option not only to contain India but also to denounce the US dominance in South Asia and also to fulfill its growing energy requirements from Persian Gulf and Central Asia.

China-India-Pakistan Triangle

China, India and Pakistan constitute a major strategic triangle in the geopolitics of Asia. The trilateral relationship that exists between India-Pakistan, Pakistan-China, and India-China is marked by enduring bitterness between India and Pakistan, strong or so called all-weather friendship between China and Pakistan, and an ambivalent friendship and discord between India and China. China and Pakistan share a history of hostility with the third side of the triangle-India. The most striking and the crucial feature of the triangle is that all the three powers possess nuclear weapons (India and Pakistan being *de facto* nuclear weapon powers while China is a recognised one with a permanent seat in the UN Security Council), and all share borders and longstanding animosities with one another.[4] China-India-Pakistan strategic triangle is mainly integral to the larger Asian landscape characterised by new security challenges and changing power dynamics. Presently, Asian states are facing major challenges such as entrenched territorial and maritime disputes, sharpening competition over scarce natural resources especially energy and water, poverty, rise of extremism, historical legacies that weigh down all important interstate relations, and the increasingly fervent nationalism. Though the Asian states are coming together economically and are becoming more interdependent through trade, investment, technology and tourism; but they are not coming together politically. The widening gulf between politics and economics divides Asia more politically.[5]

The policies of China and Pakistan vis-à-vis each other have been greatly influenced by the Indian factor. Pakistan, through its strategic cooperation with China, wants to balance India in the subcontinent, while China perceives Pakistan as a central instrument to counter Indian power in the region which would ultimately make the ways easy for China to claim the status of an Asian and the world power. The China-Pakistan collaboration serves the interest of both by presenting India with a possible two front theatre in the event of a war with either country.[6]

In the late 1950's and early 1960's, while many factors such as the growing Indian sympathy for Tibet, the China-India boundary dispute, military frictions and the follow-on China-India war in 1962, rapidly deteriorated Sino-Indian relations, China and Pakistan on the other side reached a strategic understanding based on their convergent interests vis-à-vis India. Ever since China-Pakistan ties grew stronger, various metaphors like *Deeper than Oceans and Higher than Himalayas*, *All-Weather Friendship*, *One Nation two Countries* have been used to describe the enduring nature of China-Pakistan relationship. Maintaining close ties with China has been a priority for Islamabad and Beijing has provided extensive economic, military and technical assistance to Pakistan over the years. Many Pakistani analysts characterised China as the most benevolent, loyal and remarkably undemanding partner who always came to their rescue at times of severe crisis by providing valuable moral, diplomatic and material support without any strings attached. They argue that Pakistan's relationship with China comes up from the need to counter Indian dominance in the subcontinent.[7] Not only Pakistan, but China is also benefiting from its close cooperation with Pakistan as Pakistan has long served as a conduit for Western technology to flow into China, to fulfill China's growing energy requirements from Persian Gulf and Central Asia, and China also used Pakistan as a front in the arms trade with several Middle Eastern countries. In fact, it was Pakistan that in the early 1970s enabled China to cultivate its ties with the West and the US in particular, becoming the conduit for Henry Kissinger's landmark secret visit to China in 1971 and has been instrumental in bringing China closer to the larger Muslim world.

The geopolitical realities of the post-Cold War era prompted India and China to adopt a reconciling attitude towards each other in order to seek out a more stable and mutually advantageous relationship. Despite the rivalry and disagreement on a number of issues, China and India started normalising their relations so as to achieve their long-term goals of socio-economic development. China started showing declining interest in Pakistan because its South Asian policy now aimed at adopting an even handed approach towards the longstanding disputes in the region. Therefore, the post-Cold War developments had apparently compromised Pakistan's strategic importance to China as Devin T. Hagrety argues that these developments led to the 'relative neglect' in China regarding its entente with Pakistan.[8] However, owing to Pakistan's geopolitical significance for China, the strategic relevance of the China-Pakistan cooperation has not been severely affected.

Though the Chinese analysts believe that their foreign policy towards the subcontinent has been always guided by the five principles of peaceful coexistence but maintaining close ties with Islamabad has been the priority for China. Anil Joseph Chandy argues that despite evidence of a bias in China's foreign policy behaviour that favours Pakistan over India, the mantra of peaceful coexistence is always projected as the guiding principle of Chinese policy.[9]

The India-China boundary dispute and the fundamentally conflicting views about the nature of China's relations with the South Asian countries continue to be the main stumbling blocks that undermine the Sino-Indian rapprochement. China's strategic projects in South Asia including new ports in Sri Lanka and Pakistan, new transportation links with Myanmar, Nepal, and Pakistan, aroused the fear of encirclement in India and sharpened the geopolitical competition between India and China. For India, China's longstanding and cordial partnership with Pakistan has been and remains a major obstacle in the way of improving ties with Beijing. Though Beijing attempted to develop parallel relations with both India and Pakistan, India, however, looked at China-Pakistan relations very disapprovingly and viewed it as an exclusively anti-India partnership. While bilateral relationship between China and Pakistan has its own resonance, India weighs heavily in this narrative of strategic nexus.[10] In their own ways, each is using the other to balance India and indeed, preventing India's dominance of South Asia by strengthening Pakistan has been a strategic priority for China. Despite the growing concerns about Pakistan because of the rise of extremism and an increasingly unstable and politically dysfunctional state, China will not abandon its relations with Pakistan. As Mohan Malik argues:

"China's all-weather relations with Pakistan will remain the most important factor in Beijing's South Asia policy- If Beijing downgrades ties with Islamabad, Pakistan may become destabilised, or may completely slide into the American camp, or may come to terms with Indian predominance; all three supposed outcomes are detrimental to China's core security interests... Unless Pakistan descends into total chaos and anarchy and is seen as posing a serious threat to China's vital interests Beijing will not give up on its most allied ally in Asia."[11]

Though both China and India have benefited from the rising trade relations, the development has not, however, eliminated the security concerns that the two countries perceive from each other. Protracted mistrust, growing suspicions of each other and a burgeoning strategic rivalry between Asia's two rising powers will continue to inflict considerable restraints on the scope and pace of normalisation. Beijing's strategy to pursue economic ties with India while hedging its security bets by having close ties with Pakistan and pursuing other regional security engagements clearly indicates that China continues to perceive India both as a major economic opportunity and a source of increasing security concern. Therefore, the security dilemma in India-China relations has neither disappeared completely nor is likely to, though the levels of engagement between India and China have expanded considerably.[12] The fear of losing control over the restive province of Tibet and Xinjiang coupled with the geo-strategic imperative to balance growing Indian power motivate Chinese efforts to improve ties with India in tandem with its parallel efforts to bolster Pakistan's capabilities – militarily, economically and politically. The all-weather relationship which has its roots in the geopolitical imperative of containing India has now expanded into a multidimensional partnership that encompasses the transnational issues (terrorism, sea lanes safety, economic and resource security) as well as the old geopolitical concerns (India) and the new geopolitical equations (the US versus China in South West Asia).

China's Interests in South Asia: An Overview

Historically, Chinese interaction with South Asian states, notwithstanding periodic religious, commercial and cultural contacts, was minimal. China became interested in South Asian affairs more particularly after the annexation of Tibet in 1951. China's occupation of Tibet and the subsequent solidification of Sino-Pakistan strategic cooperation allowed China to extend its reach and influence into the region where it had historically exercised little or no influence. Given China's sensitivity about Tibet which has traditionally been seen by the Chinese as their *soft strategic underbelly*, its South Asia policy had always been guided purely by its security considerations.[13] During Cold War, China feared South Asia being used as a foot-hold by anti-Chinese forces (the Western Powers). China's sense of insecurity about its fragile regions (which they believed were prone to Western influence if the Western powers got strong control over South Asian affairs), ultimately made China's

South Asian policy security-centric. Rasul B. Rais argues that initially, "the structure of three-way changes pushed China into the South Asian security system: its war with India; rivalry with Soviet Union; and Pakistan's disillusionment with the United States over the latter's military assistance to India."[14] Besides, China's strategy to limit the influence of containment policy pursued by the United States in the South Asian region during the Cold War, and secondly its concern for stability and security of the far flung and restive western periphery comprising Tibet and Xinjiang, have also significantly influenced the Chinese attitude towards South Asia. Initially China's policy of peaceful coexistence as enshrined in the Panchsheel agreement of 1954, epitomised its strategy and priority in South Asia; however, after the deterioration of Sino-India relations due to the border dispute and the vexing Tibet issue, China's policy in South Asia underwent a major shift primarily driven by the need to counterbalance India in the region. China soon embarked upon the strategy of engaging India's immediate South Asian neighbours by playing upon their complaints and grievances towards India. In cultivating India's immediate neighbourhood, China employed all available means; political, diplomatic, economic and even military.

South Asian region has an immense importance in China's strategic calculus not only because of China's turbulent western periphery, but also because of its interest in protecting its sea lanes of communication and expanding engagement with the rest of the world. During the Cold War and until the late 1980's, China appeared less concerned about India and was not convinced that relations with India would be as strategically important for China as the relations it was cultivating with other major powers. The dismissive view about India resulted from Beijing's military victory over India in 1962, and from Beijing's more impressive economic performance compared to India. On the other hand, China's rise; its mounting economic and military power; and its enduring strategic relationship with Pakistan, at all time figure prominently in India's defence and strategic foreign policy. Nonetheless, India's nuclear tests in 1998 and later its close cooperation with the United States considerably changed China's attitude towards India.

The end of Cold War and the subsequent demise of Soviet Union has opened more opportunities for China to spread its influence in the South Asian region. Post-Cold War Chinese policy towards South Asia has generally been in line with broader efforts by China to reduce tensions around its periphery in order to stabilise the peaceful international environment needed for China's grand agenda of economic development and other domestic changes and reforms. Beijing has publically emphasised on positive engagement and has endeavoured to minimise its conflicts through dialogues, high-level visits and other diplomatic measures with all the South Asian countries. Therefore, the decade of 1990's had not only awakened China from centuries of inactivity in the international arena, and saw China's unprecedented economic growth and growing international influence, but it also witnessed a major shift in China's South Asia policy which emphasised a closer relationship with its rival, India. China attempted to build a new relationship with India but not at the cost of abandoning its relations with other South Asian countries; it simultaneously pursued friendly relations with other South Asian countries. The changes that occurred in Chinese foreign policy were the manifestation of the reforms initiated by Deng Xiaoping in 1980's, who helped to steer Chinese foreign policy away from communist idealism towards socialist pragmatism.[15] As China's foreign policy in 1980's focussed much on modernisation and development, it stressed on creating a peaceful environment conducive for such an endeavour and began to highlight the importance of Panchsheel, the five principles of peaceful coexistence, and declared to the world that it would never seek hegemonism but would fight such tendencies along with other third world countries. Chinese intentions were clearly reflected by Hu Yaobang in his report to the Twelfth Party Congress in 1983, which noted:

Socialist China belongs to the Third World. China has experienced the same sufferings as most other Third World countries, and she is faced with similar problems and tasks. China regards it as her sacred duty to struggle resolutely against imperialism, hegemonism, and colonialism together with the other Third World countries.[16]

The emergence of the United States as the sole superpower after the demise of Soviet supremacy and its growing strategic presence in South Asian region became the major concern for the Chinese strategic policy-makers. Although China and Pakistan shared substantial strategic interests since the mid-1960s as part of an anti-India logic, continuing US-Pakistan alliance caused critical strategic concerns for China. Such dynamics were reinforced and compounded in the wake of 9/11 and the consequent developments like strengthening of US-Pakistan strategic partnership, the US troop presence in Afghanistan, and also by the growing US strategic links with India. China became more wary of Pakistan's internal instability which prompted it to pursue a more balanced policy towards the region and to refrain from making any commitment without carefully examining its pros and cons. China's involvement in Pakistan closely reflect Beijing's own priorities and evolving risk assessments. As Evan A. Feigenbaum argues:

China's calculus in Pakistan is becoming more diverse. The central question will be the extent to which political, and especially investment, risks begin to complicate the straightforward geopolitical calculus that has long yielded a remarkable intimacy between Beijing and Islamabad. To be sure, Beijing is too strategically tied to Pakistan — and too timid in its diplomacy, in any case — to off-load an erstwhile ally. But China is unlikely to be such an accommodating patron, either.[17]

After decades of remaining aloof from India while holding Pakistan in a warm embrace, China has now attempted to adopt a more balanced policy towards South Asia. China's even-handed approach was further nurtured by series of confidence building measures being put in place between the two great powers, China and India, since 1990's. China's stress on mutual security, mutual benefit and economic development emerged as the main components of its South Asia policy. Swaran Singh argues:

These changes in China's attitude were primarily driven by three important factors: China became more confident about its own security; launching itself on economic opening-up and modernisation drive prompted it to be more focussed on economics and on global networking than sub-regional intrigue; and lastly due to beginning of China-US entente and India-China rapprochement since 1990's."[18]

All these changes were expected to bring shift in China's South Asia policy which may ultimately weaken China's inclinations to engage India's immediate neighbourhood by offering itself to them as an alternative or counterweight against India. Post-9/11, the United States' attempts to engage both India and Pakistan caused anxiety in Beijing. China became uncomfortable with India's growing closeness with the United States and it soon revised its military contacts with Pakistan and other small South Asian states, thereby reverting back to its older method of conducting relation with South Asian states. Therefore, military relations and strategically guided policies continues to dominate China's ties with the South Asian region. India is feeling threatened by the increasing advances of China and its strategic proxies into the region – from the older-established links of China with Pakistan to newer-emerging links with other states in South Asian region. Therefore, China's strategic interests in the region have not changed significantly since the end of the Cold War; however, its economic growth, and its specific economic needs – from natural resources to transit routes – have changed the scale of its influence and the balance of its relationships in South Asia. China's priorities in the region such as, balancing a rising India, addressing terrorist threats, and expanding its economic activities, will continue to guide its policy towards South Asia in the foreseeable future.[19]

China's Response to India-Pakistan Tensions: An analysis

In the 1950's and early 1960's, China was favouring neither India nor Pakistan but insisted on resolving regional disputes bilaterally through negotiation and consultation. Chinese policy of neutrality disappointed Pakistan because Islamabad was expecting full support from China against India. Pakistan criticised it as a *communist-neutralist line*[20] and tried hard to convince PRC to review its officially neutral stance on Kashmir dispute, but Beijing refused to fall in line with Pakistan's request.[20] However, the consequences of the Chinese intervention in Tibet and the border war in 1962 engendered hostilities that not only caused the enduring enmity between Beijing and New Delhi but also concurrently brought new opportunities for China and Pakistan to develop strong strategic cooperation. China renounced its neutrality posture and started supporting Pakistan against India. Swaran Singh argues that 1962 war was the landmark event in the evolution of China's South Asian policy in general and its policy towards Kashmir issue in particular.[21]

During the war of 1965 and 1971 between India and Pakistan, China provided only rhetorical support to Pakistan and made signs of opening a second front along the Sino-Indian border. While it is widely believed that Chinese support was not restricted to mere verbal declarations, its military and nuclear technology transfer to Pakistan has played a decisive role in reducing Pakistan's power asymmetry vis-à-vis India. Moreover, Pakistan's desire for clear-cut endorsement and direct support for China in Beijing's wars with India has met with no more than rhetorical support from China as it was callously exposed in 1965 and 1971 Pakistan's war with India when China made only verbal declarations and effectively refrained from getting directly involved in the war on the Pakistani side against India. In spite of all this, China-Pakistan cooperation flourished over the decades. As Farzana Shaikh argues:

"Pakistan's willingness to accommodate a less than satisfactory partnership with China that did not directly address its security needs vis-à-vis India suggests that more is at play in Pakistan's complex relations with great powers than merely seeking military

protection from India. At issue is the recognition of Pakistan as a state that seeks international sanction to assume a role out of all proportion to its real power. Given the continuing uncertainty over its national identity and the lingering doubts over the prospects of its survival, Pakistan has come to rely on great power endorsement as a vital measure of its historical purpose."[22]

Since late 1980's, Beijing has attempted to untie itself from the India-Pakistan conflicts as Sino-Indian rapprochement progressed. Post-Cold War shifts in Chinese policy approached in the context of the continuance of several pre-existing Chinese steps towards disentanglement from India-Pakistan conflict. Unlike Mao Zedong, Deng Xiaoping soon after coming to power emphasised on improving India-Pakistan ties. The change in Chinese foreign policy was enthused by two important reasons: firstly, by China's fear of Soviet encirclement via closer Soviet-India cooperation; secondly, Deng Xiaoping's ambition to create a stable and peaceful environment necessary for economic development by reducing tensions with all of its neighbours. Deng Xiaoping's new economic policies resulted in a strategic shift not only in China's international politics but also its posture on the Kashmir issue. By the late 1990's, China's declining interest in India-Pakistan conflicts in general, and its diminishing support to Kashmir issue in particular, led to Pakistan's disappointment. Fazal-Ur-Rahman argues that:

It was very disappointing for a majority of Pakistani's, when President Jiang Zemin, while addressing Pakistan's Senate in December 1996, made no reference to the Kashmir issue but instead advised Pakistan to put the thorny issues aside in order to develop relations with India in less contentious sectors like trade and economic cooperation... indifference on Kashmir issue always hurting Pakistani's."[23]

Chinese policy of neutrality in Indo-Pakistani disputes continued with enthusiasm as Sino-Indian rapprochement gained momentum after 1988. The developments in Sino-Indian relations apparently led Beijing to adopt neutral posture in important areas of the India-Pakistan conflict. Beijing's policy makers embarked upon developing cooperative and friendly ties with both India and Pakistan and desisted from supporting one side against the other. The change in Beijing's attitude was clearly manifested during the 1990 Kashmir crisis in which China dropped its traditional stance of insisting on plebiscite vis-à-vis Kashmir issue. Instead of referring Kashmir conflict to the United Nations, Beijing stressed on solving the dispute peacefully through mutual negotiation and consultation between

India and Pakistan. Beijing advocated moderation and abstention from violence on both sides of the border.[24] Although Indian nuclear tests in 1998 posed perhaps the most serious challenge to China's even handed policy towards India and Pakistan, China, however, expressed only limited verbal offensives against India and did not go too far to destroy the embryonic Sino-Indian ties. After the crisis caused by nuclear tests had faded, Beijing's position was once again revitalised as was evident from the Chinese stand during the Kargil crisis between India and Pakistan. China refrained from supporting Pakistan's position and effectively insisted on deescalating the confrontation between India and Pakistan, and to resolve all outstanding issues peacefully through negotiation. China's noncommittal stance on the Kargil issue, argues Summit Ganguly, was the biggest diplomatic failure for Pakistan.[25] China's neutrality posture in Kargil conflict was also significantly motivated by its fear of rising extremism in Pakistan and Afghanistan as the Jihadi groups were suspected of helping the Uighur separatists against China. The rise of Taliban in Afghanistan in mid 1990's encouraged and abated the rise of radical Islamist trend which eventually made China apprehensive of it acting as a catalyst for the revival of separatism in the disturbed province of Xinjiang.[26] China had not only refrained from getting militarily involved in the Indo-Pakistan conflicts on behalf of Pakistan but has also detached itself from making any unconditional commitment that could risk China being dragged into Indo-Pakistan conflicts. While in the past China either remained evasive towards the conflict or tilted in favour of Pakistan's position in largely political rather than military gestures, it now appears more willing to encourage stability, dialogue and peaceful resolution of the Kashmir problem because of the fear that a prolonged conflict having potential to escalate into an open military confrontation between two nuclear weapons states could seriously compromise China's own fundamental security interests.

Thus from 1990's onwards, there was a discernible shift in China's position on Indo-Pakistan issues. President Jiang's call to put Kashmir issue on the backburner and instead focus on economic cooperation; Chinese neutrality in the Kargil conflict; its reluctance to support Pakistan and its insistence and endorsement of India's position that the Line of Control must be respected; and its response to 2001-2002 border crisis and November 2008 Mumbai Terrorist attacks, all gave an impression that Beijing wanted to pursue a more balanced and at best a neutral policy in the region. Given its changing regional and global role, China will not completely side with Pakistan in any dispute between India and Pakistan. However, in the recent past, certain developments like Chinese attempts to issue stapled visas to the residents of Jammu and Kashmir while making no such change for residents of so-called Azad Kashmir carrying Pakistani passports; its refusal to issue visa to Lt Gen B S Jaswal in July 2010 (the Head of the Indian Army's Northern Command) for he had commanded the army deployed in the disputed territory to suppress the Kashmiri resistant movement; and the Chinese invitation to the Mirwaiz Umer Farooq (the moderate Kashmiri leader and President of All-Parties Hurriyat Conference (APHC)) to pay a state visit to China, highlighted the Chinese intention to play a more proactive role in the Kashmir dispute and trying to abandon the policy of neutrality adopted since the 1980's.[27] Chinese invitation to Mirwaiz Umer Farooq, argues Chietigj Bajpaee, was symbolically significant for internationalising the Kashmir issue.[28] Although China had effectively called-off the stapled Visa issue and appreciated India-Pakistan's joint efforts to improve relations, but more needs to be done by China to mitigate the persistent trust deficit between India and Pakistan. Even though Pakistan and China relations may not enjoy the distinctiveness of 1960s and 1970s, but Pakistan holds its significance for China as a reliable ally internationally and a factor of security for China's Southern and Western periphery. Although, China attempted to adopt a more neutral position in Indo-Pakistani conflicts, but that was not enough to put an end to the strategic cooperation between China and Pakistan. Indeed, a fundamental change has been witnessed in China's policy regarding its position on Kashmir issue and other Pakistani diplomatic initiatives against India, but China remained adamant in its support to Pakistan for defending its national security and sovereignty. Chinese support for Pakistan's efforts to develop its military industrial base did not diminish and sales of conventional weapons did not stop with the onset of Sino-Indian rapprochement. Jingdong Yuan aptly argues:

"Despite China's varying stance on the Kashmir question over the past six decades, an underlying principle that has consistently guided China's Kashmir policy has been avoiding unnecessary entanglement in the protracted and seemingly intractable conflict between India and Pakistan. Whatever Beijing's declared position may be at any given time, it has been by and large tactical and so designed to advance China's broader geostrategic interests in the subcontinent."[29]

Terrorism: China, India and Pakistan

The issue of terrorism has added a new dimension to the already complex triangular relationship between China, India and Pakistan. Although all the three countries have been gravely affected by terrorism, it is unfortunate that among the three countries there is no common refrain to combat terrorism. After the killing of Osama bin Laden in Pakistan, New Delhi wanted Beijing to exert its clout on its all-weather friend (Pakistan), but Beijing's response, however, has not been very encouraging and has been lukewarm or rhetorical at best.[30] Instead of openly supporting Indian efforts to bring to justice the perpetrators of the Mumbai attacks, Chinese policy makers asserted that they will continuously and firmly support Pakistan's efforts in formulating and implementing an anti-terrorist strategy based on national conditions. Further they insisted that Pakistan has been at the forefront of the international fight against terrorism, and its government has been dedicated to the cause.[31] China needs to take more effective measures for preserving the stability in a volatile region so that it can pursue its own economic growth. Moreover, stabilisation of Pakistan is imperative for building a stable Xinjiang as a destabilised Pakistan could prove a disaster for territorial integrity of China.

China's counter-terrorism concerns stem from its restive western Xinjiang region bordering northwest Pakistan. Most of the people in China's Xinxiang province, other than Han people, are of Islamic religious faith. China has long been facing threats of ethnic separatism from these Islamic, largely Turkic peoples of Xinjiang province. These challenges increased during the late 1980s and early 1990s as the *mujahedeen* struggle in Afghanistan against the Soviets came to prominence. Xinjiang is home to nearly 9 million Uyghur's, a Muslim people of Turkic origin, among whom separatist sentiment is dominant. In the 1980s, hundreds of Uyghur's crossed into Pakistan, enrolled in radical *madrassas* (religious schools), and fought the Soviets in Afghanistan. After Soviet withdrawal from Afghanistan, China became increasingly concerned about the Uyghur separatist problem in Xinjiang and the apparent inability of Pakistan to control these militant groups. Among these militant groups some have joined violent Uyghur ultra-nationalist groups against China, thus, threatening China's territorial integrity and control.[32] China responded with increased domestic repression and started supervising religious institutions and extremist activities in Xinjiang.[33] Beijing, in the mid and late 1990's, adopted three important methods to responded to this increased menace of separatist activity: Firstly, Beijing intensified cooperation with Russia and the newly independent states of Central Asia which ultimately embodied in the Shanghai Cooperative Organisation of Russia, China, Kazakhstan, Kyrgyzstan and Tajikistan. Secondly, Beijing began stressing on Pakistan to take measures in order to end the training of Chinese citizens from Xinjiang in camps of Islamic schools in either Pakistan or Afghanistan. Thirdly, Beijing began using carrots and sticks in an effort to persuade the Taliban regime to cease and desist all training camps for Muslims from Xinjiang.[34]

Between 1990 and 2001, these groups carried out approximately 200 attacks in China that killed 162 people. Consequently, China pressurised Pakistan to launch a crack down on militant groups it suspected of supporting and arming separatists in Xinjiang; closed the Karakorum Highway and curtailed border trade for several months to stop the destabilising flow of fighters. Pakistan denies that it is supporting the separatist elements against China and assured that its strategic ties with China are more important than its religious ties with Uyghur's. Consequently, Pakistan, since late 1990's, has increasingly taken strict measures to lessen China's fears.[35]

In post-9/11 era, China's anxiety about the growing US presence and influence in Pakistan and Afghanistan and Washington's strong ties with both India and Pakistan (India as a natural ally and Pakistan as a major non-NATO ally), reinforced China-Pakistan strategic cooperation. Therefore, the changed strategic landscape restored Pakistan's geostrategic significance for China. Though, China and the United States had worked closely in 1980's and together supported Pakistan to oust the Soviets; however, since 9/11 Chinese analysts became deeply apprehensive about the US presence in Central Asia. From a Chinese perspective, September 11 and the subsequent global campaign on terror constitute a double-edged sword, presenting both opportunities and challenges. For optimists, counter-terrorism provides a functional field in which China and the US can cooperate which can in turn facilitate an improvement in their relationship. Moreover, counter-terrorism cooperation with the US can provide China with more leeway in dealing with Xinjiang, Tibet and Taiwan. On the other hand, the pessimists hold the view that the US military presence in Central, South and South-East Asia may undermine Chinese influence in these regions and make it more difficult for China to achieve its security, economic and energy objectives in the future.[36]

Pakistan's decision to side with the United States in the War on Terror initially worried Chinese policy makers. However, Pakistan through the exchange of high-level visits assured China that Pakistan would not allow its cooperation with the United States under any circumstances to undermine Chinese strategic interests. Post-9/11, Pakistan vowed that it will wholeheartedly support China's battle to strike against the East Turkestan terrorist forces. Notwithstanding Pakistan's full cooperation, China remains deeply concerned about the long-term implications of the growth of extremism in Xinjiang.[37] China's growing anxiety regarding extremism in Pakistan may provide an opportunity not only for Washington but also for India to work more closely with Beijing in encouraging more effective Pakistani counter-terrorism policies. The instability in Pakistan threatens the safety and security of Pakistan's nuclear weapons. New Delhi expects Beijing to show sensitivity to India's concerns and to exert pressure on Pakistan to stop the terrorist activities against India. Indeed, China could play a more effective role in ensuring stability in Pakistan because it enjoys widespread credibility in Pakistan. Besides, for the sake of its own geopolitical and geostrategic interests in Pakistan, China has to work for the advancement of stability in Pakistan.

Conclusion

As it is clear that China has its own security agenda for the South Asian region, China's own regional and global priorities will, therefore, determine the nature of its involvement with India and Pakistan for the foreseeable future. In the present context, given the geopolitical and geo-strategic realities, Beijing's interest lies in facilitating reconciliation between New Delhi and Islamabad, because any potential military confrontation between the two nuclear armed states (India and Pakistan) could cast a profound negative impact on China's security in the region. It is widely believed that neither an all-out war between India nor Pakistan nor Pakistan's collapse would serve Beijing's grand strategic objectives.

The nuclear triangle of China-Pakistan-India presents a unique example of its kind in which three nuclear armed neighbours share disputed borders that have witnessed numerous wars and continued tension. China became increasingly concerned about nuclear weapons in South Asia, particularly after the rising wave of extremism in Pakistan, as it has direct national stakes in the stability of nuclear South Asia. Any possible nuclear conflict between India and Pakistan may ultimately drag China into it. The spectre of nukes in the hands of extremist groups who are always eager to export extremism and terrorism adds an element of instability to the regional situation. Given the rising threat of extremism and the apparent instability in Pakistan, China's first concern will be to de-escalate any crisis that may crop-up between India and Pakistan before it translates into nuclear war. China and the United States should work jointly in regional crisis management as it is in the interest of both to avert any nuclear exchange between India and Pakistan. China should adopt a position identical to its policy in the 1950's with a view to maintain good neighbourly relations with both India and Pakistan because only a stable South Asia could serve Beijing's long-term interests.

References

1. Sumit Ganguly, *Conflict Unending –India Pakistan Tension since 1947*, New Delhi: Oxford University Press, 2002, pp. 1-10.
2. S. M Burke, *Pakistan's Foreign Policy: An Historical analysis*, London: Oxford University Press, 1973, p. 108.
3. Aparna Pande, *Explaining Pakistan's Foreign Policy: Escaping India*, London: Routledge, 2011, p. 116.
4. Chintamani Mahapatra, "India-China-Pakistan Triangle: The US Factor," *Indian Foreign Affairs Journal* Vol. 6, No. 4, October-December 2011, pp. 408-410.
5. Brahma Chellaney, "The China-India-Pakistan Triangle: Scenarios for the 21st Century," *CERI Strategy Papers*, No. 8, September 2010, p. 2 Found at http://www.sciencepo.fr/ceri/en/printpdf/2115 accessed on 20 February 2013.
6. John W. Garver, *Protracted Contest: Sino-Indian Rivalry in the Twentieth First Century,* Seattle: Washington University Press, 2001, p. 188.
7. Anwar H. Syed, *China and Pakistan: Diplomacy of an Entente Cordiale*, London: Oxford University Press, 1974, pp. 8-10 see also Rasul B. Rais, *China and Pakistan: A Political Analysis of Mutual Relations*, Lahore: Progressive Publishers, 1977.
8. Devin T. Hagrety, "China and Pakistan: Strains in the Relationship," *Current History*, September 2002, p. 284.
9. Anil Joseph Chandy, "India, China and Pakistan," in Kanti Bajpai and Amitabh Mattoo (eds.), *The Peacock and the Dragon: India-China Relations in the 21st Century*, New Delhi: Har Anand Publications, 2000, p. 302.
10. Harsh V Pant, "The Pakistan Thorn in China-India-US Relations," *The Washington Quarterly,* Vol. 35, No. 1, 2012, p. 84.
11. Mohan Malik, China and India: Great Power Rivals, London: First Forum Press, 2011, p. 191.

12. Jonathan Holslag argues that a persistent security dilemma exists between India and China. See Jonathan Holslag, "The Persistent Military Security Dilemma between China and India", *The Journal of Strategic Studies*, Vol. 32, No. 6, December 2009, pp. 811-840
13. Swaran Singh, "Sino South Asian ties: Problems and prospects," Strategic Analysis, Vol.24, No.1, 2000, p. 32.
14. Rasul B Rais, "South Asia and Global System: Continuity and Change," in Shelton U Kodikara (ed), *External Compulsions of South Asian Politics*, New Delhi: Sage, 1993, p. 37.
15. Mahinda Werake, "China and South Asia in the Eighties," in Shelton U Kodikara (ed), *External Compulsions of South Asian Politics*, New Delhi: Sage, 1993, p. 79.
16. As quoted in Mahinda Werake, "China and South Asia in the Eighties," p. 80.
17. *Evan A. Feigenbaum,* "China's Pakistan Conundrum The End of the All-Weather Friendship," *Foreign Affairs,*2011, pp. 2-3 found at http://www.foreignaffairs.com/articles/136718/evan-a-feigenbaum/chinas-pakistanconundrum accessed on 16 December, 2012.
18. Swaran Singh, *China-South Asia: Issues, Equations, Policies*, New Delhi: Lancer Books, 2003, p. 337.
19. *Andrew Small*, "Regional Dynamics and Strategic Concerns in South Asia: China's Role," *CSIS Paper (Centre for Strategic and International Studies),* Washington, D.C, January 2014, pp. 2-3.
20. S.M Burke, *Pakistan's Foreign Policy: An Historical Analysis*, op. cit., pp. 217.
21. See Swaran Singh, *China-South Asia: Issues, Equations, Policies,* op. cit., p. 78.
22. Farzana Shaikh, *Making Sense of Pakistan*, London: Hurst and Company, 2009, p. 196.
23. Fazal-ur-Rahman, "Pakistan's Relations with China," *Strategic Studies*, Vol. 21, No. 4, Winter 1998, pp. 85-86.
24. John W. Garver, .Sino-Indian Rapprochement and the Sino-Pakistani Entente,. *Political Science Quarterly*, Summer 1996, pp. 323-347.
25. Sumit Ganguly, Conflict Unending –India Pakistan Tension since 1947, op. cit. p. 120.
26. Ehsan M. Ahrari, "China, Pakistan and the Taliban Syndrome," *Asian Survey*, Vol. 40, No. 4, July-August 2000, pp. 658-671.
27. Ishtiaq Ahmad, "The Role of China and Sino-Indian Rivalry in the Kashmir Dispute," Paper Presented in an International Conference on *Asian Powers in Kashmir*, London: Royal United Services Institute (RUSI) for Defense and Security Studies, 25th January 2011, pp. 1-9.
28. Chietigj Bajpaee, "China-India Relations: Regional Rivalry Takes the World Stage," *China Security*, Vol. 6, No. 2, 2010, p. 5.

29. Jingdong Yuan, "Beijing's Balancing Act: Courting New Delhi, Reassuring Islamabad," *Journal of International Affairs.* 64(2) (Spring-Summer 2011), p. 39.
30. Rup Narayan Das, *India-China Relations: A New* Paradigm, IDSA Monograph Series No. 19 May 2013 p. 81.
31. *Ibid.*
32. on Uyghur problem in Pakistan-China relations see Ziad Haider, "Sino-Pakistan Relations and Xinjiang's Uyghurs: Politics, Trade and Islam along the Karakoram Highway," Asian Survey, Vol. XLV, No. 4, pp. 522-545 see also Preeti Bhattacharji, 'Uighurs and China's Xinjiang Region', Council of Foreign Relations, 29 May 2012, Found at http://www.cfr.org/china/uighurs-chinas-xinjiang-region/p16870.
33. Lillian Craig Harris, "Xinjiang, Central Asia, and the Implications for China's Policy in the Islamic World,". *The China Quarterly*, No. 133, March 1993, pp. 111-129.
34. John W. Garver, "The Future of the Sino-Pakistani Entente Cordiale," in Michael R. Chambers (ed.), South A*sia in 2020: Future Strategic Balances and Alliances*, United States: Strategic Studies Institute, November, 2002, pp. 430-431 see also M. Ehsan Ahrari, *Jihadi Groups, Nuclear Pakistan, and the New Great Gam*e, Carlisle Barracks: Strategic Studies Institute, U.S. Army War College, August 2001, pp. 32-33.
35. Ziad Haider, "Sino-Pakistan Relations and Xinjiang's Uyghurs: Politics, Trade and Islam along the Karakoram Highway," op. cit.
36. For Chinese assessment of US policy towards South Asia in post 9/11 see Zhang Guihong, "US Security Policy towards South Asia after September 11 and its Implications for China," *Strategic Analysis*, Vol. 27, No. 2, April-June 2003, pp. 145-171.
37. Rajshree Jetly, "Sino-Pakistan Strategic Entente: Implications for Regional Security," *ISAS Working Paper*, No. 143, 14 February 2012, p. 10.

12

India-Afghanistan Relations Post-9/11 and Unending Indo-Pak Rivalry in Afghanistan

Reyaz Ahmad Ganaie

"Ever since India's independence, we have grown closer to each other, for a variety of reasons. The long memory of our past was there, and the moment it was possible to renew them, we renewed them. And then came mutual interest, which is a powerful factor".[1]

Indian Prime Minister, **Jawaharlal Nehru**

Introduction

The formation of the national unity government in Afghanistan – as envisaged in the power-sharing deal brokered earlier by US Secretary of State, John Kerry – marked the end of the months-long political stalemate. The political impasse, stemming from an alleged fraud in the presidential run-off elections, proved to be a major impediment in the process leading to the first democratic transition in Afghanistan. The political impasse engendered the possibility of renewing inter-ethnic conflict in Afghanistan besides impeding the flow of financial assistance from United Nations and the US post-2014. Even though the consensus among the two presidential candidates on forming the unity government is dubbed as a major success for US diplomacy, experts, however, seem to be critical of the US-brokered power-sharing agreement for they believe, and rightly so, that such precarious political deals nullify the essence of nascent democratic process in Afghanistan and invalidate the legality of elections.[2] In fact, the extra-constitutional political haggling helps the Taliban in promoting their narrative of elections in Afghanistan being a farce besides gives credibility to their claim that, in the end, it is the United States which chooses the winner and adjusts the results accordingly.[3] To prevent the surfacing of a similar political standoff, the United States and the international community must engage the two candidates carefully because political volatility at the national level can lead to a worsening of the delicate ethnic fabric in Afghanistan. In its entirety, the current political stalemate has vindicated the claim that 'Afghanistan fits a pattern of transitioning countries that have rushed to elections before their polities were sufficiently constituted.'[4]

In the backdrop of the fluidity of the prevailing situation in Afghanistan and the uncertainty of the post-2014 scenario, Afghanistan's regional neighbours, instead of espousing definitive and decisive policies, rather appear to have adopted a wait-and-watch strategy vis-à-vis Afghanistan. Even though there is little disagreement over the complex and multifaceted challenges that Afghanistan is to face beyond 2014, there is also a clear consensus among the international stakeholders and regional powers that Afghanistan holds a key geostrategic location that can be instrumental not only in promoting peace and security in the region, but can also open up avenues for trade and energy cooperation among the states in South Asia and beyond. Nonetheless, the worsening security scenario and the apprehensions of a more audacious Taliban campaign following the withdrawal of foreign combat mission is what can push Afghanistan into a dangerous spiral, which in turn could pave the way for the reversal of the gains made in the last thirteen years. Therefore, what is needed to prevent such a nightmarish situation from transpiring is continued international oversight and financial assistance and a harmonisation of interests of Afghanistan's regional neighbours.

As the deadline for the complete withdrawal of NATO-led foreign combat mission from Afghanistan approaches nearer, a military victory against Taliban seems to be an unattainable goal. The much hyped U.S-led efforts to enter into talks with the 'moderate' or 'good' Taliban has also failed to deliver any breakthrough in the Afghan quagmire. Taking these security predicaments into consideration, it seems palpable to conclude that a post-ISAF (International Security Assistance Force) Afghanistan will most likely present a scenario full of political and economic concerns which will largely be left unattended by the U.S. and its allies who seem to be in a hurry to disengage from the war torn country. One would like to see that such disengagement does not lead to same repercussions as did happen previously when U.S. abandoned Afghanistan following the withdrawal of Soviet troops way back in 1989.

The main challenges confronted by the Kabul government at present include sustaining the Afghan National Army as an institution and enhancing its counter-insurgency capabilities; consolidation of nascent democratic processes throughout the country; and most importantly, negating the Taliban influence. Meeting these challenges in a time-bound manner can prevent Afghanistan from plunging into a renewed internecine conflict. India, in the capacity of a large aid donor and a potent regional ally, has contributed considerably in order to meet these challenges. However, such broad based engagement is not necessitated by only humanitarian concerns or a sense of altruism per se, but the geo-strategic location of Afghanistan embodies a number of strategic interests for India.

Although the reconstruction efforts undertaken by India have garnered appreciation from all stakeholders, its expanding presence within Afghanistan has, however, been resented by Islamabad as a conscious step intended to encircle Pakistan.[5] Initially, the United States allowed for a limited Indian involvement in Afghanistan confining its engagement to humanitarian assistance and infrastructure related activities. However, lately, a discernible shift in the U.S policy, seeking a larger role for India points towards the possibility that India may step into the role of, as Leon Panetta once remarked, "the net provider of security from Indian Ocean to Afghanistan and beyond."[6] While the situation inside Afghanistan remains in a flux, India has to strike a proper balance in its Afghan policy that simultaneously aims at sustaining the momentum of the reconstruction process and, more importantly, seeks to benefit from the position it has been able to achieve in order to secure its vital interests in the region without antagonising other regional neighbours particularly Pakistan.

A Historical Overview of India's Engagement in Afghanistan

Afghanistan-India relations go beyond the limits of cordial relationship that the two countries' governments have enjoyed in the past. Afghanistan and India have remained interacting with each other through the means of trade and commerce and also through their many shared cultural values and commonalities. India and Afghanistan signed a Friendship treaty way back in 1950.

Signed between Prime Minister Jawaharlal Nehru and the Afghan Ambassador Najibullah Khan in New Delhi on January 4, 1950, the treaty envisaged a commitment for everlasting peace and friendship 'with a view to the common benefit of their people and the development of their respective countries.'[7] The treaty laid the foundation for the development of a close bilateral relationship for the decades to come. India, therefore, enjoyed excellent diplomatic ties with all Afghan governments, starting from King Zahir Shah's tenure to the successive regimes including those that were hoisted on the country following the Soviet invasion in December 1979. The moment Pakistan came into being, New Delhi-Kabul relations gained impetus because both the countries shared territorial dispute with Islamabad. Furthermore, Kabul's opposition to Pakistan's stand on the Kashmir dispute laid a strong foundation for India-Afghanistan relations. Indian government continued to assist Afghanistan even during the tumultuous decade of anti-Soviet war. India maintained its influence in Afghanistan through investments in developmental activities including irrigation, agriculture and hydro-electric projects. Nonetheless, the decade of Soviet intervention witnessed India's Afghan policy as oscillating between the avowed principle of Non-Alignment on the one hand and the zeal to gain geopolitical leverage on the other. Initially, India opposed the Soviet intervention in Afghanistan and called for the withdrawal of the Soviet troops from Afghanistan. However, realising that the withdrawal of Soviets would serve Pakistan's interests by virtue of the ascendance of Pakistan-backed Mujahideen factions in Afghanistan, India chose to abstain on key U.N. resolutions calling for the complete Soviet withdrawal from Afghanistan. India chose to turn a blind eye towards Soviet occupation of Afghanistan because it feared a Mujahedeen victory in Afghanistan would become the basis for Pakistan to gain greater geopolitical leverage in the region.[8] Furthermore, the scale of military assistance Pakistan received from the United States and the latter's policy of turning a blind eye towards Islamabad's covert nuclear weapons programme shaped India's Afghan policy during that decade. India's main concern was the revitalisation of Washington's security links with Pakistan, which India contended could alter the natural balance of power in the region in favour of Pakistan. India was the only country outside of the Warsaw Pact bloc that maintained cordial ties with the Soviet-backed regimes in Afghanistan.[9] Geopolitical realities rather than the grandiose rhetoric of Non-Alignment guided India's Afghan policy during this epoch. The advent of Taliban in 1996, however, resulted in complete rupture in Indo-Afghan relations as Taliban shared close liaison with Pakistan's military and Intelligence establishment. What left India worse off in the coming years was India's decision to enter into a working relationship with the Northern Alliance which stood opposite to the Taliban. India established links with the anti-Pashtun Northern Alliance so as to negate the possibility of Afghanistan falling under the command of Taliban forces who were acting at the behest of Pakistan's security establishment. Following the ouster of Taliban in late 2001 by the U.S. led coalition in response to the 9/11 Attacks, India was swift in renewing its diplomatic ties with Afghanistan. Immediately after Karzai took the reins of Afghanistan, India's Minister for External Affairs, Jaswant Singh, flew to Kabul to participate in Interim Government's inauguration and to re-open the Indian embassy, which closed on the eve of the Taliban's seizure of Kabul in 1996.[10] Since then India's relations with Afghanistan have improved considerably for a number of factors facilitated the renewal of diplomatic ties. First, India kept its post-9/11 Afghan policy completely in sync with the principles mandated under the Bonn Agreement of 2001. Second, unlike Pakistan, Indo-Afghan relations are not hampered by the existence of a contiguous and contested border. Third, India was able to garner official support from the Kabul government because many members of the Northern Alliance which India supported in the mid-1990s became members of the Interim Government or held influential provincial posts.[11]

Avoiding any sort of military engagement, India adopted the 'Soft Power Approach' towards Afghanistan, sticking to civilian issues rather than military matters. With the inception of the Interim Government led by Hamid Karzai, Prime Minister A.B. Vajpayee immediately announced a U.S. $100 million in reconstruction aid to Afghanistan. Since 2001, India has already pledged more than $2 billion on various projects, emerging as the fifth largest bilateral donor to Afghanistan. India's assistance was largely directed towards education, health and infrastructure related activities. This civilian-centric policy laid a strong foundation for a deep mutual trust. A look at recent public opinion polls in Afghanistan illustrates the apparent positive sentiment that Afghans hold for India and its people. Among local Afghans, India's assistance and investment in establishing basic facilities like schools, hospitals and transportation has earned it a place of pride, and is therefore seen positively throughout Afghanistan. Specifically, India has till now successfully constructed the 218-km long highway linking the town of Zaranj near the Iranian border to Delaram in the northeast Afghanistan despite periodic attacks on Border Roads Organisation (BRO) personnel. India has also played a significant and commendable role in constructing roads which have improved Afghanistan's connectivity with strategic ports thereby reducing Kabul's dependence on Pakistan.[12] India has so far been able to increase Afghanistan's connectivity with the Iranian port of Chabahar which has led to an indirect decline in Afghanistan's dependence on Pakistani ports of Gwadar and Karachi.[13] India's effort at developing the Chabahar Port in Iran is also based on the fact that it provides India with the most viable option of gaining access to Afghanistan since Pakistan has refused to provide land transit to Indian goods bound for Afghanistan through its territory.[14] In July 2013, Indian Ambassador to Afghanistan, Amar Sinha, noted that India is fully committed to the development of Chabahar Port as it represents the best option for the transit of Indian goods to Afghanistan.[15] India used the port in 2012 to deliver humanitarian aid to Afghanistan demonstrating that the sea-route access to Afghanistan through Pakistan is not the only option available to India in the long run.[16] Furthermore, India has accomplished the task of constructing Afghanistan's new parliament building and the construction of Salma Dam project in Herat from which a power transmission line to Kabul has also been set up. Moreover, India has successfully renovated the damaged Indira Gandhi Institute of Child Health and has regularly dispatched teams of doctors to Herat, Mazar-e-Sharif and Kandahar to attend to the massive medical needs of Afghanistan. India has also granted 500 scholarships annually to Afghan students under the auspices of Indian Council of Cultural Relations (ICCR).

While the war in Afghanistan seems nowhere near the end, India's civilian centric policies have gained wide currency and appreciation at official level and among local populace as well. President Karzai has time and again reiterated his government's admiration for India's policies in Afghanistan. Since 2001, several high level official visits from both countries have strengthened the case for closer and enhanced cooperation between the two countries. For instance, India and Afghanistan signed a Preferential Trade Agreement (PTA) in 2003, aimed at removing all obstacles in the way of increasing mutual trade and commerce. This agreement made India one of the major trading partners of Afghanistan and its fifth largest source of imports. Similarly, in 2005 when Indian Prime Minister Manmohan Singh met Afghan President Hamid Karzai in Kabul they agreed on expanding bilateral cooperation to wide ranging areas including development, defence, education, energy, trade, combating terrorism and working towards greater economic and cultural integration of South Asia. Prime Minister Manmohan Singh's perfectly timed visit, just three weeks before the September 2005 parliamentary elections in Afghanistan, pointed towards India's desire for a tangible and a long-term engagement in Afghanistan.[17] Indian Prime Minister reaffirmed India's commitment towards Afghan reconstruction process and pledged an additional financial assistance of US $ 50 million to Afghanistan. Besides announcing 500 scholarships for Afghan students to pursue higher education in India, India also announced that it will adopt hundred (100) villages in Afghanistan to promote and enhance integrated rural development by introducing solar electrification and rainwater harvesting using technologies that have already proven to be successful back in India. India also threw its support behind Afghanistan's entry into SAARC as a full-fledged member.[18] On October 4, 2011, India and Afghanistan signed a milestone agreement on "Strategic Partnership" that included inter-alia provision for both security and economic cooperation, training and equipping of Afghan National Security Forces, provision of economic aid and assistance, development of mining and energy production, and establishment of 'strategic dialogue' between their national security advisers to provide a framework for cooperation in the area of national security.[19] The fact that Afghanistan signed such a broad-based agreement for the first time in the region underlines the finely tuned and deepening ties between Afghanistan and India.[20] Commenting on the importance of India's renewed engagement with Afghanistan and India's readiness in assisting Afghanistan in the future, Indian Prime Minister Manmohan Singh said: "Our cooperation with Afghanistan is an open book. We have civilisational links, and we are both here to stay. India will stand by the people of Afghanistan as they prepare to assume the responsibility for their governance and security after the withdrawal of international forces in 2014."[21] India has also been extensively involved in building institutional capacity by way of training Afghan diplomats, doctors, paramedics, entrepreneurs, lawyers, judges and Afghanistan's government officials. The recent dialogue between Indian Prime Minister Manmohan Singh and Afghan President Hamid Karzai in November 2012 in New Delhi provided further impetus to the bilateral partnership. Both leaders agreed on the need for deepening economic cooperation in areas ranging from agriculture, small business to mining and infrastructure. Hamid Karzai, in a bid to woo Indian investors remarked: "We would like to welcome you on red carpet and others on grey carpet. If you don't arrive on the red carpet it will get dusty. Therefore, do hurry up and take advantage of the opportunities in Afghanistan."[22] Karzai recently participated in the inaugural ceremony of inception of Narendra Modi as the Prime Minister of India. As the new government settles down in New Delhi, both sides must look forward to rejuvenate their bilateral ties and to further consolidate and sustain the cordiality that has so far been achieved over the past 13 years.[23] Foreign Minister Sushma Swaraj's visit to Kabul on September 10, 2014 marked the first formal diplomatic interaction between the two countries since the inception of the Modi government. Her visit focussed on improving strategic cooperation with the Kabul government and to work closely for the consolidation of stability and security in Afghanistan. Swaraj's visit is an indication that Modi government is keen in taking forward the bilateral relations to a much higher level in the years to come. New Delhi's status as a regional friend and a decidedly non-western power could give it some staying power with the candidates which in turn could pave the way for close Indo-Afghan ties in the years to come.[24]

Indo-Pak Rivalry in Afghanistan and its Impact on Pakistan-Afghanistan Relations

Whereas Taliban's ouster marked an end to the four-year repressive rule by the fundamentalist regime backed by Pakistan, it also gave birth to new complexities rooted primarily in pre-9/11 geopolitical realities of the region. Rivalry among South Asian and Central Asian neighbours of Afghanistan began to manifest itself more clearly when it came to their conflicting interests and objectives in post-Taliban Afghanistan. In a bid to carve out for themselves a niche in the changed geopolitical dynamics in Afghanistan, the policies adopted by these countries only exacerbated Afghanistan's problems of reconstruction and hindered its march towards peace and stability. Most notable among these regional rivalries is the contest between India and Pakistan to gain influence in Afghanistan. Typically, India's interests in Afghanistan have been viewed through the prism of Indo-Pak rivalry. This rivalry has largely been driven by real or imagined security threats and has plotted Afghanistan as a field for both countries to vie for influence in that country.[25] India and Pakistan have typically approached Afghanistan as a zero-sum dynamic in which loss for one side implies gain for the other.[26] Both sides have always tried to restrict each other from gaining a strong foothold in Afghanistan. While India managed to build friendly relations with Afghanistan after 9/11, Pakistan, in contrast, sought to checkmate India's influence in Afghanistan primarily because Islamabad sees Afghanistan as Pakistan's strategic backyard. The rivalry immediately rejuvenated itself following the ouster of Taliban regime in late 2001. It is against this backdrop that India's Afghan policy since 9/11 has aimed at limiting Pakistan's influence and ensuring that any regime around the order of Taliban is not allowed to gain foothold inside Afghanistan. These two objectives remain the top priority for India's Afghan policy.

Soon after the Taliban were ousted and Hamid Karzai was inaugurated as the leader of the Interim Administration, India reopened its embassy (in Kabul) and four consulates (in Jalalabad, Mazar-i-Sharif, Herat and Kandahar) in Afghanistan. India's support to Karzai Administration and its growing influence in Afghanistan reinforced Pakistan's security paranoia. Pakistan alleged that India's primary motive in Afghanistan was not to contribute towards the reconstruction of the war torn country but to stir up unrest within Pakistan with the help of Afghan authorities (particularly the Afghan intelligence agency). Pakistan was particularly incensed at the reopening of Indian consulates close to Pakistan's border in the provinces of Jalalabad and Kandahar. Pakistan alleged that India's lavish diplomatic presence in Afghanistan was aimed at supporting subversive activities inside Pakistan. President Musharraf voiced Pakistan's concern over India's presence in Afghanistan when he said: "India's motivation in Afghanistan is very clear, nothing further than upsetting Pakistan. Why should they have consulates in Jalalabad and Kandahar, what is their interest? There is no interest other than disturbing Pakistan, doing something against Pakistan."[27]

Pakistan's interventionist policy towards Afghanistan seems driven, at least in part, due to India's growing presence in Afghanistan. It is towards the goal of thwarting India's presence and influence in Afghanistan and to create a regime that will forge foreign policies favourable to Pakistan that Islamabad has continued to support the Afghan Taliban, the Haqqani network and other extremist outfits who, in varying degrees, work at the behest of Pakistan's security establishment.[28] Even though, the policy of sponsoring insurgency in Afghanistan has left Pakistani society more vulnerable to violence and extremism, the security establishment in Pakistan has, however, relentlessly pursued its interventionist policy in Afghanistan by using the Taliban as a proxy force. Commenting on the aspect of the continuity in Pakistan's Afghan policy post-9/11, Steve Coll argues that the, "geopolitical incentives that have informed Pakistan's alliance with the Afghan Taliban remain unaltered. Pakistani generals have retained a bedrock belief that, however, unruly and distasteful Islamist militias such as the Taliban may be, they could yet be useful proxies to ward off a perceived existential threat from India. In the Army's view, at least, that threat has not receded."[29] The Indo-Pak rivalry has thus continued to thrive despite many attempts by the Kabul government and the international community aimed at attenuating the mistrust and security paranoia between the two nuclear armed South Asian neighbours. Karzai tried to assuage Pakistan's reservations regarding India's expanding influence in Kabul by assuring Musharraf that he was, "very specific in telling the Indians that they cannot use Afghan soil for acts of aggression against another country."[30] Karzai's verbal assurance was too inefficient a tool to end Pakistan's suspicion about India's presence in Afghanistan. Afghanistan once again became a playfield for competing regional neighbours. The ensuing rivalry not only became a source of unending strife and violence but also hindered the reconstruction activities in Afghanistan. Further, India's active presence in Afghanistan made it rather difficult for Pakistan and Afghanistan to build a cordial bilateral relationship following the ouster of Taliban. The revival of the alleged 'quasi-alliance' between New Delhi and Kabul was seen by Pakistan as reason enough to continue with its policy of sheltering and supporting Afghan Taliban. This presumed connivance between India and Afghanistan (at the expense of Pakistan's strategic interests in the region as Pakistan alleges) continues to be a major irritant in Pakistan-Afghanistan relations.

While on the one hand, India views good relations with Afghanistan as a means to check the terrorist threat looming large from the Af-Pak region, it is also interested in retaining Afghanistan as a friendly state from which it has the capacity to monitor Pakistan and even cultivate assets to influence activities in Pakistan.[31] On the other hand, Pakistan has suffered from the historic paranoia of being trapped in a pincer movement should India be able to gain political and military space inside Afghanistan. Therefore, a friendly political dispensation in Kabul, often referred to as strategic depth, is viewed by Pakistan as essential to escape the strategic dilemma of being caught between a powerful adversary in India in the east and an irredentist Afghanistan with claims on the Pashtun dominated areas in the west.[32] Having a Pashtun-dominated pro-Pakistan political dispensation in Kabul has always been a central premise of Pakistan's Afghan policy, because policy makers in Pakistan view it as a means to secure long-term security on its western border since Islamabad is always faced with a problem-prone eastern border with India.[33] To that extent, Pakistan has been and still continues to be a Pashtun power broker in Afghanistan.[34] In this backdrop, Pakistan has resented the Indian involvement in Afghanistan since 9/11 as it amounts to, as Islamabad contends, a loss of vital strategic space. Pakistan's Afghan policy since 9/11 has carried an integral and fundamental component of ensuring protection of Pakistan's influence and space within Afghanistan against an alleged Indian encroachment, and the *modus operandi* to safeguard this objective has been Islamabad's continuing support to pro-Pakistan proxies (Taliban and allied factions) who act at Pakistan's behest. This has led some scholars to view Pakistan's Afghan policy as being singularly concerned with India's involvement in Afghanistan and less focused on preserving Islamabad's regional geopolitical interest. In Islamabad's Afghanistan calculus, protecting itself against Indian encroachment takes precedence over pursuing Pakistan's broader geopolitical and economic goals; and the basis for this flawed prioritisation stems from the fact that Pakistan's security establishment plays a predominant role in decision-making process, which has historically emphasised the primacy of security related matters over all other aspects of foreign policy.[35]

Pakistan has on various occasions alleged that Indian intelligence personnel particularly RAW (Research Analysis Wing) officials have – in connivance with Afghan intelligence officials – actively engaged in instigating Baluch separatism inside Pakistan and provided support to the TTP (Tehreek-i-Taliban Pakistan). Pakistan has also accused Afghanistan of conniving with Indian intelligence officials in fomenting unrest in the restive Baluchistan province of Pakistan. If WikiLeaks revelations are to be considered a reliable source of information, then Pakistan's accusations against Afghanistan seem to be valid to a certain extent. It was revealed by a leaked cable that Karzai had admitted in January 2007 of having sheltered more than 200 Baluch nationalists and their families who had fled Pakistan.[36]

The dominant narrative prevailing within Pakistan's security establishment is that while Afghan army cannot threaten Pakistan's security in a conventional warfare, what threatens Pakistan's regional interests, however, is the possibility of Afghanistan being used by Islamabad's neighbours (Iran and India) to prosecute their hostile policies vis-à-vis Pakistan. This is the strategic framework which helps one understand the reason for Pakistan's resentment against India's increasing influence in Afghanistan. In July 2006, former Pakistan senator and Chairman of the Standing Committee on Foreign Affairs, Mushahid Hussain, accused India of using its embassy and consulates in Afghanistan for training Baluch dissidents from Pakistan. He accused the Afghan security apparatus (the Afghan National Police and the Border Security Forces) of facilitating the visits of Indian diplomatic staff and intelligence officials into Pakistan's tribal areas, and assisting them in arranging meetings with pro-Afghan dissidents.[37] The rhetoric that India manipulates its presence inside Afghanistan to stimulate unrest inside Pakistan's borders is ubiquitous within Pakistan's mainstream media (especially the Urdu print media which reflects more clearly the mindset of the security establishment). For instance, M. Maqbool Khan Wazir, writing in the official publication *IPRI,* a state-sponsored think tank, attempts to defend Pakistan's allegations by asserting that India's involvement in instigating and assisting the insurgency in Pakistan's FATA and Baluchistan has been substantiated by credible evidence collected by Pakistani law enforcement agencies which confirmed that 'Indians were not only involved in providing comprehensive financial support to terrorists in Pakistan but were also providing them with arms, equipment and technical support.'[38] Nonetheless, it is clear that the basis of Indo-Pak rivalry in Afghanistan is rooted more in their conflict-ridden bilateral relationship and misgivings of the past rather than on India's anti-Pakistan agenda in Afghanistan. Regarding the veracity of the claims on which Pakistan and India engage in this blame-game, American scholar Christine Fair maintains that the mutual recriminations levelled by the two sides (India and Pakistan) are nearly impossible to verify. However, it can be said that Pakistan's most sweeping claims are ill founded while at the same time India's claim to complete innocence is also unlikely to be true.[39] These accusations have fuelled a renewed Indo-Pak rivalry in Afghanistan often resulting in terrorist attacks at Indian personnel and installations in Afghanistan allegedly done at the behest of Pakistan.

A vital element of this rivalry has been the conflict of interests and the divergence of policies adopted by India and Pakistan vis-à-vis Afghanistan. India's interests in Afghanistan stand in sharp contrast with those of Pakistan's and are virtually antithetical. India has been deeply concerned by the limits put on its activities and presence by the U.S. on account of the security threat perceived by Pakistan which have considerably constrained the ability of the former to contribute towards stabilisation in Afghanistan. India strongly believes that U.S. should not give any undue concessions and disproportionate importance to Pakistan and its military, often seen by the west as indispensible to Afghan peace process, as India is concerned by the close ties that Pakistan shares with Taliban. Any move by the United States intended to give more space to Pakistan's military, India contends, is going to jeopardise the entire effort of ushering Afghanistan into a stable and democratic state. In response to India's contention, Pakistan believes that the reluctance on the part of the Afghan government or the United States to address Pakistani misgivings increases the possibility that India will continue to expand its presence in Afghanistan which can facilitate New Delhi's ability to manipulate the end game negotiations and the post-settlement dispensation in Kabul.[40] Pakistani security analysts are of the view that the U.S. withdrawal from Afghanistan will lead to the entrenchment of India's presence in Afghanistan. They argue that India has successfully convinced the United States and allies of its ability to fill the power vacuum in Afghanistan.[41] While it is true that India has been able to craft for itself a significant space within Afghanistan, Pakistan has tried to fend off the perceived threat by questioning the motivations behind India's growing presence in Afghanistan. It must be noted, however, that any attempt by either of the two states to completely sideline the other is surely going to be detrimental to the security of the entire region in general and to the rebuilding process of Afghanistan in particular. Efforts aimed at advancing their parochial interests would make it difficult for Afghanistan to achieve a measure of stability.[42]

Even though there is enough evidence to show that Indo-Pak rivalry in Afghanistan has intensified since 9/11, Pakistan has, nevertheless, come to appreciate and acknowledge the fact that it has little leverage to convince the international community to restrict India's growing presence in Afghanistan. Islamabad has also tacitly acknowledged that India's efforts of reconstructing infrastructure in Afghanistan are praiseworthy. Therefore, Pakistani elite has accepted that India has a significant role to play in Afghanistan's economic progress and prosperity. However, Pakistan is likely to undo this policy posture should it feel that a post-2014 scenario is tilted in favour of India. Pakistan would like to see that the space gained by India within Afghanistan is not used to pursue security-driven agendas against Pakistan. As the endgame in

Afghanistan unfolds, Pakistan must be watching cautiously the changing dynamics within Afghanistan because it is unlikely that Islamabad will let India gain an upper-hand once foreign troops withdraw from Afghanistan. India must restrict itself to the tasks it has been doing meticulously for the last thirteen years, while Pakistan should also try to contribute meaningfully towards the reconstruction process in Afghanistan without being singularly concerned about India's presence there. As the army in Pakistan stands opposed to the idea of Pakistan's civilian government's efforts of normalising ties with India[43], there is every possibility that Indo-Pak rivalry in Afghanistan will continue to remain a crucial factor in determining, at least in part, the contours of Indo-Pakistan relations, and to a large extent the course of Pakistan-Afghanistan relations. However, such a scenario is bound to exacerbate the tension between the two nuclear-armed neighbours while also hindering the post-withdrawal reconstruction in Afghanistan.

The success of India's quite diplomacy in Afghanistan in the last thirteen years notwithstanding, India's choices of engaging Afghanistan beyond 2014 – in concert with its strategic interests in the Af-Pak region – are limited. While one can argue that the U.S. withdrawal from Afghanistan is going to be rewarding for India since Pakistan will not be in a position to milk financial and military resources from the United States under the guise of being a counterterrorism ally of U.S. led coalition. There is, however, a realistic understanding within India's strategic circles that India has little capacity to alter the strategic landscape within Afghanistan in its favour. The best India can do is to is to leverage its soft power so as to ensure the deepening and expanding of its ties with Afghanistan.

India cannot expect a dramatic rise in the quality of its engagement with Afghanistan beyond 2014. Neither should it allow its influence to dwindle as a result of the U.S. withdrawal from Afghanistan. India must realistically appreciate the fact that Pakistan's role in resolving the conflict in Afghanistan shall remains essential. Therefore, India needs to formulate its Afghan policy commensurate with this understanding in order to keep alive the cordiality in India-Afghan relations while at the same time trying to prevent the emergence of an intensified turf battle with Pakistan. Such a policy will retain relevance irrespective of the nature and consequences of the U.S. withdrawal.[44]

Given the fact that the security scenario in Afghanistan is most likely to deteriorate following the U.S. troop withdrawal, India must seek to engage all ethnic factions in Afghanistan without being seen as tilted in favour of a particular ethnic community.[45] Building rapport with the new regime in Kabul and trying to forge linkages with the youth in Afghanistan (through increased scholarship programmes and liberal visa regimes) can certainly facilitate the cementing of India-Afghan relations in the years to come. Once the new government takes charge in Kabul, India must try to carry forward the understanding that has been reached upon between the governments of India and Afghanistan during the last thirteen years. And the best approach to facilitate the continuation of that affinity is for India to continue with its aid and assistance programmes in Afghanistan. Financial assistance will be the key to the consolidation of India-Afghan relations beyond 2014, because Afghanistan will need foreign assistance to keep the state institutions functioning (particularly the Afghan National Army). India's soft-power approach (even though it may not yield quick strategic gains) together with its government-to-government financial assistance, will continue to be the best policy option available to India in the foreseeable future in order to sustain the cordiality in Indo-Afghan relations, and also as a means to sustain and enhance its influence in and around Afghanistan.

Conclusion

Very recently, India's ambassador to Afghanistan Amar Sinha criticised Pakistan for its suspected proxy war tactics and encouragement for terrorism in Afghanistan. He emphasised that Pakistan is trying to use Afghanistan as its combat zone while doing nothing to eliminate the terrorist sanctuaries on its soil. Ambassador Sinha's accusations were swiftly refuted by in a statement released by Pakistan's embassy in Afghanistan maintaining that India's accusations are 'baseless and unfounded.'[46] These mutual accusations are an indication that Indo-Pak rivalry in Afghanistan stands far from resolved. What is more important is that this enmity can only get worse once the withdrawal of foreign forces is complete. The post-withdrawal situation in Afghanistan may be used by Afghanistan's regional neighbours to advance their own interests at the expense of Afghanistan's stability. In such a scenario, India must cautiously formulate its Afghan policy with an emphasis on engaging all ethnic groups in Afghanistan so as to gain wider acceptability among Afghans as a friendly neighbour. India needs to cooperate with other regional neighbours in order to address the pressing issues in Afghanistan and support Kabul government in its efforts towards rebuilding and reconstruction of the war-weary country. A stable and democratic Afghanistan will not only serve India's interests within Afghanistan in the long run, but can also limit Pakistan's manoeuvring of religious extremism as a state policy. The security vacuum in post-2014 scenario may offer Pakistan-based anti-India extremist groups a strategic space to organise and plan their attacks without much scrutiny. In the absence of the security cover that the U.S. troops and ISAF were able to provide in Afghanistan for the last thirteen years, India's interests and installations inside Afghanistan might become vulnerable to attacks orchestrated and schemed by Pakistan's security establishment and carried out by their proxies. For this reason, India's post-2014 Afghan policy should aim at mitigating the possibility of Afghanistan again becoming sanctuary for extremist outfits who, more often than not, take diktats from Pakistan's ISI.

References

1. For the full text of Nehru's speech see A. Appadorai (1985), *Select Documents on India's Foreign Policy and Relations 1947-1972,* Vol. II, New Delhi, p. 5.
2. While the deal initially stipulated a recount of valid votes so as to determine the winner of the presidential election, the continuing disagreement between the two candidates, however, forced the United States Secretary to propose a power-sharing arrangement, wherein the winner of the vote will convene a Loya Jirga so as to create a position of Prime Minister for the runner up candidate or his nominee. There is still disagreement over the powers and functions of the proposed post. See May Jeong, "Afghanistan's presidential rivals reach agreement after Kerry flies into Kabul," *The Guardian*, August 8, 2014.
3. Loannis Koskinas, "The Only Choice Left for Afghanistan," *Foreign Policy*, September 11, 2014.
4. Sarah Chayes, "Afghanistan is not ready to vote" Bloomberg, October 20, 2013.
   Found at: http://www.bloomberg.com/news/print/2-13-10-20/afghanistan-isn-t-ready-to-vote.html
5. Sumit Ganguly, "India's Role in Afghanistan," January 2012, CIDOB Policy Research Project, p. 1. Found at: http://www.idos.org/es/ontent/download/.../SUMMIT_GANGULY.pdf
6. Julian E. Barnes, "U.S Seeks Larger Role for India," *The Wall Street Journal*, June 6, 2012, p. 9.
7. Text of the Treaty of Friendship accessed from the website of Ministry of External Affairs, Government of India. Found at: http://www.mea.gov.in/bilateral-documents.htm?dtl/6584/Treaty+ of+ Friendship (Accessed on 14 July 2014).

8. Raghav Sharma (2011), "India's relations with Afghanistan," in David Scott (ed.) *Handbook of India's International Relations*, New York, Routledge, pp. 107-108.
9. Rasul Bakhsh Rais (September 1993), "Afghanistan and the Regional Powers," *Asian Survey*, Vol. 33, No. 9, p. 913.
10. C. Christine Fair (Spring 2011), "Under the Shrinking U.S Security Umbrella: India's Endgame in Afghanistan," *The Washington Quarterly*, Vol. 34, No. 2, p. 180.
11. Harsh V. Pant (Spring 2011), "The Afghanistan Conflict: India's Changing Role," *The Middle East Quarterly,* Vol. XVIII, No. 2, pp. 31-32. Found at: http://www.meforum.org/2895/India-Afghanistan (Accessed on June 5, 2013).
12. Zahid Ali Khan (Winter 2012-2013), "Post 9/11 Development of Indo-Afghan Ties: Pakistan's Concerns and Policy Options," *Regional Studies*, Vol. XXXI, No. 1, p. 83.
13. *Ibid.,* pp. 83-84.
14. Armayan Bhatnagar and Divya John (October 2013), "Accessing Afghanistan and Central Asia: Importance of Chabahar to Inida," *Observer Research Foundation Special Report*, Issue No. 3, p. 7.
15. "India says Iran's Chabahar Port best for transit of goods to Afghanistan," Press TV, July 18, 2013.
16. Rani D. Mullen and Sumit Ganguly, "The Rise of India's Soft Power," *Foreign Policy*, May 8, 2012.
    Found at: http://www.foreignpolicy.com/articles/2012/05/08/the_rise_of _indian_soft_power (accessed on 12 July 2014).
17. Zahid Shahab and Stuti Bhatnagar (April 2007), "Pakistan-Afghanistan Relations and the Indian Factor," *Pakistan Horizon*, Vol. 60, No. 2, p. 166.
18. Amiya Chandra (2007), "India and Afghanistan: Renewing Economic Relations," in K. Warikoo (ed.) *Afghanistan: Challenges and Opportunities*, Vol. 2, New Delhi, Pentagon Press, pp. 182-183.
19. Found at: http://www.Indo-Afg/India,%20Afghanistan% 20sign%20 strategi%20pat%20-%20WSJ.com.htm.
20. Ashraf Haidari, "Afghanistan is seeking to strengthen regional partnerships in a post-NATO era," *The Diplomat*, July 5, 2014.
21. Rama Lakshmi, "India and Afghanistan sign security and trade pact," *Washington Post*, October 4, 2011.
22. The Hindu, 13 November, 2012.
23. Ashraf Haidari, "Afghanistan is seeking to strengthen regional partnerships in a post-NATO era," *op. cit.*
24. Ankit Panda, "What Role Can India Play in Defusing Afghanistan's Election Crisis?," *The Diplomat*, September 10, 2014.
25. Gautam Mukhopadhaya, "India", in Ashley J. Tellis and Aroop Mukharji (eds.), "Is a Regional Strategy Viable in Afghanistan," *Carnegie Endowment for International Peace*, 2010, p. 27.

26. Larry Hanauer and Peter Chalk (2012), *India's and Pakistan's Strategies in Afghanistan: Implications for the United States and the Region*. Santa Monica: RAND Corporation, Occasional Paper, p. 1.
27. Parvez Musharraf as quoted in "Two Hundred Percent, There Won't Be War," *Outlook*. Full interview available at: http://www.outlookindia.com/article.aspx?220543-0 (Accessed on February 15, 2014).
28. See C. Christine Fair (2014), *Fighting to the End: The Pakistan Army's Way of War*, Oxford, Oxford University Press, pp. 1-2.
29. Steve Coll, "Don't Look Back," *The New Yorker*, March 1, 2010. Found at: http://www.newyorker.com/talk/comment/2010/03/01/100301 taco_talk_coll (Accessed on April 28, 2014)
30. Ahmed Rashid, "Karzai Pledges Good Relations but Demands Pakistan Stop Extremists," *The Nation*, July 22, 2003.
31. C. Christine Fair (2010), "India in Afghanistan and Beyond: Opportunities and Constraints," *Century Foundation Report*, p. 8.
32. Riffat Hussain (2002), "Pakistan's Relations with Afghanistan: Continuity and Change," *Strategic Studies,* Vol. 4, p. 22. Found at: http://www.issi.org.pk/journal/2002_files/no_4/article/3a.htm (Accessed on 3 June 2011).
33. Humera Iqbal, "Pak-Afghan Ties in the Light of Pak-US Strategic Dialogue," p. 17. Found at: http://www.irs.org.pk/afghanistan/spn10.pdf (Accessed on 2 August 2014).
34. "Afghanistan: The Problem of Pashtun Alienation," *International Crisis Group Asia Report No. 62*, 5 August 2003, p. 23.
35. Larry Hanauer and Peter Chalk (2012), *India's and Pakistan's Strategies in Afghanistan: Implications for the United States and the Region*. op. cit., p. 2.
36. *Ibid.*
37. C. Christine Fair, "Under the Shrinking U.S Security Umbrella: India's Endgame in Afghanistan," The Washington Quarterly, op. cit., pp. 184-185.
38. M. Maqbool Khan Wazir (Winter 2011), "Geopolitics of FATA after 9/11," *Islamabad Policy Research Institute (IPRI) Journal*, Vol. 11, No. 1, p. 71. As cited in C. Christine Fair (2014), *Fighting to the End: The Pakistan Army's Way of War*, Oxford, Oxford University Press, p. 119.
39. C. Christine Fair (2010), "India in Afghanistan and Beyond: Opportunities and Constraints," *Century Foundation Report*, pp. 13-14. Also see C. Christine Fair (January 2014) "Securing Indian Interests in Afghanistan Beyond 2014," *Asia Policy*, No. 17, pp. 28-29.
40. Moeed Yusuf, Huma Yusuf and Salman Zaidi (2011), "Pakistan, The United States, and the Endgame in Afghanistan: Perceptions of Pakistan's Foreign Policy Elite," *A Jinnah Institute Research Report, Jinnah Institute of Peace*, p. 23.
41. Usman Saeed (June 2012), "Indian Interests in Afghanistan," *Hilal*, Vol. 48, No. 12, pp. 14-15.

42. Larry Hanauer and Peter Chalk (2012), *India's and Pakistan's Strategies in Afghanistan: Implications for the United States and the Region*, *op. cit.*, pp. 1-3.
43. Hussain Haqqani, "A bubble called Pakistan," The Indian Express, August 8, 2014.
44. For a detailed analysis of India's options in Afghanistan beyond 2014, see "Afghanistan: Post-US Drawdown and India," *Indian Foreign Affairs Journal*, Vol. 6, No. 3, pp. 239-271.
45. Marine General Joseph Dunford, while handing over the command of ISAF troops in Afghanistan on 26 August 2014, said that the Afghan security forces will be put to test in 2015 once the Taliban launch their offensive following the U.S. troop withdrawal. The security situation has further been compromised by the slow pace of the training of Afghan forces as a result of the months-long political stalemate over the results of 2014 presidential elections. See Lolita C. Baldor, "US Commander: Afghans face Taliban Test in 2015," *Associated Press*, August 27, 2014.
46. "Pakistan Rejects Indian Ambassador Accusations," *TOLO News*, August 16, 2014.

13

Promotion of Democracy by India and the U.S. in the Af-Pak Region: An Analysis

Dr Josukutty C.A.

Abstract

The U.S led intervention in Afghanistan was not only an effort to uproot terrorism from Afghan soil but also an attempt to cultivate democracy in the Af-Pak region. It has been argued that strategic and security interests of India and the U.S. converge in this region at multiple levels, with the primary focus on fighting terrorism and promoting democracy. It has been assumed that the collaborative efforts by the world's oldest democracy (USA) and the largest democracy (India) could strengthen their bilateral relations and mitigate conditions of terrorism in South Asia. This presumption is oriented by the basic tenets of democratic peace theory-that democracy is useful in resolving crisis and bettering relations between and among nations. But the collaborative efforts in the Af-Pak region has neither promoted democracy nor strengthened Indo-US relations in the expected lines.

Introduction

Terrorism is a major threat to world peace and security of nations in contemporary times. The menace of terrorism can be eliminated only through concerted efforts of the international community. Both India and the US are victims of terrorism and they have pledged to work together to fight it. India has been considered as an ally of the U.S. in this endeavour. Democracy is considered as an important means to counter terrorism. India and the United states are considered to be 'natural allies' primarily on account of their common democratic beliefs and practices. The Af-Pak region, a hot bed of international terrorism, is a major theatre where India and the US have found convergence of interests for working together to realise objectives such as fighting terrorism, promoting democracy and strengthening bilateral relationship. Democracy promotion and nation building have been declared two important objectives of U.S. led intervention in Afghanistan. It is presumed that the collaborative efforts by the world's best/oldest democracy (USA) and the largest democracy (India) in the region could strengthen their bilateral relations and mitigate conditions of terrorism. The paper attempts to examine two pertinent issues. One, whether attempts of democracy promotion by India and the US helped to fight the challenge of terrorism in the region? Two, does the collaborative endeavour by India and the U.S. contributed to strengthening Indo-US bilateral relationship? The ensuing discussion is based on the assumption of 'democratic peace theory' that democracy is useful in resolving crises, including terrorism and bettering relations between and among nations. In the course of the paper, the basic tenets of democratic peace theory, role of democracy in Indo-US relations, the impact of Indo-US joint efforts on democracy promotion in the Af-Pak region and, Indo-US relations are discussed.

Democratic Peace

Democratic peace theorists posit that wars rarely occur between democracies and constitutional republics would be pacifist. Although "peace among men living side by side is not the natural state," the checks and balances of republican constitutions would prevent adventurous rulers from committing their nations to war, and the submission of each republican government to international law would obviate the impetus for wars (Kant, 1957:10). This is attributed to the domestic norms and institutions that exist in democratic politics and that constrain their recourse to force when a conflict of interests arises between them. (Bremer, 1993:231-49, Huth and Allee 2002, Oneal and Russet 2001)). The rationale is that the domestic norms and institutions of democratic states interact in such a way that neither state will resort to violence to settle any conflict of interests that arises between them. In democratic states, the prevailing norm requires citizens to settle disputes between them without using force. In other states, however, force is more often the weapon of choice (Maoz and Russet, 1993:624-38). Leaders and decision makers in democracies are constrained by a number of checks and balance factors to use force for conflict resolution.

An adjoining and interpretative argument of democratic peace theory is that democracy leads to less terrorism. The more democratic a country becomes, the less likely it is to produce terrorists and terrorist groups. Democracy encourages the development of secular, nationalist, and liberal political organisations to fight terrorism. It is reasoned that, promoting freedom will produce peace. These tenants echo an important position of liberal theorists that the aggressive instincts of authoritarian leaders and totalitarian ruling parties make for war and liberal states, founded on individual rights such as equality before the law, free speech and other civil liberties, private property, and elected representation are fundamentally against war (Doyle 1986:1151-1169).[1]

Democracy in the Af-Pak Context

South Asia, particularly the Af-Pak region, has been criticised for its democratic deficits. Lack of democracy and weak democratic institutions is one of the reasons for wars and the transformation of the region into the terror headquarters of the world. The philosophical and ideological basis of the formation of Pakistan and the prominent role that military has come to play in its politics has sidelined democracy as a factor in nation building in Pakistan. Pakistan has to this day not had a civilian government peacefully succeeded by another civilian government as the result of free and fair elections except the PPP government from 2009 to 2013 (Blackwill and Chandra 2011). It has been using its extended religious identity with Afghanistan to sharpen the ideological battle against India. Afghanistan also has very little experience and tradition in democracy. At present it is reverberating with theocracy based on religious fundamentalism and grand visions of recreating the modern Khaliphate of the political Islam variety under the tutelage of Taliban. Historically too, the geo-politics of the region has never been a fertile ground for democracy to flourish. Therefore, there are fundamental differences over running the government and managing social and inter-religious relationships. The relationship among countries of the region particularly with India is seriously affected by this non-democratic context.

There are many reasons for the undemocratic culture of Af-Pak region. Lack of political development, the absence of proper democratic institutions and procedures, irreconcilable national identities, weak economies and poor intra-regional trade, unsettled border disputes, and lack of regional institutions to settle violent disputes account for undemocratic nature of the region (Paul, 2005:3). Three solid pillars of Kantain peace – institutions, democracies and economic interdependence need to be developed in this region. The emergence of strong democratic states and faster economic growth and interdependence among countries of South Asia can lead to peace and change the dynamics of the region (Paul and Mc Lauchlin 2011:305). Shared democratic norms and institutions would constrain recurrence of violent engagement and terrorism. The undemocratic context of the region has three features with adverse impact on India's security-One, Intensive Indo-Pak rivalry two, cross border terrorism related conflicts in Kashmir and three, the degeneration of the region as the epicenter of international terrorism.

Democracy Factor in Indo-US Relation

During the cold war, despite being democracies, India and the US were virtually on the opposite sides of world politics primarily due to their differing ideological positions. India was committed to non-alignment and anti-imperialism whereas the US was driven by anti-communism and alliance politics. The practical positioning of this differing perception was the US tilt towards Pakistan and a pro-Soviet India. According to Dennis Kux the root cause of disagreements between India and the US during the cold war days was the clash over national security issues of prime significance to each country- for India, the US arming and aligning with Pakistan-India's principal security threat and for the US, India's relationship with the USSR, the major threat to American perceptions of global security and peace (Kux, 1993:447-8). This clash of interest was visible in the pro-Pakistan position of the US on the Kashmir issue, Pak-US military alliances, their joint mission in fighting the Soviet occupation of Afghanistan and in strengthening the China-Pak axis. These differences were so pronounced that they evolved into strategic complications and threatened the stability of South-Asia by sharpening Indo-Pak rivalry.

In spite of these glaring differences, there was a feeling of goodwill towards each other even during days of deep tension and disinterest. In a speech to the US Congress in 1949 Nehru had indicated, "Friendship and cooperation between our two countries are natural", (Embassy of India 1949). Democracy was perceived to be strong enough a factor in India, for the USA to be genuinely invested in building upon its economy and society through development assistance that helped India at different times to avoid famine, launch green revolution, tackle malaria and educational expansion. According to David M. Malone the US has always viewed Pakistan as military ally and India as political ally (Malone, 2011:171). Gary Guess suggests that the US maintained a two-pronged strategy of engagement in South Asia that involved the simultaneous building of an alliance with Pakistan and promoting close political and economic ties with India (Kundu 2005:171). This is attributed to India's democratic credentials and the tacit appreciation the US has for it (Malone, 2011:162).[2]

The end of cold war and the subsequent changes have reinforced and synergised Indo-US relations on a democratic edifice by common interests and ideals in manifold ways. Leaders of both the countries have evoked, time and again, the significance of democracy as a factor of strategic significance in the relationship. In 1998, Prime Minister Atal Bihari Vajpayee stated that India and the United States, as the world's largest democracies, were "natural allies", a term subsequently adopted by President Clinton and Bush (Indian Embassy, 1998). Defending India's nuclear test U. S. Senator Mack emphasised India's commitment to peace in contrast to Chinese undemocratism and commented, 'We have a common bond with the Indian people based on a commitment to democracy, freedom, and the rule of law', (U.S. Congressional Record, 1998). The visit of President Bill Clinton in 2000 had created tremendous goodwill in the relationship by placing democracy at the centre of India-U.S. relations. Prime Minister Manmohan Singh declared in February 2005 that "Liberal democracy is the natural order of political organisation in today's world. All alternate systems, authoritarian and majoritarian in varying degrees, are an aberration," (Singh, 2005a). The July 18, 2005 joint statement by Indian Prime Minister Manmohan Singh and the U.S. President George W. Bush in the landmark Indo-U.S. civilian nuclear agreement recognised democracy as a guiding principle for building a peaceful, prosperous, inclusive and sustainable world (IDSA, 2010). They also emphasised their countries' joint "obligation to the global community to strengthen values, ideals, and practices of freedom, pluralism, and rule of law", and agreed to assist states seeking to democratise (U.S. Department of State, 2005). In his speech to the US Congress on 19th July 2005, Manmohan Singh emphasised the coincidence of values and strategy in the new India-USA relationship. He said, "there are partnership based on principle and there are partnership based on pragmatism. I think we are at the juncture where we can embark on a partnership that can draw both on principle as well as pragmatism" (Singh, 2005b). In a testimony before the House International Relations Committee in 2006, Secretary of State Condoleezza Rice stated the United States has invested heavily in India's rise through economic assistance, defence training and transfer, and civilian-nuclear energy cooperation — to help incorporate India into what she calls 'the tent of responsible democracies that wish to be anchors of stability and the promotion of democracy and peace in the world (Rice, 2005). In 2007 Nicholas R. Burns (Burns, 2007:145) wrote that promotion of Democracy and freedom around the world,' should be essential component of the new USA-India relationship. The US considers India's identity as a "multi-ethnic and multi-religious and pluralistic" democracy the "foundation for our partnership in regional and global affairs", while Indian leaders declare "our common commitment to democracy, pluralism, and prosperity" the basis for Indo-American cooperation on global issues (Hindustan Times, 2005).

India and the US are partners in many global democracy promotion endeavours. They became founding members of the Community of Democracies in 1999 and UN Democracy Fund in 2005 to promote representative institutions and human rights worldwide. The US and India have been working together to promote political reconciliation in Sri Lanka and for the restoration of democracy in Nepal and Bangladesh. Above all, India is increasingly becoming an important partner in the democratic reconstruction of Afghanistan.

On the whole, unlike the cold war years, democracy has become a common asset of the relationship that have placed India at the core of new networks of strategic cooperation weaved by the US among Asia's leading democracies. It has helped India and the US agree and work together internationally at many levels-democracy, market capitalism, rule of law, fighting terrorism, the UN charter and all regimes or webs of international law (Armitage, Richard L., Burns, R. Nicholas and Fountain, Richard, 2010). With the rapid rise of religious fundamentalism and terrorism, both the countries have a common interest in promoting liberalism, political moderation and peaceful change. Both India and the U.S. support the ideas and principles of 'democratic peace'. A report by the Centre for New American Security says "The United States and India should work together to spread the culture of democracy in lands where it does not yet exist", (Armitage, Richard L., Burns, R. Nicholas and Fountain, Richard, 2010). In these and other ways, the liberal-democratic identities of America and India have reinforced strategic and economic interests to draw the two nations closer together in an era of uncertainty ....and growing threats from failing states and terrorism (Green, 2008:9). Indian strategists argue that a future balance of power in which democratic India constitutes a principal pole would better protect the liberal values embodied by Indian society than a future order in which an authoritarian China enjoyed hegemony in Asia (Raja Mohan, 2004, Chellany 2006).[3]

The growing ideological affinity has its positive resonance on US policy towards India on Pakistan and Afghanistan. The United States shares with India common objectives regarding Pakistan- a moderate Pakistan that is a responsible nuclear steward, that confronts extremism within its borders and stops supporting terrorism outside of its territory, and that also plays a positive role in maintaining the stability of Afghanistan (Raja Mohan, 2007:99-115). Similarly there is an explicit pro-US tilt in India's foreign policy. In 2001 India was one of the few countries to support the Nuclear Missile Defense Initiative by the US. The formulation of the Next Step in Strategic Partnership (NSSP) in 2004 and the July 18, 2005 initiative on civilian nuclear cooperation further strengthened the relationship. The partnership assumed a comprehensive character that covered economy, energy security, democracy promotion, defence cooperation, disaster relief, maritime cooperation, nuclear cooperation, high technology and space cooperation. The Civilian Nuclear Agreement of 2008 and the U.S.-India Strategic Dialogue (annual) that began in June 2010, the establishment of the U.S.-India Homeland Security Dialogue in 2011 are quality steps in improving the relationship. The elaborate Joint Statement issued at the end of the strategic dialogue in June 2012 makes the context very clear, "The U.S. and India have a shared vision of peace, stability, and prosperity in Asia, the Indian Ocean region, and the Pacific region and are committed to work together, and with others in the region, for the evolution of an open, balanced and inclusive architecture", (Sreenivasan, 2012).

Counter Terrorism and Democracy Promotion in the Af-Pak

One of the primary objectives of US intervention in Afghanistan was democracy promotion and nation building in that country. The counter terrorism measures initiated in the Af-Pak region on the aftermath of the attack on World Trade Centre offered a great opportunity for India and the US to jointly fight terrorism and promote democracy in the region.

A democratic, stable and secure Afghanistan was high on the agenda when counter terrorism measures were initiated and Taliban was deposed. Obama, before occupying the presidency, was an ardent advocate of the need for building a just, secure and democratic Afghanistan (Obama, 2007). As international forces toppled the Taliban in 2001, the coalition's leaders emphasised that, besides defeating Al-Qaeda and the Taliban, this was an effort to create a new future for the Afghan people a future based on democracy. When the combined forces entered Afghanistan in October 2001, British Prime Minister Tony Blair said at the time ".... to the Afghan people we make this commitment. The conflict will not be the end. We will not walk away, as the outside world has done so many times before", (Fly, 2012). Equal emphasis was given to free its people from despotic Islamic rule. The National Security Strategy, of the USA-2010, emphasised in no uncertain terms the need to deny al-Qaida a safe haven, deny the Taliban the ability to overthrow the government, in Afghanistan (White House, 2010).

Afghanistan is one of the few countries where India has enthusiastically intervened to promote democracy as a factor for nation building, peace and stability in the region. India has already poured billions of dollars into reconstruction and development aid in Afghanistan, entered into a strategic partnership agreement and has committed to training Afghan security forces.[4] India took the initiative to organise an Investment Conference in New Delhi on June 2012 as a measure of nation building in Afghanistan. The two countries have decided to hold a regular strategic dialogue with the aim of intensifying mutual efforts towards strengthening regional peace and security.[4]

Gradually the agenda for democracy promotion receded to the background in the Af-Pak region. Much was expected from president Obama's approach to world politics. But the Af-Pak Policy, Obama's signature foreign policy initiative towards Afghanistan initiated in 2009 (Cooper, 2009) and the decision to withdraw US forces by the end of 2014, jeopardised democracy promotion in the region mainly at two levels. One, centrality of Pakistan in fighting terrorism in the region and two, reconciliation with Taliban and their prospective induction as the future administrative dispensation in Afghanistan.

Centrality of Pakistan

The Af-Pak policy emphasised the centrality of Pakistan in fighting terrorism in the region. The very nomenclature 'Af-Pak' points to the fact that Af-Pak region remains the epicentre of violent extremism and the U.S. sees it as 'as a common, interrelated problem' (Ghosh, 2009). The Af-Pak policy reiterates the link between Afghanistan and the unsettled relationship between India and Pakistan on Kashmir. This link is the key factor that roadblock democracy promotion in the region. A state of permanent tension in the LOC between India and Pakistan is projected by the latter as the major hurdle for constructive action against the terrorists in the Af-Pak border region. Pakistan worries more about its threat from India than from extremists from within and around its borders. Its policy towards Taliban is steered by its antagonistic relationship with India. To avoid losing the strategic advantage against India, Pakistan has devised a two-track policy in fighting terrorism. On the one hand, they have been fighting terrorism along with the international community and on the other hand, supporting and promoting the same terrorists whom they said to have been fighting. Pakistan is proving to be the biggest stumbling block for a solution in Afghanistan. The US could not do much on Pak duplicity as, according to Shashi Tharoor, (Tharoor, 2012: 52) Islamabad remains logistically indispensible for the US. The US considers an undemocratic Pakistan a better ally to fight terrorism than a democratic India.

The key role for Pakistan in the Af-pak region in the US scheme of things underlines the view that Afghanistan must be insulated from a potentially harmful Indian-Pakistani rivalry as it was necessary to take care of Pak strategic interests. General Mc Chrystal in his Commanders' Initial Assessment Report in 2008 said that India's rising influence in Afghan is likely to 'exacerbate regional tensions' and Pakistan is likely to take countermeasures (Mac Chrystal, 2009:19). The US accepted Pakistan's strategic interest at the costs of India's interests in the region and in Kashmir. And therefore, the US was eager to limit India's role in Afghanistan to economic and humanitarian diplomacy. This has adversely affected Indo-US joint-endeavour of democracy promotion and fighting terrorism.

Reconciliation with Taliban

The Af-Pak policy envisages reconciliation with moderate Taliban. The U.S. hopes to drive a wedge between what President Obama described as "uncompromising" Taliban and al-Qaeda leaders on the one hand, and less implacable insurgents who may be more inclined, for the right price, to make a deal with Western forces or the Afghan government on the other hand (Ghosh, 2009). It is a plan to reintegrate the rank and file Taliban fighters in to the political mainstream of Afghanistan.

The accommodation plan is a two-track program. One is reintegration of fighters — to entice the Taliban's rank-and-file fighters to lay down their weapons and rejoin Afghan society. The core of this policy is a vast jobs programme (induction into local police force), security guarantee, and amnesty for the Taliban fighters (Rod and Alissa, 2010). The logic is that there are lots of low-ranking Taliban foot soldiers within Afghanistan who are fighting essentially for money and that really don't care about the ideologies. If better incentives are offered, they are not going to be committed unto death for the Taliban, per se (Biddle-Gwertzman, 2009). The other is reconciliation with Taliban leaders and allow them to play a political role. In exchange, both rank-and-file Taliban fighters and leaders would have to pledge to renounce violence, separate completely and permanently from Al-Qaeda and accept the Afghan constitution (Rubin, 2010). The Plan also includes turning some of the tribes as potentially the best hope for success against the resurgent Taliban.

Impact on Democracy

The centrality of Pakistan in fighting terrorism and the policy of integration and reconciliation with Taliban work against democracy and strategic relationship between India and the US. It goes against the consensus built by the international community to focus on institution building, demobilisation of existing militia, and the recreation of stable and democratic Afghanistan (Chellany, 2009). All these promises remain unfulfilled and the U.S. is spearheading an effort to make peace with the Islamists fundamentals it promised to free Afghan from. It would reinstate the religious radicals to the seat of power in Afghanistan. Taliban continues to be conservative, obscurantist, anti-democratic and is driven by the idea of political Islam towards the grand goal of establishing a Modern Caliphate. Any attempt by the moderate Taliban to genuinely collaborate in the stabilisation and democratisation of Afghanistan is likely to be sabotaged by the hardliners.

The assassinations of former Afghan President Barhanuddin Rabbani, Maulvi Arsala Rahmani of Afghanistan's High Peace Council, the attack by Afghan National Police Force on the allied forces (green-on-blue attacks) and numerous other terror strikes are indicative of the dim future that lie ahead (Roggio and Lundquist, 2012).[5] The plan to work with tribal groups are likely to backfire as local militias and tribal chiefs are notorious for their shifting loyalties and reluctance to any central national authority. The British and Soviet experiences had proved that no strategy that relied on tribal or religious groups have succeeded in establishing peace and stability in Afghanistan. The plan to differentiate between moderate and extremists Taliban, split them politically and conduct factional negotiations has not succeeded. In fact, the decision to negotiate with the Taliban has given them the much needed legitimacy. The US attempts to negotiate directly with Taliban to the exclusion of Pakistan, has not produced the desired results (Jacob, 2009). The high precision drone attacks would harden fundamentalist elements to seek and justify anti-democratic alternatives. The emergence of Yusuf-al-Qaradawi, a Doha based Islamist Scholar, as a key negotiator proves India's fears of jihadi groups like Lashkar-e-Taiba and Jaish-e-Muhammad would find new sanctuaries in a future Afghan regime that includes the Taliban (Swami, 2011).

These developments show that democracy have not been a serious factor in the counter terrorism strategy. The shared values and interests that brought India and the US together would not be a part of the ensuing dispensation in Afghanistan. A democratic India is now expected to play a role that would not displease the undemocratic elements in the Af-Pak region. This secondary and nominal role for democracy in the counter terrorism strategy was never corrected rather it was increasingly undermined over the years. The United States has been rather reluctant to discuss democracy in Pakistan in its dialogue on shared political values with India.[6] At same time, it was eager to involve India to address the democratic deficiencies in other neighbouring countries and elsewhere. Where as the US found it necessary to deal with Pakistan in an entirely different manner (Rja Mohan, 2005). It means that it is not in US interest to antagonise powerful elements in Pak for the sake of democracy promotion (Markey, 2009).[7] At the same time it wants India as a partner to share the burden of fighting terrorism and for realising other strategic objectives. This has given rise to many potentially divisive strategic issues that adversely affect the promotion of democracy. The emerging scenario (particularly after the US withdrawal), will not, in the near future strengthen democracy neither in Afghanistan nor in Pakistan. The major reason is that a military-theocratic-anti-India Pakistan would find a Taliban dominated undemocratic Afghanistan as the best strategic asset against India. India and the US failed to evolve a democracy based strategic approach in Afghanistan and therefore the Af-Pak strategy is a big blow to democracy promotion and peace in the region.

Impact on India-US Relations

The Af-Pak region has been time and again referred to as a site where India and the US share a host of common interests in fighting terrorism and promoting democracy. The Indo-US relations have not improved in any substantial way as a result of their joint endeavours in the region. Contrary to expectations and claims both the countries could not serve their strategic interests the way it was envisaged. Rather the US was insensitive to India's core strategic interests.

India has strategic, security and economic interests in the region. Strategically India, wants to maintain a strong presence in the region as a regional power and as a gateway to Central Asia and West Asia. From a security point of view India is eager to ensure that Afghan territory is never used against it either by Pakistan or by terrorist groups for anti-India activities including cross border terrorism. Equally important is India's economic and energy interests in the region. A key goal of Indian policy is to have a stable arrangement for trade, particularly energy transit involving India, Afghanistan, Iran, Pakistan, Central Asian countries and Russia. The US interests in the region include preventing the region's use as a base for terror groups to attack the United States and its allies, ensuring that nuclear weapons do not fall into the hands of terrorists and protection of vital interests in the region as a global power in relation to China, Iran and other Islamic countries in the West Asia, Central Asia, Russia (David, 2011).

The protection of India's interest in the region is determined primarily by two factors. One, U.S. policy towards Pakistan vis-à-vis India in the context of fighting terrorism and two, Pakistan's role in any future dispensation in Afghanistan. The U.S. policy towards Pakistan vis-à-vis India in the context of counter terrorism measures have been disappointing. Pakistan's duplicity and double standard in fighting terrorism is no secret. The Director of the Pakistan Institute for Peace Studies in Islamabad, Muhammad Amir Rana, openly said that the terrorists could be Pakistan's ally in Afghanistan at some point in future, so it made no sense for the military to take them on at this point (Curtis 2011:79-89). The U.S. is reluctant to go beyond a point to put pressure on Islamabad to change its policies towards India or in its fight against terrorism. The Taliban and Al-Qaeda combine which include the Haqqani Network and the Mullah Omar-led Quetta Shura Taliban, safely housed in Pakistan, have close links with terrorist groups like Maulana Abdul Wahid Kashmiri's Lashkar-e-Toiba, and Masood

Azhar's Jaish-e-Mohammed that have been particularly active in Pakistan and their main aim is to integrate Jammu and Kashmir with Pakistan (Lambah 2009). They collaborate on logistics, training, recruiting and fundraising with the militants in Kashmir and other parts of India. The US has done little to dismantle these safe havens or force Pakistan to take action against them (Majidyar, 2012). The CIA-led drone strikes have largely targeted al-Qaeda leaders. For India, both Taliban and Al-Queda are equally dangerous. The US decision to withdraw from Afghanistan by the end of 2014 fits Pak plans and expectations in Afghanistan. The key role assigned to Pakistan in the fight against terrorism would enable Pakistan to regain its strategic asset in Afghanistan against India.

Generous aid by the US to Pakistan is another factor that goes against India's interests. A Congressional Research Service Report-2012 reveals that the US State Department has waived legal requirements that made the multi-billion dollar aid to Pakistan possible (Swami 2012). The State Department opined that they continue with the aid to Pakistan to protect US national interest. This aid, both economic and military, would be generously distributed to terrorists headquartered in Pakistan fighting against India in Kashmir. The report further substantiates that of the some \$2.1 billion in foreign Military financing provided to Pakistan from 2002 to 2010, a part of it has been used to purchase equipments that could be used against India (Swami, 2012). There is every reason to observe that the US has again started the old game of 'balancing' India and Pakistan to deal with the geo-political complexes of the region. The situation is similar to what Denis kux observed two decades ago that the US has ignored the essential precondition for an enduring relationship with India- of the US respecting India's security sensitivities in relation to Pakistan (Kux, 1993:45).

The US has not taken into consideration India's core security concerns while assigning Pakistan a key role in the counter-terrorism strategy in Af-Pak region. On the whole, the US continues to be an adversarial factor in Indo-Pak relationship. So long as Washington continues to be soft on Pakistan and ignores its India specific terror outfit, democracy, peace and stability will never become a reality in the region and India-US will remain mere partners devoid of any strategic substance in the relationship. Obviously, it goes against promotion of democracy in the region and any further improvement in Indo-US relationships. Above all, US policy towards the Af-Pak region is turning out to be the biggest challenge to stability in the region.

Democratic Peace in the Region?

The democratic peace theory has not worked in the Af-Pak context in terms of promoting democracy, fighting terrorism and improving Indo-US relations. The collaborative efforts by the two leading democracies –India and US- failed to promote democracy in the region. The major reason is that both the countries were driven more by their own realist national interest and not a genuine desire to promote democracy- the US, among other things, the compulsion to withdraw by 2014 (necessitated by the pressures its troubled economy) and India the plan to transform Afghan its strategic asset against Pakistan. Democracy promotion and fighting terrorism, though apparently seemed to converge the interests of India and the US, on the ground it worked in cross purposes particularly with regard to their immediate strategic interests. Gradually democracy promotion and nation building receded to the background. It raises a few pertinent questions as to whether convergence of long term strategic interests among countries is essential for collaborative democracy promotion by countries. Also it needs to examine the prospects of joint democracy promotion by developed and developing democracies.

Conclusion

The joint counter-terrorism measures by India and the U.S. in the Af-Pak region was expected to free the region of terrorism, promote democracy and strengthen the relationship between India and the U.S. After twelve years of fighting terrorism and democracy promotion, establishing a stable democratic national government in Afghanistan capable of delivering essential public goods and fighting terrorism with legitimacy is nowhere in sight. The key factor that affects Indo-US relationship and terrorism in the region is the US policy towards Pakistan. The US has overlooked Pak duplicity in promoting terrorism. When more effective steps were required against Pak sponsored terrorism, the US was selective in not taking action against India specific terrorists in that country. Not only that, despite Pak duplicity in fighting terrorism, the US continued to assign it the central role in fighting terrorism and extended liberal military and economic aid. India's core national security interests are at stake from Pak sponsored terrorism. In Afghanistan, apart from the initial rhetorical statements on democracy promotion and nation building, nothing concrete was materialised in realising democracy. The undemocratic, non-secular, theocratic and mono-cultural future dispensation that the US has compromised with in Afghanistan nullifies the grand schemes of democratic nation building and fighting terrorism in the region. Democracy as a factor has been under-utilised in Indo-US relations and in fighting terrorism in the Af-Pak region. Therefore, it has failed to strengthen Indo-US relations and neutralising terrorism in the region.

Notes

1. Democratic peace theorists posit that when the citizens who bear the burdens of war elect their governments, wars become impossible. Furthermore, citizens appreciate that the benefits of trade can be enjoyed only under conditions of peace. Thus the very existence of liberal states, such as the U.S., Japan, and our European allies, makes for peace. In a time when wars over dynastic succession were fought with mercenaries, Kant thought that if the consent of citizens were required for the declaration of war, none would be declared because citizens would be cautious about having to fight, paying the costs of war, having to repair the devastation of the fighting and "loading themselves with a heavy national debt that would embitter peace itself and that can never be liquidated on account of constant wars in the future." Under a constitution that is not republican, on the other hand, the war would not require sacrifice of the ruler. "He may, therefore, resolve on war as on a pleasure party for the most trivial reasons, and with perfect indifference leave the justification which decency requires to the diplomatic corps who are ever ready to provide it." (Kant. p. 13) Checks and balances should make constitutional republics more pacific toward all nations, not just toward like governments.
2. The importance of democracy in the relationship was emphasized in 1978 when the U.S. president Carter and Indian PM Desai exchanged visits.
3. Indo-US relationship is characterised as the D-2, referring to current status and future prospects of evolving a strong partnership between the two most significant democracies, as the most important strategic alliance of coming decades than the G-2 vision which refers to the alliance of two biggest economies—US and China.
4. India, with a commitment of $1.2 billion through 2013, is already the sixth largest donor to Afghanistan and the largest regional donor.

5. Green-on-blue attacks are attacks on Coalition forces by Afghan forces. These attacks have become a major threat in the eleven year-old war in Afghanistan. In 2012 such attacks accounted for 15 per cent of Coalition deaths.
6. The US is high on rhetoric about the lack of democracy and its values in Russia, China, Burma and the Middle East. It was also very timely in criticising India's for its reluctance in promoting democracy in Burma.
7. Analysts like Markey Daniel (2009) are of the view that Washington should aim to develop far closer cooperation with the Pakistani military and intelligence services, including more extensive training and, where mutually acceptable, regular joint operations and extensive intelligence sharing is possible.

References

Armitage, Richard L., Burns, R. Nicholas and Fountain, Richard, (2010): "Natural Allies, A Blueprint for the Future of U.S.-India Relations", *Centre for New American Security (Report)*, retrieved from *http://www.cnas.org/files/documents/publications/CNAS_ Natural% 20Allies_ ArmitageBurnsFontaine.pdf#page=1&zoom= auto,0,792,* accessed on 24-06-2013.

Biddle and Gwertzman (2009): "Obama's Afghanistan-Pakistan Strategy: A Reasonable First Step", retrieved from http://www.cfr.org / publication/18982/obamas_afghanistan pakistan_ strategy.html, accessed on 6-4-2009.

Blackwill, Robert D. and Chandra, Naresh, (2011): "The United States and India; A Shared Strategic Future", *Council on Foreign Relations and Aspen Institute India, Joint Study Group Report*, September, retrieved from *http://i.cfr.org/content/publications/attachments/USIndia_ jointstudy group_ IIGG.pdf, accessed on 14-4-2013.*

Bremer, Stuart A. (1993): "Democracy and Militarised Interstate Conflict, 1816–1965", *International Interactions*, No.18, pp. 231–49.

Burns, Nicholas R. (2007): "America's Strategic Opportunity with India", *Foreign Affairs*, Vol. 86, No. 6, p. 145.

Chellaney, Brahma (2006): "Asian Juggernaut: The Rise of China, India, and Japan", Harper Collins, New Delhi.

Chellaney, Brahma (2009): "Why U.S. Policy risks repeating history", *The Hindu*, 3rd March. Cooper, Schmitt (2009): "Plan would narrow goals in Afghan", March 28, retrieved from *iht.com/articles/2009/03/28/america/policy*, accessed on 15-4-2010.

Curtis, Lisa (2011): "Afghanistan-Pakistan: Lessons Learned and Future Directions", in *Counter-Terrorism in South Asia, ORF-Heritage Dialogue*, KW Publishers Pvt. Ltd., New Delhi, retrieved from http://

www.observerindia.com/cms/export/orfonline/modules/orfpapers/attachments/kaustav_1374143885446.pdf, accessed on 27-8-2013.

David, W. Barno (2011): "2014 and Beyond: U.S. Policy Towards Afghanistan and Pakistan" *Testimony before the House Foreign Affairs Committee Subcommittee on the Middle East and South Asia*, Center for a New American Security. November 3.

Doyle, W. Michael (1986): "Liberalism and World Politics", *The American Political Science Review*, Vol. 80, No. 4, pp. 1151-1169.

Embassy of India (1949): "Jawaharlal Nehru's speech in the US House of Representatives and the Senate", (13th October), Washington D C, retrieved from *www.indiaembassy.org/ indusrel/ india_us/nehru_congress_Oct_131949.htm* accessed on 15-3-2012.

Fly, Jamie M. (2012) : "Remembering why we are fighting in Afghanistan" Thursday, April 19, retrieved from *http://shadow. foreign policy.com/posts/2012/04/19/Remembering_ why_we_are_ fighting_in_Afghanistan,* accessed on 23-05-2013.

Ghosh, Bobby (2009): "Obama Afghanistan Plan Breaks Old Ground", *Foreign Affairs,* retrieved from *http://www.foreignaffairs.com/articles/64932/john-mueller/how-dangerous-are-the-taliban?,* accessed on 3-6-2009.

Green, F. Michael and Twining, Daniel (2008): "Democracy and American Grand Strategy in Asia: The Realist Principles Behind an Enduring Idealism" , *Contemporary Southeast Asia*, Vol. 30, No. 1, p. 9.

Hindustan Times. (2005), US Secretary of State Address Press Conference in New Delhi, Transcript, March 16.

Huth, P. and Allee, Todd (2002): "The Democratic Peace and Territorial Conflict in the Twentieth Century", Cambridge University Press, New York.

IDSA (2010): *India–United States 2020, United States, Europe, Nuclear Cluster*, Summary, Policy Brief 11, October 29, retrieved from http://idsa.in/policybrief/IndiaUnitedStates2020, accessed on 24-04-2013.

Indian Embassy (1998): "Speech of Atal Bihari Vajpayee at the Asia Society", (28 September) New York, retrieved from *<http://www.indianem hassy.org/nspecial/cahinet/Primeminister/pm(asiasociety).htm>;* accessed on 14-5-2013.

Indian Embassy (2000): "President William Clinton address to the Joint Session of the Indian Parliament", New Delhi, 22 March, retrieved from *<http://www.indianemhassy.org/indusrel/clinton_india/clinton_parliament_march_22_2000.htm>.* accessed on 15-2-2013.

Jacob, Happymon (2009): "Afghanistan, Taliban and the Southern Asian Geopolitics", *IJPAIR*, Kottayam, Vol. 2, No. 1.

Kant, Immanuel (1957): *Perpetual Peace,* Liberal Arts Press, Indianapolis, (first published 1795)

Kundu, Apurba (2005): "The National Democratic Alliance and National Security", in K. Adney and L.Saez (Eds.), Coalition *Politics and*

Hindu Nationalis, Rout ledge, London, (pp. 212-36) in Malone, M. David (2011): *Does the Elephant Dance: India's Foreign policy*, OUP, New Delhi.

Kux Dennis (1993): "Estranged Democracies: India and the United States", Sage publications, New Delhi.

Lambah, S.K. (2009): "A Comprehensive Strategy in a Regional Context"; Statement made as Special Envoy of the Prime Minister of India at The Hague,International Conference on Afghanistan: 31st March. Annual Report 2009-10, Ministry of External Affairs, Government of India. Retrieved from *http://www.mea.gov.in/mystart.php?id=500415660.*, accessed on 14-03-2012.

Machrystal, Stanley (2009): "Commander's Initial Assessment, International Security Assistance Force Afghanistan", August 30, *http://articles.cnn.com/2011-05-24/opinion/bergen.taliban.talks_1_taliban-leader-taliban-foreign-ministry-islamic-emirate? _s=PM: OPINION.*, accessed on 24-12-2011.

Majidyar, Ahmad, (2012: "5 ways to help fix Afghanistan" Special to CNN, retrieved from *http://globalpublicsquare.blogs.cnn.com/2012/10/01/5-ways-to-help-fix-afghanistan/?hpt=hp_bn13,* accessed 7-05-2013.

Malone, M. David (2011): "Does the Elephant Dance: India's Foreign Policy", OUP, New Delhi.

Maoz, Zeev, and Russett, Bruce (1993): "Normative and Structural Causes of Democratic Peace, 1946–1986", *American Political Science Review,* Vol. 87, No. 3, pp. 624–38.

Markey, Daniel (2009): "From Af-Pak to Pak-Af; A Response to the New U.S. Strategy for South Asia", *Council on Foreign Relations*, pp. 1-15.

Raja Mohan, C. (2004): "Crossing the Rubicon: The Shaping of India's New Foreign Policy", Palgrave Macmillan, New York.

Raja Mohan, C. (2005): "PM Steps Out of Third World Shadow", *Indian Express,* September 15.

Raja Mohan, C. (2007): "Balancing Interests and Values: India's Struggle with Democracy Promotion", *The Washington Quarterly,* Vol. 30, No. 3, pp. 99-115.

Obama, Barack (2007): "Renewing American Leadership", *Foreign Affairs*, July/August retrieved from *http://www.foreignaffairs.org/20070701faessay86401-p60/barack-obama/renewing-american-leader ship.html, accessed on 22-2-2009.*

Oneal, John R, and Russett, Bruce (2001): "Clear and Clean: The Fixed Effects of the Liberal Peace", *International Organization*, Vol. 55, No. 2, pp.469-485.

Paul, T. V. (2005): "State Capacity and South Asia's Perennial insecurity Problems", in Paul *T.V. (Ed.) South Asia's Weak States;Understanding the Regional Insecurity Predicament*, (ed.), Oxford, New Delhi.

Paul, T.V. and Theodore McLauchlin, (2011): "Transforming South Asia; Is a Pluralistic Security Community Feasible?" in T.V Paul, (Ed.), *South Asia's Weak States; Understanding the Regional Security Predicament*, Oxford, New Delhi.

Rice, Condoleezza (5 April2006): "U.S.-India Civilian Nuclear Cooperation Agreement", Testimony Before the House International Relations Committee, 5 April, Washington, retrieved from http://www.state.gov/secretary/rm/2006/64146.htm, accessed on 25-06-2013.

Rod and Alissa (2010): " Karzai Closing in on Taliban Reconciliation Plan", retrieved from http:*//www.nytimes.com/2010/01/18/world/asia/18afghan.html?ref=asia,* accessed on 18-1-2010.

Roggio, Bill and Lundquist, Lisa, (2012): "Green-on-blue attacks in Afghanistan:" August 23, retrieved from http://www.longwarjournal.org/archives/2012/08/green-on-blue_attack.php, accessed on 9-7-2013.

Rubin, J. Alissa (2010): "Afghanistan Set to Push a New Reconciliation Plan", retrieved from *http://www.nytimes.com/2010/01/28/world/asia/28afghan.html?ref=global-home*, accessed on 28-1-2010.

Singh, Manmohan (2005): "PM's Speech at India Today Conclave", 25 February, New Delhi, retrieved from www.pmindia.nic.in/speech/content.asp?id=78 accessed on 25-03-2013.

Singh, Manmohan (2005a): "PM's Remarks at the Launching of UN Democracy Fund", 14.

September, New York, retrieved from www.pmindia.nic.in/speech/content asp?id=193 , accessed on 25-06-2013.

Singh, Manmohan (2005 b): "Address to the joint session of the United States Congress", 19th July, Washington DC, reproduced in Seminar, No. 560 (April 2006).

Srennivasan, T.P. (2012): "India and America's Growing Partnership", retrieved from *http://the diplomat.com/2012/09/03/view-from-delhi-the-us-rebalance/2/?all=tru,* accessed on 25-06-2013.

Swami, Praveen (2011), "Mediator in Taliban –U.S. Talks backed Kashmir Jihad", *The Hindu*, December 28.

Swami, Praveen (2012): "U.S. waived counter-terror conditions for aid to Pakistan, new official report states", *The Hindu*, October 6.

Tharoor, Shashi (2012): "Pax Indica: India and the World of the 21st Century", Penguin Books India, New Delhi.

U.S. Congressional Record (1998, June 16): " *Proceedings and Debate of the 105th Cong.*, 2 Session", Senator Mack, United States Government Printing Office, Vol.144, part 9, Washington.

US Department of State (2005): "U.S.-India Global Democracy Initiative", 18 July, retrieved from www.state.gov/p/sca/rls/fs/2005/49722.htm, accessed on 25-06-2013.

Varadarajan, Siddarth (2009): "From de-hyphenation to dual hyphenation", *The Hindu*, March 30.

White House (2010 May), "National Security Strategy", Washington, retrieved from *http://www.whitehouse.gov/sites/default/files/rss_viewer/national_security_strategy.pdf*, accessed on 15-4-2011.

14

India and Bhutan: Striving for a Better Future

Sarish Sebastian

Introduction

Choosing his first ever foreign visit abroad, Indian Prime Minister Narendra Modi selected Bhutan as his destination. This step itself makes clear about the strategic and cultural importance of the tiny Himalayan kingdom in the north-east boarder of the country. Though there were no important agreements signed on this visit, the prime minister's short visit marked a high regard for the smallest state in the South Asian community over the extended international community. He stated that both India and Bhutan are made for each other and India stands committed to Bhutan's happiness and progress. He also added that though government in India has changed, Bhutan remains a priority for New Delhi and it will strengthen the past relations for a comprehensive partnership, strengthen development cooperation and further enhance economic ties.

The initiatives taken by the new Prime Minister Narendra Modi shows the peaceful co-existence of both India and Bhutan in the past. Since independence, Bhutan was a close friend of India which hardly poses any challenges to the nation. The rulers of Bhutan ensured that the nation always maintained a free and legitimate government which upholds the principle of GNH and peace. Though in the recent past there was first ever crack in India-Bhutan relations related to the withdrawal of subsidies from kerosene oil, LPG and excise duty refund by the ministry of external affairs, India.

sThough some criticised the situation as ill-timed considering it to be a policy lapse by the Indian government, as the second general election was about to take place, while others interpreted this issue as a reactionary and response towards the former Prime Minister, Jigme Thinley's closeness to China. Though this issue did create political ripples in the landscape of Bhutan, the relations between both the countries moved smooth and steady.

Historical Background

India's policy towards the Himalayas had a history ever since the ancient Hindu kings as strategic framework of keeping this region as an integral part of India's defence structure. The geo-strategic position of Bhutan and Nepal has transformed the relations of India towards the region into a vital importance to India's defence and security since independence. On the other hand, there is no doubt that for both the Himalayan Kingdoms, i.e., for Nepal and Bhutan, security imperatives are at the core of the close relationship with India in terms of its security interests and territorial integrity. In the long-standing political disputes and border confrontations between India and China, Bhutan have been a part of India's strategic defence plan since independence. The events that took place in the Tibet region had a major effect on India-Bhutan relations in the past. In the year 1951, when Tibet was taken over by the Chinese Communists, Bhutan moved towards her southern neighbour India for more external help and relations to avoid such a condition like Tibet.

In Indian geo-politics, Bhutan occupies a strategic position in the Himalayas on northern border. With respect to the border issues with China, it is natural for India to maintain a friendly relation with Bhutan as the tiny Himalayan kingdom is sandwiched between the two Asian giants. A conscious policy of isolation by the rulers complemented by formidable geographical barriers enabled the kingdom to maintain its independence throughout its history. The relations between India and Bhutan can be traced back to the entry of Guru Rinpoche to Bhutan from India in 747 A.D. In spite of the policy of isolation from the rest of the world, under the Shabdrungs and first two Druk Gyalpos, Bhutan kept her foreign relations only with India. A formal treaty based relation was begun in 1910, when the King signed a treaty with British India. Even during the periods of isolation, Bhutan had maintained good relationship with India, especially with the bordering states such as Ladakh, Lahaul, Spiti and Kinnaur in the West and Sikkim, Cooch Behar and Northern

Assam in South-East. Under the treaty of 1910, the British Government agreed not to interfere in the internal affairs of Bhutan and the Bhutanese government agreed to be guided by the advice of the British government in regard to its external relations. After the independence in 1947, Indian government signed a new treaty with Bhutanese government on 8 August, 1949. Under this treaty, India played a major role in Bhutan's foreign relations with the rest of the world. Though the treaty gives some sort of restrictions in the nation's foreign relations, India respected Bhutan's sovereignty and aspiration and in fact supported the nation for establishing diplomatic relations with other nations.[1]

The Treaty of 1949

On August 8, 1949, aiming for peace and cooperation and non-interference in each other's internal affairs, India and Bhutan signed the Treaty of Friendship. However, updating the 1910's treaty with the British India, Bhutan agreed to let India "guide" its foreign policy and both the nations would consult each other closely on foreign and defence matters. The treaty of 1949 also established a free trade and extradition protocols between both the nations. The second half of the 20th century saw a major increase in India's economic, military and development aid to Bhutan that helped the modernisation of its economy, security and military, political system and the society. By the end of the 20th century, Bhutan began to express its dissatisfaction in being assisted by Indian Government in its foreign affairs. Though the relations between the nations remained closer, the Royal Government of Bhutan expressed a need to amend some parts of the treaty to enhance the nation's sovereignty. Bhutan slowly gained its momentum of an independent actor in the international relations by joining the UN in 1971 and signing a new treaty with Bangladesh in 1972. The move towards being an independent actor in the international relations does not create any issues with the treaties signed with India in 1949. Both the nation's relations have not been affected by concerns over the treaty provisions.[2]

The Treaty of 2007

The Treaty of 1949 was amended and renegotiated relating to the promotion of and fostering the relations of friendship and neighbourliness between India and Bhutan and signed a new treaty of friendship called the Indian-Bhutan Friendship Treaty in 2007. This treaty was signed in New Delhi on February 8, 2007 and came into force following the exchange of Instruments of Ratification between the two governments in Thimphu on March 2, 2007. Through this new treaty the Government of the Republic of India and the Government of the Kingdom of Bhutan reaffirmed their respect for each other's independence, sovereignty and territorial integrity. Though this treaty changed many of the previous articles, both the nations tried to retain the historical relations that have existed between our two countries by recognising deep satisfaction the manner in which these relations have evolved and matured over the years into a model of good neighbourly relations.

The India-Bhutan Friendship Treaty of 2007 gave Bhutan a complete sovereign power in its foreign affairs. The Treaty of 2007 is fully committed to further strengthening the enduring and mutually beneficial relationship between India and Bhutan, based on genuine goodwill and friendship, shared interests, and close understanding and cooperation. The new treaty replacing the provision of requiring guidance from the Indian Government was removed and granted complete freedom over arms import. In the year 2008, the Indian Prime Minister Dr Manmohan Singh visited Bhutan and expressed strong support for Bhutan's move towards democracy and encouraged deeper bilateral foreign relations.[3]

Recent Trends in Indo-Bhutan Relations

Since the establishment of a parliamentary democracy in 2008, the relationships between India and Bhutan reached in to a new level of cooperation and friendship. The relationship between both countries further increased with the tradition of regular visits of the high-level officers. The State Visit of His Majesty the King Jigme Khesar Namgyel Wangchuck to India from 21st to 26th December, 2009 was his first such visit to a foreign country since his coronation as the King of Bhutan in 2008. Later from 5th to 7th October, 2010, the King visited India during which University of Calcutta conferred upon him the Honorary Doctorate Degree of Law. His Majesty the King again visited India from 20-29 October, 2010 for the National Defence College's (NDC) golden jubilee celebrations as Special Guest of Honour. His Majesty the King Jigme Khesar Namgyel Wangchuck and Her Majesty the Queen Jetsun Pema Wangchuck paid a State Visit to India from October 23-31, 2011, the first foreign visit after the Royal Wedding on 13th October 2011. The King His Majesty the King Jigme Khesar Namgyel Wangchuck was the chief guest for the 64th Republic Day on 26th January, 2013. On January 14, 2013, the Indian External Affairs Minister, Salman Khurshid, was on an official visit to Thimpu strengthening the ties between both the nations.

After the 16th Lok Sabha election, the new Prime Minister Narendra Modi made his maiden visit to Bhutan from 15 to 16 June, 2014. He was accompanied by External Affairs Minister Sushma Swaraj, National Security Adviser Shri Ajit Doval, Foreign Secretary Sujatha Singh and other senior officials of the Government of India.

At present India is more concerned about the political issue of Bhutan's recent talks with China and the internal security concerns of both India and Bhutan. Another important matter of concern between India and Bhutan was the internal security issues that gained importance at recent time as Bhutan witnessed occasional incidents of IED blasts in 2012 and increased activity of insurgent groups across the India-Bhutan border. A healthy relationship between the nations is important at the present conditions and given its strategic importance, India cannot ignore the tiny kingdom and should always be sensitive to its relations to create a long-term relation.[4]

Economic Relations

Over the last few decades, India has provided assistance to Bhutan mainly in the social sectors such as education and human resource development, health, agriculture and roads. Gradually, the economic relations between Bhutan and India collaborated on mutually beneficial projects like hydropower development and industrial projects. These projects are taken outside the Five Year Plan programmes and considered beneficial to both the nations especially to India. Such a mutual beneficiary projects will assure business opportunities in the manufacturing and other industries in both India and Bhutan.[5]

Though Bhutan began to get foreign aid from other nations after joining the UN, India continued to be the major donor of external aid to Bhutan. The Fiscal Year 2009-10 started with an approved budget of Nu 26,304.310 million, out of the Government received a total grant of Nu 11,118.877 million representing about 16.6 per cent of the GDP recording an increase of 69.1 per cent. The major increase in the receipt of grant from Government of India by 66.2 per cent and other donors by 74.87 per cent was due to the contribution towards the relief fund for the flood and earthquake amounting to Nu 710.707 million besides receipts in-kind.

The Fiscal Year 2010-11 started with an approved budget of Nu 31,586.779 million which was revised to Nu 35,237.088 million. The Government received a total grant of Nu 10,497.727 million which is about 13.7 per cent of the GDP. The Government of India

Table1: Comparison of International Assistance (Grants) Received

Particulars	*Nu in millions*				
	2008-09	*2009-2010*	*2010-11*	*2011-12*	*2012-13*
(a) GOI	**4394.879**	**7306.388**	**7882.768**	**9003.442**	**4693.402**
1. Program Grant	1400.000	1400.000	1400.000	1400.000	1050.000
2. Project Grant	2994.879	5906.388	6482.768	**7603.442**	**3643.402**
i. Cash	2994.879	4984.063	5282.768	7603.442	3643.402
ii. Kind	-	922.325	1200.000	-	-
(b) Other Donors	**2180.19**	**3812.489**	**2614.959**	**3498.078**	**4869.234**
1. Program Grant	189.079	569.326	381.161	321.654	1568.453
2. Project Grant	1991.111	3243.163	2233.798	3176.424	3300.781
i. Cash	1920.582	2594.114	1837.207	2455.872	3083.181
ii. Kind	70.529	649.049	396.591	720.552	217.600
Total	**6575.069**	**11118.877**	**10497.727**	**12501.52**	**9562.636**

Source: Ministry of Finance, Government of Bhutan.

contributed Nu 7882.768 million with an increased of 7.9 per cent from the previous financial year. This was due to the incorporation of in-kind assistance received for the double lining of Babesa–Phuentsholing highway. The FY 2011-12 started with an approved budget of Nu 37,923.257 million out of Nu 9003.442 million has been provided by the Government of India. During the FY 2012-13, the Government of Bhutan received a total grant of Nu 9,562.636 million which is about 9.2 per cent of the GDP, out of which, a total of Nu 4693.402 million was received from the Government of India which is almost 47.9 per cent less from the previous Financial Year grant allocation, i.e. Nu 9003.442 million.

A detailed statement of International Assistance (Grants) received in-cash and in-kind for the FY 2008-09 to 2012-13 from Government of India and other International donors are presented in Table 1.

Today, India stands as the biggest development partner of Bhutan. In the year 2011, bilateral trade between India and Bhutan reached Rs 61.6 billion which constituted 72 per cent of Bhutan's total imports and 85 per cent of its exports. Almost 70 per cent of the kingdom's trade is with India and as of the statistics of 2011, a large amount of development budget of India's Ministry of External Affairs goes to Bhutan. For the year, 2010-2011 Bhutan received almost Rs 1723 crore as loan from India in which most of the amount goes to development programmes. The visit of Salman Khurshid in 2013 was also a beginning process of India's help towards Bhutan's "Eleventh Five Year Plan".[6]

India's assistance to the Tenth Five -Year Plan (2008-13) of RGoB

While addressing a Joint Session of the Bhutanese Parliament in May 2008, the then Prime Minister Dr Manmohan Singh announced that India's total bilateral economic commitment to Bhutan's Tenth Five Year Plan (2008-13) worth Nu 3400 crores, for funding projects in key socio-economic sectors such as agriculture, ICT, media, health, hospitals, education and schools, capacity building, energy, culture and infrastructure etc. Some of the important projects executed under the Tenth FYP include construction of the Supreme Court, strengthening of Constitutional Offices like the Royal Audit Authority, Election Commission, Anti-Corruption Commission and Office of Attorney General, renovation of important Dzongs, preparation of DPRs for the new power projects, widening of major roads, scholarships and expansion of tertiary educational institutions.

The overarching mechanism for discussing India's bilateral assistance to RGoB including PTA, Programme Grant, SDPs, Chiphen Rigphel and BIMS, is the Annual Plan Talks or India-Bhutan Development Cooperation Talks. The Indian side is headed by Joint Secretary (North) and the Bhutanese side by their Foreign Secretary. The Ninth India-Bhutan Development Cooperation Talks were held in Thimphu, on 5th April, 2013. To monitor implementation and fast track the progress of developmental projects particularly projects funded under the PTA, there established a Project Monitoring Committee (PMC) which meets regularly. The last PMC meeting was held in Thimphu, on 25th November, 2012. The PMC meetings are co-chaired by Director (North), MEA, GoI and Secretary, Gross National Happiness Commission (GNHC) of Bhutan.

Project Tied Assistance (PTA)

Under the project tied assistance, Nu 20,000 million was committed under the Tenth Five Year Plan. Around 71 projects were undertaken in key socio-economic areas of agriculture, ICT, media, health, tertiary education, school education, scholarships, labour and human resource development, roads, energy, civil aviation, urban development, road safety and transport, judiciary, culture, constitutional offices and media. Each of these projects has a specific scope of work, work plan and fund utilisation plan. The projects are executed by the RGoB, except for two road projects – Phuentsholing-Thimphu II and Damchu-Chukha bypass – which are being executed by Project DANTAK of the Border Road Organisation of India.

Small Development Projects (SDP)

Small Development Projects are short gestation and community-oriented projects in areas such as drinking water schemes, irrigation channels, farm roads and other infrastructure. Funds under Small Development Projects (SDP) are mainly used for infrastructure development in rural areas of Bhutan which are planned and implemented by the local governments based on the priorities and needs of their respective communities. Focused on basic socio-economic development, these projects are found to be an effective tool for addressing rural poverty as they have a direct bearing on the lives of the grassroots people. Under the SDP, some 1800 projects were completed in the Tenth Five Year Plan.

Programme Grant and other Grants

Programme Grant is a development subsidy that is released in quarterly instalments of Rs 35 crore. GOI's total commitment for PG in the Tenth FYP is Rs 700 crore. In addition to the Plan commitment of Rs 3400 crores, GoI also funded two major capacity building projects of Bhutan in the ICT (Rs 205 crore Chiphen Rigphel/ Total Solutions Project and health sectors (establishment of Bhutan Institute of Medical Sciences).[7]

Eleventh Five Year Plan 2013-18

A planned development in Bhutan began in 1961 with the introduction of the Five Year Plans in the country. The first two Five Year Plans from 1961-71 were fully funded by the Government of India. Over the years, the assistance from the government of India has increased steadily from Rs 107 million in the First Five year plan to Rs 9000 million in the Eighth Five Year Plan. For the Tenth Five Year Plan India had contributed 23 per cent of the total budget of 14800 million.

Under the current 11th Five Year Plan, out of the total committed external assistance of Nu/Rs 66 billion, India's contribution is Rs 45 billion (excluding the Rs 5 billion committed for the Economic Stimulus Plan), which is about 68 per cent of the total external assistance, 21 per cent of the Plan outlay of Rs 213 billion, and 49 per cent of the capital expenditure of Nu 92 billion. During the visit of the Prime Minister of Bhutan, Lyonchhen Tshering Tobgay to India from August 30 to September 4, 2013, Government of India's Assistance Package for Bhutan's 11th Five Year Plan for the period July 1, 2013 to June 30, 2018, was

Table 2: India's Contribution to Bhutan's Five Year Plans

Five Year Plans	*Total Allocations*	*India's Contribution*	*% of India's Contribution*
1961-66 (1st Plan)	10.72	10.72	100
1966-71(2nd Plan)	20.22	20.22	100
1971-76 (3rd Plan)	47.52	42.66	90
1976-81 (4th Plan)	1,10.62	85.30	77
1981-87 (5th Plan)	4,44.05	134.0	30.2
1987-92 (6th Plan)	9,50.00	4,00.00	42.1
1992-97 (7th Plan)	23,50.00	7,50.00	31.9
1997-02 (8th Plan)	4000.00	1050.00	26
2002-08 (9th Plan)	8900.00	2610.14	29.33
2008-13 (10th Plan)	14800.00	3400.00	23
2013-18 (11th Plan)	6600.00	4500.00	68

Source: http://www.indianembassythimphu.bt/goi_assistance.html

agreed upon. Additionally, GOI agreed to provide as Rs 500 Crore as Economic Stimulus Package, to boost the Bhutanese economy and help the RGOB to tackle the liquidity shortage. Table 2 gives an overall idea of India's contribution to Bhutan's Five Year Plans from 1961 to 2018.

Hydropower Projects

Hydropower cooperation with Bhutan is a classic example of win-win cooperation, providing clean electricity to India, generating export revenues for Bhutan, and further strengthening our bilateral economic linkages. Three hydro-electric projects (HEPs) totaling 1416 MW, viz., the 336 MW Chukha HEP, the 60 MW Kurichu HEP, and the 1020 MW Tala HEP, are already operational in Bhutan and are supplying electricity to India. Three more HEPs totaling 2940 MW, i.e., the 1200 MW Punatsangchu-I HEP, the 1020 MW Punatsangchu-II HEP and the 720 MW Mangdehchu HEP, are under construction, and are scheduled to be commissioned by 2018.

The framework "Inter-Governmental Agreement between the Royal Government of Bhutan and the Government of the Republic of India concerning development of Joint Venture Hydropower Projects through the Public Sector Undertakings of the two Governments" was signed on 22 April, 2014 in Thimphu by Mr Sonam Tshering, Secretary, Ministry of Economic Affairs, Royal Government of Bhutan and Shri P.K. Sinha, Secretary, Ministry of Power, Government of India.

The GOI had funded a number of projects under the cooperation between the two nations such as the Chhukha (336 MW), Kurichhu (60 MW), and Tala (1020 MW) Hydro Power Projects; the Penden and Dungsam Cement Projects; and the Paro Airport Project.[8] Some of the completed or ongoing GOI funded Mega Projects are: Chukha Hydro Electric Project (CHEP), Kurichhu Hydro Electric Project (KHEP), Tala Hydro Electric Project (THEP), Punatsangchhu-I Hydro Electric Project (PHEP), Dungsam Cement Plant and Penden Cement Plant.

Let us examine some of the ongoing hydro-electric projects in Bhutan funded by the Government of India.

1. Mangdechhu Hydroelectric Project

Mangdechhu Hydroelectric Project (720 MW) is one amongst the ten hydroelectric Projects planned under the 10,000 MW hydropower development by the year 2020 programme of Royal Government of Bhutan supported by the Government of India. An agreement for execution of Mangdechhu Hydroelectric Project was signed between the two governments on 30th April, 2010 at the approved cost of Nu/Rs 33821.58 million (March 2008 price level) to be funded by GoI as 30 per cent grant and 70 per cent loan at 10 per cent annual interest to be paid in thirty equated semiannual installments. The tentative project cost has now become Nu/Rs 38006.90 million. The Mangdechhu Hydroelectric Project Authority was subsequently constituted on 8th June 2010. The Authority comprises of Chairperson and four members nominated by the Royal Government of Bhutan and three members nominated by the Government of India. The Project Management is headed by the Managing Director, who is being assisted by a Joint Managing Director, Director (Technical) and Director (Finance). NHPC Limited, a Central Public Sector Undertaking of GoI is the Design and Engineering consultant to the Project. The project is scheduled for commissioning by September, 2017.

2. *Punatsangchhu-I*

Punatsangchhu-I is the first Project of the 10,000 MW initiative taken by the Royal Government of Bhutan (RGoB) and the Government of India (GoI) in May 2008, for development by 2020. The Punatsangchhu-I Hydroelectric Project (1200 MW), a milestone in Indo-Bhutan relations, is presently the largest hydropower project undertaken in the Himalayan Kingdom of Bhutan by the RGoB and the GoI. The Project, an environment-friendly run-of-the-river scheme, is located on the left bank of the Punatsangchhu in Wangduephodrang Dzongkhag in Western Bhutan. The Project will utilise 357 m fall available in about 11 km river course.

Agreement between the GoI and the RGoB for implementation of the Punatsangchhu-I Hydroelectric Project was signed on 28 July, 2007 by H.E. Shri Pranab Mukherjee, Hon'ble Minister for External Affairs on behalf of the GoI and H.E. Lyonpo Khandu Wangchuk, Hon'ble Minister for Foreign Affairs on behalf of the RGoB. Punatsangchhu-I Hydroelectric Project Authority (PHPA), an autonomous body was set-up for implementation of the Project on 05 October, 2007.

The project sanctioned at a cost of Nu 35.15 billion excluding IDC on December 2006 price level with installed capacity of 1095 MW (now revised to 1200 MW) is being funded by the GoI: 40 per cent grant and 60 per cent loan @ 10 per cent interest p.a. repayable in 12 equated annual installments commencing one year after the mean date of commercial operation. Based on the approval of the

RGoB for relocation of Dam site (conveyed on June 27, 2008) and recommendations of the TCC the PHPA approved re-location of the dam and revision of the station capacity from 1095 MW to 1200 MW during its third Meeting held on 08 August, 2008 and fixed the Zero-Date (Date of start) of the Project as 11 November, 2008.

WAPCOS Ltd. (Ministry of Water Resources, Government of India) is the engineering design consultants to the Authority. The premier organisations of Government of India, e.g., Central Electricity Authority, Central Water Commission, Central Water and Power Research Station, Central Soil and Materials Research Station, Geological Survey of India and Survey of India make their valuable expertise available to the Project through WAPCOS.

3. Punatsangchhu-II

Punatsangchhu-II is the second Project of the 10,000 MW initiative taken by the Royal Government of Bhutan (RGoB) and the Government of India (GoI) in May 2008, for development by 2020. Agreement between the GoI and the RGoB for implementation of the Punatsangchhu-II Hydroelectric Project was signed on 30 April, 2010 by H.E. Shri S.M. Krishna, Hon'ble Minister for External Affairs on behalf of the GoI and H.E. Lyonpo Khandu Wangchuk, Hon'ble Minister for Economic Affairs on behalf of the RGoB. On the same auspicious day, the foundation stone of the Project was laid jointly by H.E. Dr Manmohan Singh, Hon'ble Prime Minister of India and H.E. Jigmi Y. Thinley, Hon'ble Lyonchhen of Bhutan.

The Project is located on the right bank of Punatsangchhu along the Wangdue-Tsirang highway between 22 km and 35 km downstream of Wangdue Bridge. The dam site is about 94 km from Thimphu and connected by a highway. The project sanctioned at a cost of Nu 37.78 billion excluding IDC on March 2009 price level with installed capacity of 990 MW (now revised to 1020 MW) is being funded by the GoI: 30 per cent grant and 70 per cent loan @ 10 per cent interest p.a. repayable in 30 equated semi-annual installments commencing one year after the mean date of commercial operation.

Punatsangchhu-II Hydroelectric Project Authority (PHPA), an autonomous body was set-up for implementation of the Project on 08 June, 2010. The project implementation started on 17 December, 2010 with a completion schedule of seven years including two years of infrastructure development.

WAPCOS Ltd. (a Government of India Undertaking) are the engineering design Consultants to the Authority. The expertise of premier organisations of CEA, CWC, Central Water and Power

Research Station (CWPRS), Central Soil and Materials Research Station (CSMRS), GSI and Survey of India (SoI) are made available to the Project through WAPCOS.[8]

Future Perspectives of Indo-Bhutan Relations

With the establishment of a new central government in India after the 16th Lok Sabha election, the world community in general and both India and Bhutan governments in particular are looking towards a better future for the bilateral relation between the countries. Accompanied by the External Affairs Minister Sushma Swaraj, National Security Adviser Shri Ajit Doval, Foreign Secretary Sujatha Singh and other senior officials of the Government of India, the Prime Minister of the Republic of India Shri Narendra Modi paid a State Visit to Bhutan in June 2014. The visit of the Prime Minister to the tiny Himalayan Kingdom was significant, unlike any other previous ministers, as it is his first visit abroad after he was sworn-in as the Prime Minister of India on 26 May, 2014 in New Delhi. The visit reinforced the tradition of regular high-level exchange between the two countries and it helped to uphold and strengthen the special and unique age-old friendship between Bhutan and India. The Prime Minister held official talks with His Majesty Jigme Khesar Namgyel Wangchuck, the King of Bhutan and His Majesty Jigme Singye Wangchuck, the Fourth Druk Gyalpo and the Prime Minister of Bhutan Lyonchhen Tshering Tobgay to discuss issues of mutual interests. Narendra Modi also addressed the Joint Sitting of the Parliament of Bhutan in the Gyalyong Tshogkhang on 16 June, 2014 which helped to address various issues of mutual interests and a perspective for strong future relations.

The visit of the Prime Minister proposed new ideas for enhancing cooperation with Bhutan, while asserting that commitments made by the previous government will be fulfilled. The visit of Indian delegates proposed to hold a joint sports festival between Bhutan and the northeastern states of India, establish e-libraries in 20 districts in Bhutan and set up a university on Himalayan studies. India wanted to complete the power projects implemented both by the present as well as the previous UPA government would be completed speedily. The Foreign Affairs Minister Sushma Swaraj said that establishing e-libraries in 20 districts by GOI will help the nation as it make available around two million books to the youth of Bhutan. Both the countries leaders tried to resolve the concept that the Himalayas Divide, and stated that in fact the Himalayas are uniting as these region share a common legacy and need for development of the ecology of the region. The Prime Minister's statement that the names of the two countries start with the letter 'B' and Bharat should stand for Bhutan and Bhutan for Bharat, made clear how close both the countries are.

The new government began a new era for India-Bhutan relations, strengthening the economy of both the countries and helping to develop the nations mutually. As a beginning, the Prime Minister unveiled the Foundation Stone of the 600 Megawatt Kholongchu Hydropower Project which is a Joint Venture project between the Indian and Bhutanese PSUs, SJVNL and Druk Green Power Corporation.

Major Outcomes of the Visit by the New Prime Minister Shri Narendra Modi

Following are the major outcomes of the recent visit made by the present Prime Minister Shri Narendra Modi on June 2014:

(i) Both the leaders recalled the strong historical ties of friendship and understanding that existed between the governments and peoples of the two countries. The two sides exchanged views and held discussions on bilateral relations and economic cooperation as well as cooperation in regional and multilateral forums. The discussions between the leaders reaffirmed their commitment to further strengthen the special friendship between the both the countries.

(ii) Lyonchhen Tshering Tobgay, the Prime Minister of Bhutan, on behalf of the Royal Government and people of the country conveyed his appreciation to the Government and people of India for the generous developmental assistance provided since the First Five Year Plan in 1961 till now. He expressed satisfaction over the all round socio-economic development achieved by the nation with the assistance and support of Indian government.

(iii) The Prime Minister of Bhutan, Lyonchhen Tshering Tobgay, thanked the Government of India for the allocation of Rs/Nu 45 billion for the 11th Five Year Plan and Rs/Nu 5 billion for the economic stimulus plan of the Royal Government of Bhutan. Prime Minister Shri Narendra Modi reassured the commitment of the Government of India to support Bhutan for the successful implementation of the 11th Five Year Plan as well as the other developmental activities of the Royal Government of Bhutan.

(iv) Indian Prime Minister on behalf of the Government of India, expressed satisfaction at being a privileged partner of Bhutan in its socio-economic development, and reassured India's continued commitment to capacity building especially in the education and IT sectors in Bhutan.

(v) The two sides acknowledged the importance of cooperation and mutual benefit arising from the hydropower sector between the two countries and expressed satisfaction on the progress being made in this regard. They reiterated their commitment to achieving the 10000 MW target.

(vi) The two leaders expressed satisfaction with the completion of the Supreme Court building and the imminent commencement of the construction of the Kholongchhu Hydroelectric Project.

(vii)The two sides recalled the free trade arrangement between the two countries and the expanding bilateral trade between the two countries and its importance in further cementing the friendship between the two countries. Government of India conveyed its decision to exempt Bhutan from any ban or quantitative restrictions on exports of following items: Milk powder, Wheat, Edible oil, Pulses and Non-basmati rice. The two sides also agreed to further promote trade and investments between the two countries.

(viii) In keeping with the emphasis on capacity building and education, Prime Minister Shri Narendra Modi announced the doubling of the Nehru-Wangchuck scholarship to Rs/Nu 20 million per year. Government of India would also provide grant assistance for the establishment of the digital section/E-library in the National Library of Bhutan and in all 20 districts of Bhutan.

(ix) The two sides expressed satisfaction with the cooperation between the two countries related to their mutual security. They agreed to continue with their close coordination and cooperation with each other on issues relating to their national interests, and not allow each other's territory to be used for interests inimical to the other.

(x) The visit of Prime Minister Shri Narendra Modi to Bhutan further strengthened the close bonds of friendship and cooperation between the two countries and promised to continue and strengthen the bond between India and Bhutan in the future.[9]

Conclusion

India always remained committed to its support to Bhutan in its efforts towards economic, social and political development for a comprehensive partnership. The bilateral relations between the two countries gained momentum in the areas of hydropower development, information and communication technology, health, industry, education and culture. During the past decades, these relations were further consolidated with regular exchange of high-level visits and strengthening of bilateral cooperation between both the nations. In the near future, with the contentious state of Indo-China relations, Bhutan with its strategic location will find a major role in India's security interests. Any change or development in the Indo-China relations will also have a greater impact on India-Bhutan relations as well. The recent border talks between Bhutan and China on January 2010 over the disputed claims boarder line in North Western Bhutan and in a surprise move in 2012, the then Chinese Premier Wen Jiabao and his Bhutanese counterpart, Jigmi Y Thinley met on the sidelines of the UN Conference on Sustainable Development at Rio De Janeiro for a talk related to border issues and maintaining peace between both the countries generated a fear on Indian leaders over the security matters.[10] The bilateral relations between Bhutan and China will surely be a concern for the nation's closest friend India in the near future.

Choosing Bhutan as his first foreign visit destination, the Prime Minsiter Shri Narendra Modi again proved to the world community that it is not the geography or economy matters, but the everlasting friendship and peace between the nations that keep India and Bhutan together. Both the nations are now striving to strengthen the glorious past relationship between India and Bhutan for a better future and comprehensive partnership in economic, social and political development.

References

1. Council on Foreign Relations, *Bhutan's Road to Democracy*, Interview with Prime Minsiter Jigme Y. Thinley by Jayashree Bajoria, September 25, 2008. Available at: http://www.cfr.org/publication/17331/bhutans_road_to_democracy.html
2. Embassy of India, Thimphu, *Treaty between India and Bhutan 1949*. Available at: http://www.indianembassythimphu.bt/treaty.htm
3. Treaty between India and Bhutan, 2007. Available at: http://www.bhutandnc.com/Treaty.htm
4. Bisht, Medha (2013), Jigme Khesar Namgyel Wangchuk's Visit to India: Towards an Assuring Alliance, Institute for Defence Studies and Analysis, February 1, 2013. Available at: http://www.idsa.in/idsacomments/Jigme Khesar Namgyel Wangchuks Visitto India_MedhaBisht_010213
5. Choden, Tashi, (2004), Tashi Choden, (2004), *Indo-Bhutan Relations Recent Trends*, Journal of Bhutan Studies, Volume 11, p. 115.
6. Bisht, Medha (2013), Jigme Khesar Namgyel Wangchuk's Visit to India: Towards an Assuring Alliance, Institute for Defence Studies

and Analysis, February 1, 2013. Available at: http://www.idsa.in/idsa comments/Jigme Khesar Namgyel Wangchuks VisittoIndia_ MedhaBisht_010213
7. Embassy of India, Thimphu, India's assistance to the Tenth Five – Year Plan (2008-13) of Royal Government of Bhutan. Available at: http://www.indianembassythimphu.bt/relationpages.php?rid=8
8. Embassy of India, Thimphu, Ongoing Hydropower Projects in Bhutan. Available at: http://www.indianembassythimphu.bt/relationpages.php?rid=1
9. Embassy of India, Thimphu, Bhutan-India Joint Press Statement on the State Visit of Prime Minister of India Shri Narendra Modi to the Kingdom of Bhutan from 15-16 June 2014. Available at: http://www.indianembassythimphu.bt/events.php?eid=46
10. DNA Webdesk (2014, June16), China expresses happiness over Narendra Modi's visit to Bhutan, growing bilateral ties, *Dnaindia.com*. Available at: http://www.dnaindia.com/india/report-china-expresses-happiness-over-narendra-modi-s-visit-to-bhutan-growing-bilateral-ties-1996062

15

India-Nepal Relations: Pursuit of Proactive Partnership

Anshuman Behera

India-Nepal relationship has been a long standing history of mutual interdependence and (dis)trust. The relationships between both the countries are characterised mainly by three factors. They are: the long and open border between two countries, socio-cultural and historic ties and mutual interdependence. Despite strong cultural, emotional and historic links, India and Nepal have not been able to maximise their interests. Ever since the end of British rule in India political regimes have changed in Nepal, as the governments in India, nothing substantial has changed in India-Nepal relationship. What could best describe the relationship is that India and Nepal have remained as 'uneasy friends'.[1] Though both the countries have been able to maintain the relationship despite the asymmetry in size, yet they cannot be called as all weather friends. It could be called as a relationship of "falling-apart-and pooling-together".[1]

Of many other important factors, the political and security considerations dominated the India-Nepal relationship for over last six decades. The political masters of India have not really been able to handle the Nepal case with care. From India side Nepal has often been seen as a small and dependant neighbour and India continues to have a big brotherly attitude towards Nepal. For Nepal the over size of India is a matter of hallucination. Political instability has been a stable feature of Nepal politics and to a great extent affected the bilateral relationship. India is being widely held responsible for the political instability by various political constituencies, strengthening the trust deficit. India card is being played by different political constituencies to maximise their political interests. As a typical case in point, India's attempts to reach out different political constituencies backfired.

As mentioned earlier, the political situation in Nepal plays an important role so far the India-Nepal relationship is concerned. Ever since the Maoists of Nepal laid down their arms and entered into a peace talk in the form of Seven Party Alliance (SPA), there have been signs of positive political development in Nepal. Nepal has shown exemplary maturity accepting the former armed rebels, Maoists, into the mainstream politics. Nepal has been successful to have an elected Constituent Assembly (CA) to draft a constitution. Though there continues a deadlock over drafting the constitution within a stipulated time frame, many are hopeful that Nepal will be able to overcome the deadlock soon. As positive political developments are unfolding and Nepal is heading towards a stable government there is a huge potential for better relationship between India and Nepal.

This chapter makes an attempt to critically analyse different phases of India-Nepal relationship. In the process of doing so it also aims to highlight the lost opportunities by both the countries in making the relationship better. The positive developments in New Nepal have lot of important things to offer to India. Similarly India must see Nepal on equal footing and engage with it in a positive manner which will benefit both the countries.

Phases of India-Nepal Relationship

The first phase of India-Nepal relationship from 1950 to 1955 could be viewed as mutual interdependence in terms of security and economic interests between two countries. Chinese occupation of Tibet in 1949 determined the India-Nepal relationship to a great extent. India desperately needed to engage Nepal to check Chinese influence beyond Tibet. Similarly, the Rana regime in Nepal, which was protected by the British India, wanted to develop strong ties with India. Growing anti-Rana protests in Nepal was also an important factor which forced the regime to come closer with India. Under this backdrop both countries went ahead in signing the 1950 Treaty of Friendship and Peace. Some scholars believe that the Rana regime in Nepal which believed in an isolationist policy was left with no options but to go for the Treaty. According to Lok Raj Baral, "any Nepal ruler could have done the same as the Ranas did, through the Ranas were under dire need of cultivating India for the survival of the beleaguered regime as well as to insulate Nepal from the threat of communism".[2]

The 1950 Treaty of Peace and Friendship is considered to be the bedrock on which India-Nepal relationship is built. The treaty was marked by the convergence of security and economic interests. It outlined more of India's security interest and Nepal's economic interests, hence laid the foundation of special relations between the two countries. This treaty could be seen as a 'virtual imitation' of the 1923 Treaty between the British India and the Rana regime.[4] The treaty provides that both countries would have understanding leading to mutual security, and would inform each other of any misunderstanding between two with any other country which may cause a threat to the friendly relations. According to this treaty, both countries would not engage a foreigner whose activities would be perceived prejudicial to the security of other. Another important provision of the treaty enshrined in Article 6 is to give residential status and equal opportunity to the citizens of both the countries in each other's territory.

So far the convergence of economic interests of both the countries are concerned, a Treaty of Trade and Commerce was signed on July 31, 1950. This treaty allowed Nepal to have transit facilities through Indian Territory for import and export of goods. During this period virtually all the Nepalese trade took place through India. Apart from these two treaties both the countries also decided to have joint border checkpoints along Nepal's territory with Tibet (China). India provided wireless assistance to the Nepalese military personnel to man these checkpoints. Indian Military Mission was set up to train the Nepalese Army. India maintained its security interests firmly with Nepal as the strategic competition between India and China heightened.

Second Phase of India-Nepal Relationship: 1955-1990

The second phase of India-Nepal relationship from 1955 to 1990 was crucial for both the countries as trust deficit between the two developed like never before. This was the phase of trust deficit, divergence of security and economic interests, Nepal's close proximity with China and assertion of Nepali nationalism. During this period a number of political developments in the South Asian region also affected the relationship between India and Nepal. Nepal developed a sense of fear psychosis over Sikkim's accession to India on May 16, 1975 and India's silence over Soviet's occupation over

Afghanistan. On the other hand-Nepal's close proximity with China after the Sino-Indian war in 1962 did not go well with India's interest.

Political developments at the domestic level in Nepal in 1955 changed the rules of the game. Let it be mentioned here that India played a vital role in bringing an end to the Rana regime in 1951 and establishing a democratic order and a constitutional monarchy with King Tribhuvan as head of the state. With the death of King Tribhuvan, king Mahendra ascended to the throne in 1955. King Mahendra believed in self-image of Nepal and asserted Nepal nationalism. Self-image and nationalism was only possible by reducing its dependence with India, hence laying the foundation of anti-India sentiment. Introduction of democracy in Nepal with India's active support in 1951, there emerged a contradiction between the democrats and the monarch. This contradiction added to the suspicion and bitterness between India and Nepal. According to Padmaja Murthy, till 1990, a singular contradiction running through Indo-Nepal relation was the desire of the Monarchy to wield power and the belief in India that only a democratic government would give Nepal stability.[5] Even though after sometimes India supported the monarchy, the suspicions continued.

Nepal's experience with democracy was short lived as King Mahendra diluted the democratically elected bodies and took over power in December 1960. A Party-less Panchayat Democracy was introduced which invited open and strong criticism from India leading to further deteriorated relationship between two countries. The China factor played a crucial role in this juncture. King Mahendra believed that in order to reduce Nepal's dependence on India, diversification of aid and trade was required. China, in this regard, was a natural choice for Nepal. The China card was played mainly for two important reasons by King Mahendra. The first reason was to have an independent foreign policy of Nepal without taking India into consideration and the second was to use it as a pressure tactic on India.

The China factor became important in India-Nepal relationship. China continues to be of the major irritants between two countries. Between 1956 and 1989 China provided Nepal with grant assistance for 42 projects, 36 of which were completed by the latter year. These included construction of roads, irrigation canals, hydropower, brick and paper making plants, sugar and textile mills. Since 1981 the Chinese firms have also bid for various contract projects and undertaken labour cooperation, technical consultancy and joint ventures. By late 1989-Chinese firms had signed 85 contracts worth $ 137 million for work in Nepal, five Chinese companies maintained offices in Kathmandu and more than one thousand workers and experts were working in Nepal.[3] While Nepal was using its China card against India, China had also its vested interest to engage with Nepal. The Khampa Rebellion in 1959 against the Chinese occupation of Tibet was a turning point of Chinese policy towards engaging Nepal. China wanted to keep the King of Nepal in good humour so that the king didn't allow the anti-China revolts originating from Nepalese districts bordering Tibet.

Nepal's attempt to dilute the security interest of India touched new height when King Birendra, who succeeded King Mahendra, ordered to purchase arms from China in 1988. From Indian point of view such a move by Nepal was against the spirit of 1950 Treaty of Friendship and Peace. But according to Nepal, it was forced to go for China as India was not able to meet its request. According to Nepal in 1972 and 1976 when Nepal asked to purchase antiaircraft guns but New Delhi declined on the grounds that Nepal did not need them. Similarly, in the early 1980s, Nepal approached India regarding the purchase of anti-aircraft guns, but for several years there was no reply from India.[4] The first consignment of arms from China included was light arms and ammunitions, uniforms and boots and 16 anti-aircraft guns.

As Nepal was getting closer to China, it tried to dilute the security interest of India. The role and importance of the Indian Military Mission in Nepal was reduced and reorganised in 1958. In 1970, Nepal asked India to withdraw its military personnel from Nepal-India check posts. Meanwhile, the trade and transit treaty, considered to be beneficial to Nepal's economic interests, which expired in 1970 could not be renewed for one year. In 1975, King Birendra's appeal to the international society to declare Nepal as a 'Zone of Peace' was not liked by India. Though it was not at all endorsed by India, Nepal kept on pushing this proposal in various internal platforms for next 15 years with active support from China. However, by 1990, 112 countries had endorsed the proposal.

The Indian 'blockade' of transit routes for Nepal in 1989 was another chapter of strained relationship during this period. Nepalese trade and transit with India and other countries used to be regulated by a series of treaties signed successively in 1950, 1960, 1971 and 1978. The last treaty expired on March 23, 1989. India took a tough stand against Nepal's close proximity with China and its attempts to dilute the security interests of India. In a letter to the Commerce Minister of Nepal on March 1, 1989, the Indian embassy in

Kathmandu mentioned that the 1978 Treaty of Trade and Transit would expire on March 23, 1989. India on March 23, 1989 blocked 13 out of 15 transit points on its border with Nepal. Two transit points at Raxaul and Jogabani were left open. Though the 'blockade' sounded illegal, yet India was able to defend its stand as India was not a signatory to the 1965 International Convention on Transit Trade of Landlocked countries, or to the United Nations Convention on the Law of the Sea, both of which guarantee certain transit rights to land locked countries. The message from the India was loud and clear that was "be prepared to reciprocate if you want special privileges".

Third Phase of India-Nepal Relationship: 1990-1996

The Third Phase India-Nepal relations continued from 1990 to 1996. This phase could be called as the beginning of positive bilateralism. By 1990, there was a perception in India that the democratic forces, which were banned by the King since 1959, needed to be strengthened. The idea behind supporting the democratic forces was that these forces would be better allies of India than the king. During this period in Nepal there emerged a democratic movement against the Monarchy popularly known as the 'Jana Andolan'. The political parties of Nepal were successful in establishing a multi-party democratic set up with a limited monarchy. India extended its full support to the multiparty democracy in Nepal and for the election.

The new and democratically elected Prime Minister (PM) of Nepal, Krishna Prasad Bhattarai visited India in June 1990. This was a major development so far the bilateral relationship was concerned. The Joint Communiqué issued at the end of his visit attempted to iron out the differences between the two countries. Important outcomes of this visit were: both countries agreed to respect the security concerns and not to allow any activities in their respective territory which would go against the security interest of other, India agreed to have to separate treaties on trade and transit matters, an agreement was signed to control illegal trade across the open border and both sides agreed to have bilateral cooperation in harnessing common water resources for mutual benefit. To strengthen the new chapter of positive ties with Nepal, the Indian PM, Chandra Sekhar visited Nepal in February 1991.This visit was followed by Prime Minister P V Narasimha Rao in October 1992. In 1993, King Birendra Shah of Nepal also visited India to strengthen the relationship. As step forward to strengthen the ties between

India and Nepal, P V Narasimha Rao made clear to Manmohan Adhikari that, India would deal with Nepal as a country, irrespective of the political and ideological complexion of the party in power or the (alleged) pro or anti-India leanings of the Prime Minister of the day. He also outlined that India did not expect reciprocity in an arithmetical sense, there had to be reciprocity at least in spirit, and certainly in core areas of relationship.[5]

Though this phase was looking promising for stronger ties between two countries, India was not able to manage the rising anti-India feeling among various power structures in Nepal. The political parties who were supported by India during the Jana Andolan turned to be questioning 'India's involvement in internal affairs of Nepal'. Issues such as the 1950 treaty of Friendship and Peace were point of discussion to raise the anti-India sentiments. Political parties in opposition often used this treaty for their own political mileage which till today continues to be dominant feature of Nepali political parties. The China factor remained as a major irritant in India Nepal relations in this phase.

Civil War in Nepal and India-Nepal Relationship

The multi-party democracy that was set up in 1990 got the strongest opposition from the Communist Party of Nepal-Maoist (CPN-Maoist) on February 13, 1996. The CPN-Maoist waged a 'People's War' against the democratically elected government in Nepal and against the Monarch. The armed rebellion which was initially considered as a law and order problem by the Nepali government turned into a full scale civil war in the successive years changing the political situation in Nepal. The decade long civil war in Nepal caused by the CPN-Maoist was responsible to affect India-Nepal relationship to a great extent.

The anti-Indian stand of the Maoists is even clearer in their 40 points demands to the Nepali government before the emergence of the movement. A substantial portion of the 40 points demand of the Maoists covers the domination of India in Nepal in various fields ranging from nationalism to development, and from sociology to the politics of Nepal. Though anti-India stand by any constituency in Nepal was nothing new, but this was for the first time one particular constituency was loud and clear on its stand against India. The anti-India rhetoric of the Maoists was documented in their literature to maximise political mileage. According to Baburam Bhattarai:

"This way world imperialism enters Nepal by riding over Indian horse. This combined intrusion and oppression of imperialism and expansionism has not only stunted the development of Nepal's national industries but it has also created a situation where previously self-reliant industries are now beginning to get liquidated one after another."[9]

He went on to say that:

"In this over all context there is no doubt that 180 years of uninterrupted semi-colonial relation with India expansionism has had very negative and destructive effect on the development of internal class relations and socio-economic structures and in essence in the development of national capitalism in Nepal. That is why it is one of the most important objectives of Maoist people's war to break the chains of semi-colonialism and to usher in a new type of national capitalism (or New Democracy) by mobilising people of all ranks and classes suffering under all forms of semi-colonial exploitation and oppression.[10]

The emergence of Maoist insurgency in Nepal, its growth in scale and size and its anti-India stand had been really a challenge and a concern for India's age-old interest in Nepal. India was virtually trapped as there were three important power structures to be dealt with. India was in a situation of 'do something and get damned or do not do anything and get damned'. So far India's response towards such a situation in Nepal was concerned, India did not take the problem seriously till 2001. For the first five years of the civil war India viewed it as an internal matter of Nepal.

India responded to the Maoist problem in Nepal once the peace talks between the government of Nepal and the CPN-Maoist broke down in September 2001. Another factor which made India serious to respond to the Maoist Problem was the involvement of external powers in Nepal especially the United States of America (USA). India was the first country to declare the CPN-Maoist as a terrorist group and supported the democratic institutions in Nepal. Prime Minister of India, Atal Bihari Vajpayee, called up the PM of Nepal and the King offering assistance in their fighting against the Maoists. In May 2002, the Army Chief of India, General S. Padmanabhan paid a visit to Nepal and promised the Royal Nepal Army more military assistance. He observed that: "We can provide training assistance whenever required and anything Royal Nepal Army requires. India willstand by Nepal in every possible way. If there is a requirement of military assistance we will be glad to share what we have with Nepal".[6]

India's Nepal policy was guided by the principle of "Twin Pillar Policy". The Twin Pillar Policy of India towards Nepal supported a multi-party democracy and a constitutional monarchy. India's Twin Pillar Policy was more of a convergence with the King as the Army of Nepal was under his direct control. India's indirect support to the king invited criticism both from the political parties and the Maoists. King Gyanendra's visit to India added to the suspicion of both the political parties and the Maoists. The Political parties developed a fear psychosis that India was trying to re-establish the Monarchy with full power. Baburam Bhattarai in his criticism to Gyanendra's visit said that:

"The heightened bonhomie between the ruling Hindutva forces in India and the so-called incarnation of Vishnu within the Nepalese Royal palace during and after Gyanendra's visit to India. It is there for all to see. The ban imposed on the All India Nepalese Unity Society under the draconian POTA on July, arrest and deportation of four journalists were clearly designed to appease the monarchy.[7]

The political parties also suspected India's commitment against the CPN-Maoists as the Maoists used Indian Territory as safe havens. The Twin Pillar Policy back fired for India. India was not able to satisfy any one of three power structures in Nepal. India's vehement criticism against the Royal take over in 2002 and 2005 was against the interest of the King. The King went ahead to win the support of China when India decided to stop arms supply to Nepal after the Royal take over in 2005. India's decision to stop arms to Nepal invited criticism not only from the King but also from Nepal Army. Though India's commitment for democracy was reflected in this move, yet it did not succeed in getting full support from the political parties. This phase from 1996 to 2005 was the most critical for both the countries as they failed to take the relationship to new heights. India was virtually in trap and was held responsible, virtually, for all the mishappenings in Nepal.

The Post-Civil War and India-Nepal Relations

Let it be mentioned that whenever there was a regime change in Nepal, India always played a vital role for the change. After the Royal take over by King Gyanendra in 2005, India supported the political parties to negotiate with the Maoists to bring an end to the decade old violence in Nepal. On November 22, 2005 seven political parties of Nepal (Seven Party Alliance) along with the Unified Communist Party of Nepal (UCPN) signed a 12-point agreement with active mediation of India. The Comprehensive Peace Agreement (CPA)[8] signed on November 21, 2006, which succeeded the 12-point agreement put an end to the civil war and brought the Maoists into mainstream. Following the successful signing of the CPA, the Constituent Assembly (CA) was elected with 601 members in April 2008.[13] Originally, the CA was given tasks of drafting a constitution for Nepal and giving a logical conclusion to the peace process. The first CA successfully integrated the People's Liberation Army with the Nepal Army before its term expired on May 25, 2012. Nepal went for a second CA election on November 19, 2013. The second CA is expected to draft a constitution by November 2014. Since April 2008, the Political situation in Nepal has remained unstable. In these seven years time, Nepal has been witnessing constant interruption in smooth functioning of the CA in drafting the constitution. One of the major factors for delay in constitution drafting process has been the change of governments almost in regular interval. Nepal has seen six Prime Ministers in these seven years period. The worst ever political horse-trading took place when Madhav Kumar Nepal resigned as the PM on July 1, 2010. There continued a seven-month long political deadlock and the political parties were finally able to elect Jhala Nath Khanal as the prime minister only after more than 20 rounds of prime ministerial elections. Khanal, who became PM on February 6, 2011, had to resign on August 14, 2011. Baburam Bhattarai succeeded him on August 28, 2011 and continued till May 27, 2012.[9]

Just like its past experiences, India, in the post-civil war period faces a dual problem. One the one hand, Nepal recognises that India has played, can play and should play a positive role in bringing an end to the peace process. On the other hand, there is all around unhappiness about how India is seen to be playing this role.[10] It becomes even more difficult for India to have 'one Nepal Policy' with changing political dynamics as multiple political actors have emerged in Nepal with loads of differences with each other.[11] Though India maintains its stand that a peaceful and stable Nepal will serve the interest of both India and Nepal, Nepal always finds an Indian hand in its troubles. During this phase of post civil war Nepal the India-Nepal relationship was affected by the political instability in Nepal to a great extent. Political elites in Kathmandu strongly suspected India to be using the Madheshi groups to create political disturbances in Nepal. Nepali media also played a major role in straining the relationship. On May 17, 2012, the Consulate General of India, S D Mehta, was reported in Nepali media to have instigated the Terai political leadership for a protest for Madhesh before May 27, 2012.[12] Such media reports sparked demands from Kathmandu to recall the Consulate General.

Despite political instability in Nepal and constant India bashing, both the countries made important headways in bilateral relations. One of the positive developments in this regard was Prime Minister Baburam Bhattarai's visit on October 20-23, 2011. The issues discussed during the Nepal PM's visit took place in the backdrop of a decision taken by major political parties on October 17, 2011 and the UCPN-M's Standing Committee meeting on October 18, 2011. There was a consensus in these meetings on not raising or discussing 'controversial issues' with India, such as, the 1950 Indo-Nepal Treaty of Peace and Friendship, the Arms Assistance Agreement-1965, allowing an air marshal in Indian flights to Nepal, extradition treaty and mutual legal assistance treaty. In view of the above, the delegation led by Bhattarai was left with issues pertaining trade and commerce, health, education, infrastructure development etc for discussions with India.[13] During his visit both countries signed Bilateral Investment Promotion and Protection Agreement (BIPPA) to better the economic ties. Article 6 of the BIPPA assures investors of compensation of contracting parties in case of losses caused by "war or other armed conflict, a state of national emergency, revolt, insurrection or riot." Nepal's interest in the signing of BIPPA lies in securing huge investments from India. Some of the key issues concerning India's security like human trafficking, smuggling of arms and fake Indian currency were also discussed in this visit.

Prime Minister of India, Narendra Modi, paid a two day visit to Nepal on August 3, 2014. This visit was important as a PM of India visited Nepal after a gap of seventeen years. In his departure statement Narendra Modi said that he would "identify steps to strengthen our bilateral cooperation in key sectors, including trade and investment, hydro power, agriculture".[14] He was the first Prime Minister from any country to have addressed the law makers in Nepalese Parliament. This visit laid down some important developments for stronger bilateral ties. Nepal was acknowledged as a business partner, discussions were held to take positive steps to "review, adjust and update" the 1950 Treaty of Peace and Friendship. The Pancheswar Multi-Purpose Project (PMP) as part of the Mahakali Treaty was discussed at length. Both the countries agreed to work on the PMP. It is important to mention that the PMP has been on the drawing board for almost three decades. PM Modi stressed on tangible progress in this regard and urged for implementation of the same before the 18th South Asian Association for Regional Cooperation (SAARC) Summit at Nepal in November 2014.

Towards Progressive Partnership

India-Nepal relationship, in the post civil war period in Nepal, is moving towards progressive partnership. As mentioned before both Nepalese and Indian establishment recognise the importance of each other. In order to achieve better bilateral interests both the countries need to deal with the irritants disturbing the relations in a more matured fashion. One of the major irritant in this regard is the 1950 Treaty of Peace and Friendship. Nepal has been using this treaty to whip up anti-India sentiment. Though every political party would use this issue for their benefit, none of them, when in power, has ever discussed the issue seriously with India. India must realise that the 1950 Treaty does not really serve any of its national interests. There have been instances where the spirit of the treaty was broken by Nepalese authorities. A Treaty which was signed by the Rana Regime with India does not really hold any ground after the fall of the regime. A new treaty drafted today with mutual consent keeping in mind the strategic interests of both the countries will have more legitimacy and credibility and serve India's interest better.[15]

The China factor is another major irritant in India-Nepal relations. India for no reason gets hallucinated with Nepal's engagement China. India must realise that as a sovereign country Nepal has all the freedom and rights to engage with any other country. India must refrain from framing its policy towards Nepal on exaggerated fear of China. Given the inerasable natural, cultural and emotional links between the two countries, Nepal can ill afford to snap its relationship with India.[16] India's policy towards Nepal must be pro-active rather than as a reaction to China. India must deliver on what it promises to Nepal to prove the saying in Nepal wrong that "India promises and China delivers". Most importantly, India must see Nepal on equal footing.

Political instability in Nepal proves to an important irritant for India-Nepal relationship. It is high time for Nepal to draft a constitution and sort out unnecessary internal differences. It is time for Nepal to stop behaving like an over dependant neighbour. It should generate its own avenues and talk to India like a business partner. Nepal should understand the genuine security concerns of India emerging from the Indo-Nepal border and Nepal as well. Fake Indian Currency Notes (FICN) is mostly routed through Nepal. The Indo-Nepal border is a hub of all sorts of criminal activities. Positive cooperation from Nepal in this regard will help strengthen the bilateral ties.

Over these years, both the countries have failed to manage the perception on each other. Many a time misperceptions have the potential to strain the relationship. India, especially, must not get affected by anti-India slogans in Nepal. In most of time these slogans are for domestic consumption only. Both the countries must think beyond popular sloganeering and move towards building a progressive partnership.

References

1. See B C Upreti, *Uneasy Friends*, Kalinga Publications, New Delhi, 2001.
2. See Anil Kumar Mohapatra, "Indo-Nepal Ties: From 'Contention' to 'Course –Correction'", *World Focus*, April 2012, pp.15-23.
3. For details see Lok Raj Baral, Behind India-Nepal Relations, available at: http://www.ekantipur.com/the-kathmandu-post/2008/05/07/related_articles/behind-india-nepal-relations/146140.html, accessed on July 29, 2008
4. The 1923 Treaty was signed between the Rana regime and the British India. It was the first Treaty between Nepal and Britain to be recorded in League of Nations. This is regarded as one of the most important achievements of the Ranas as the Treaty recognised the Independence and sovereignty of Nepal.
5. See Padmaja Murthy, India and Nepal: Security and Economic Dimension, Strategic Analysis, Vol.23, No. 9, December 1999, pp.
6. For details see John W. Garver, "China-India Rivalry in Nepal: The Clash over Chinese Arms Sales", Asian Survey, Vol. 31, No. 10, October 1991, pp. 956-975.
7. *Ibid.*
8. See K V Rajan, "Nepal-India Relations", *South Asian Journal*, January-March, 2005, available at: http://www.southasia nmedia. net/Magazine/Journal/7_nepal-india_relations.htm, accessed on August 8, 2010
9. For details see Baburam Bhattarai, *Politico-Economic Rationale of People's War in Nepal*, Janadisha Publications, April, 2004, p. 63.
10. *Ibid*, pp. 64-65.
11. See "India Hounds Nepal Maoists", The Revolutionary Worker, August 2002, available at: http://rwor.org, accessed on January 10, 2006.
12. For details see Baburam Bhattarai, "Tringular Balance of Forces" *Economic and Political Weekly*, Vol. 37, No. 46, November 16-22, 2002, p. 4609.
13. The CPA promised to end the civil war, bring about political, economic and social transformation, transitional justice and sustainable peace.
14. See Anshuman Behera, "Nepal: The Constituent Assembly that was.....", June 1, 2012, available at: http://www.idsa.in/idsacomments/

NepalThe Constituent Assemblythatwas_ abehra_010612.html, accessed on September 3, 2014.

15. See Arvind Gupta, "India needs a new paradigm in its Nepal policy", August 18, 2010, available at: http://www.idsa.in/idsacomments/ Indianeedsanewparadigminits Nepalpolicy_ agupta_ 180810, accessed on October 9, 2012.
16. See Anshuman Behera, "India-Nepal relations in 2012: An Analysis", *World Focus,* December 2012, p. 102
17. For details see "Indian diplomat in Birgunj 'seeks' a 'storm' in the Madhes", The Kathmandu Post, May 17, 2012, available at: http:// www.ekantipur.com/the-kathmandu-post/2012/05/17/top-story/ indian-diplomat-in-birgunj-seeks-a-storm-in-the-madhes/ 234975.html, accessed on October 2, 2012.
18. See Anshuman Behera, "Nepalese PM's Visit to India: "Qualified Success", November 4, 2011, available at: http://www.idsa.in/ idsacomment/NepalesePMsVisittoIndia QualifiedSuccess_ abehera_041111.html, accessed on September 3, 2014.
19. See "Narendra Modi to visit Nepal today", *The Times of India*, New Delhi, August 3, 2014.
20. See Anshuman Behera, "Modi's Nepal visit shouldn't take the beaten track", *The Pioneer*, New Delhi, August 2, 2014.
21. *Ibid.*

16

The Issue of Ethnic Identity in the Indo-Nepal Relations

Amit Kumar Gupta

Introduction

Frequently asked questions to Indians of Nepali Origin (INO) in India –

- Who are you?
- Where are you from?
- Are you a Nepali from Nepal?
- Are you a foreigner?
- Are you from China?
- Are you a Bahadur or a Gorkha (here stereotyped as a chowkidar (gatekeeper))?
- Are you a Kancha (household servant) or a Daju (porter)?

Frequently asked questions to Nepalese of Indian Origin (NIO) in Nepal –

- Who are you?
- Where are you from?
- Are you an Indian from India?
- Are you a foreigner?
- Are you a madhesi (dweller of the plains)?
- Are you a Marwari or a Bihari bhaiya (brother from the state of Gujarat or Bihar – here stereotyped as a person who is looked down upon and their accent ridiculed)?

Such stereotyping of the ethnic communities (i.e., INOs and NIOs) residing both in India and Nepal has been a major source of concern and also a primary issue in the Indo-Nepal relations. Both the INOs and the NIOs are fighting for a respectful status and rights in the countries of their residence and also for the claim that they are definitely a part and parcel of the respective countries that they are residing in. In this regard Michael Hutt, according to A.C. Sinha, concludes that:

The simple fact of the matter is that a Newar or a Limbu (indigenous people of the hills having Mongoloid features) born in Darjeeling, Bhutan or Assam will always be considered 'Nepali', even if he or she adopts the label 'Gorkha' (Nepali speaking people of India) or 'Lhotshampa' (ethnic Nepalese population of Bhutan), just as Bihari or Marwari, who has no home other than Kathmandu, will always be considered 'Indian'.

The main reason cited by the two communities for such stereotyping is the Indo-Nepal Treaty of Peace and Friendship, signed in the year 1950. Among various provisions of the treaty, Article 7 is specifically considered problematic by the two communities as it reads:

The Governments of India and Nepal agree to grant, on reciprocal basis, to the nationals of one country in the territories of the other the same privileges in the matter of residence, ownership of property, participation in trade and commerce, movement and other privileges of a similar nature. (MEA)

This particular Article of the treaty provides for an open border which enables the Indian and the Nepali citizens to move freely across the border without Visa or any short of prior permission. They can reside and work in either of the country, own property, do trade or business, and have the freedom of movement throughout the country that they have migrated to. However, they are deprived of the political rights. Nonetheless, a significant number of Nepalese and Indians running into millions have benefited from the treaty.

However, the predominant losers here are those Indian and Nepali citizens, i.e., INOs and NIOs, who have their ancestral origin in the other country. For hundreds of years they are residing in the countries to which they are citizens of. However, the natives of those regions look upon them with suspect and disdain, in the sense that they are not the actual citizens of their resident countries, but are migrants from the other country as the border between the two countries are open. They are thus alleged to possess 'double homeland'. (Thapa, 2009) A majority of these communities are therefore demanding amendments in Article 7 of the treaty of Peace and Friendship of 1950, and that the borders should be regulated so as to check the free flow of people across the border. Simultaneously, there is a strong demand from the side of Nepal to check the migration of Indians into Nepal, as they are of the belief that Nepal being a smaller country in terms of size, does not have the capacity to observe more Indians into Nepal, who are migrating in great numbers and are taking control of and are dominating the Businesses and trades in Nepal. Nonetheless, India according to them must and is also capable of observing more and more Nepalese into its territory.

Nonetheless, a fact here to note is that there are historical evidences that go on to prove that there was free movement of the people between the two countries from time immemorial, which was legalised and continued by the Britishers' after the signing of the Treaty of Sugauli in 1815. According to B.C. Upreti, there were primarily three reasons for the preference of open border between India and Nepal. First, there was a need of Nepali labour to work in tea gardens and several developmental projects and also for recruitment in the armed forces, as they were considered as the martial race, which became evident to the Britishers' during the Anglo-Gorkha war of 1814, where extraordinary warfare skills of the Gorkha soldiers were proved by the fact that mere 2600 Nepali soldiers armed with traditional weapon Khukuri put up a strong fight against 4629 British soldiers who were armed with modern weaponry. (Devi, 2009). Second, the British and Indian businessmen had commercial interest and by means of open border they wanted an easy access to the Nepali markets and the raw materials, especially forest-based ones. Third, the Britishers' were also keen on getting a free access to the Himalayan peaks for the surveyors, scientists, trekkers and expeditions. Post-Independence, India by means of the Treaty of Peace and Friendship of 1950 continued with the British policy of open border with Nepal, considering the deep-rooted historical, socio-cultural, economic and political relations between the two regions.

Locating the Indians of Nepali Origin (INO) in India

The Indians of Nepali Origin, who seek to be identified by an alternate nomenclature such as Indian Gorkha, Bhargoli (Bharatiya Gorkhali), Sakhaa (friend), etc. so as not to be accused of being a citizen of Nepal, are normally claimed to have been invited by the Britishers into the British-Indian territory to join the armed forces and to work as labourers in various developmental and mining works. However, the fact of the matter is that the Kiratis (indigenous ethnic groups of the Himalayas), has been present in various parts of the Indian territory since ages and is the rightful claimants of the 'sons of the soil'. Moreover, with the implementation of the treaty of Sugauli (1815), the bordering areas of Nepal like, Darjeeling, Shimla, Nainital, Kumaon, Garhwal and parts of Sikkim were transferred to British India. With this the Nepalese residing in those areas automatically became part and parcel of British India and then of Republic of India (Devi, 2009). According to A.C. Sinha, many Indian writers of the Nepali origin, from Northeast India claim that in the ancient times there was a close ethnic link between Northeast India and Nepal. Unfortunately, however no authentic historical document exists, which could prove their age-old link. Documental evidences exist of the period after the Anglo-Burmese war of 1826, which goes on to provide an explanation as to how the Nepalese settled in the North-eastern region of India as soldiers (as members of Gorkha regiment of the British army), herdsmen, graziers, dairymen, lumber jacks, etc. In the words of A.C. Sinha:

"Among the coloured underdogs, Nepalese were the favoured ethnic stock of the white colonial rulers. Willy-nilly, they came to be identified as the "sahibs (master or owner) faithful boys"... the British also invented a myth of the Gorkha martial race. It may be pertinent that in the aftermath of the Sepoy Mutiny of 1857, the British were determined to prove that the Bengalis and high caste Hindus from the Gangetic plains were effeminate and thus unsuitable for the armed forces (mainly because they participated in the Sepoy Mutiny against the Britishers)... Meanwhile, Gorkhas, Sikhs, Marathas and others, who did not take part in the Sepoy Mutiny, were elevated to the status of 'martial race' by creating many real and putative myths and thus, they were recruited to armed forces."

As a matter of fact, the Indians of Nepali origins are those who are characterised by diversity of culture, language, religion, etc. They according to Shrawan Acharya have a high degree of mobility especially within South Asia, which has in fact further led to their diversification. The INOs can be categorised to be descendants of the Aryan and the Mongoloid communities. The Bahun, Chhetri, Newar, Kami, Sarki and Damai caste of people are primarily the descendants of the Aryan community. Similarly, the Rai, Limbu, Tamang, Sunwar, etc. caste of people are primarily the descendants of the Mongoloid community. Each of these communities and castes has their own distinct language and culture. Despite the indicated diversities, Michael Hutt has rightly pointed out that, in India, these communities have; ...attained a high degree of cultural uniformity outside Nepal, as well as a some-what higher degree of equality between castes and ethnic groups than that which obtains in Nepal. The Indian Nepalese are now unified by their use of Nepali as a common tongue (whereas, in Nepal, Nepali language is said to have been imposed as a national language by the Gorkha rulers upon their people), and by the shared experience of living as a minority community in states where they are ever likely to be categorised as foreigners.

Regardless of the bondages the Indian Nepalese consider themselves to be underdogs in India for several reasons. A.C. Sinha has cited some of the sufferings and discrimination being faced by the community within India.

Political Discrimination

The community lacks political voice and representation in the national Legislature, with hardly about six representatives out of a total of 750 seats in both the houses of the Indian Parliament. It is argued that the community representation is not just inadequate but also the representatives lack competence and sophistication to actively participate or represent the entire community in the national political platform. However, though in the State of Sikkim and the District of Darjeeling in West Bengal, they have self-governing facilities and the rule of law and the laws of the land prevails. Simultaneously, the Indian Nepali community have certain bit of representation in the state legislatures of Assam, Meghalaya, Manipur, Uttarakhand and West Bengal as per their population's proportionality. The only problem exists in their under-representation in the national politics, where they believe their concerns are simply ignored by those in majority.

Identity Crisis

The major grievance of the Indian Nepalese is that they are mistaken with the visiting Nepalese citizens of Nepal. They argue that most of the Indian communities have their home states, for example, Biharis have Bihar, Punjabis have Punjab, Bengalis have West Bengal, Marathis have Maharashtra, Tamils have Tamil Nadu and so on so forth. However, there is no home state for the Nepalese. Whenever, a question is asked to the Indian Nepalese where are they from? They have no answer and the receiving end always believe that they are from Nepal, despite the fact that these people are living in India since ages. Thus, it is visible that the Indian Nepali community is presently demanding a separate home state for the community. The movement had started earlier in the form of a forum called the All India Gorkha League (AIGL), which was established in 1923 in Dehradun (Uttarakhand). Its primary demand was a Nepali speaking state within India. During the initial phases of the 1980s, AIGL was confined merely to the Dooars region and Darjeeling District in North Bengal and was concurrently replaced by the Gorkha National Liberation Front (GNLF), which was led by a former soldier Subhas Ghising. Under Subhas Ghising a violent movement for a separate Gorkhaland state was raised, resulting in the formation of Darjeeling Gorkha Hill Council (DGHC), an autonomous administrative body for the three hill sub-divisions, Darjeeling, Kalimpong and Kurseong. Today, the GNLF has been replaced by the Semi-autonomous administrative body named, Gorkhaland Territorial Administration (GTA), which is headed by Bimal Gurung.

Though in 1992, the Government of India did recognise Nepali as an Indian language by incorporating it in the list of Indian languages in the VIIIth Schedule of the Indian Constitution. This was supposedly done so as to mitigate the anger of the Indian Nepalese. Moreover the Sahitya Academy (the official cultural body of the Government of India), does recognise Nepali literature and the Nepali authors who are constantly awarded for their contributions and meritorious works in literature and academia. Moreover, in Sikkim, various Kirati communities have been given complete freedom in order to preserve and develop their respective languages, scripts and culture. This in fact has been a welcome progress for the Indian Nepali community.

Locating the Nepalese of Indian Origin (NIO) in Nepal

According to Hrishikesh Shaha, as pointed out by A.C. Sinha, in ancient times the terai (the plain Savannas situated in Southern Nepal) region was flourishing with several well known centres of Vedic and Buddhist learning. This was possible primarily because the great Magadh Empire or the Gupta rulers and many other dynasties of main land India had their sway in Nepal for the most part in the terai region. The present status of Nepal's terai region was determined by Treaty of Sugauli (1815), under the terms of which Nepal was to surrender the entire terai region to the Britishers. However, slowly and gradually, Nepal recovered the terai region as a reward for its services to the Britishers during the Sepoy Mutiny of 1857 in India.

The majority of people residing in the terai region are the Madhesis who are predominantly of Indian origin. It is alleged that these Madhesis or the Nepalese of Indian Origin (NIOs) are land-hungry emigrants from India, who came and settled in the terai region after the Sepoy Mutiny. However, as mentioned earlier, history is evident that many of these NIOs have been residing in the terai and other regions of Nepal from time immemorial and are in fact the rightful claimants of the 'sons of the soil'. However, the NIOs have suffered from a continuous sense of discrimination, exploitation and ensuing deprivation. An old appellation of 'Timiharu Madhesis' (you are Madhesis) is very common in the region. The tragedy of the Madhesis according to A.C. Sinha does not end here, as it is also evident that the people of Bihar and Uttar Pradesh in India treat them (the NIOs) as uncouth and even avoid marital relationships with them.

According to Nihar R. Nayak, the NIOs have felt this discrimination from the end of the Nepalese government due to the following few reasons:

Firstly, the NIOs were debarred from citizenship certificates, under the Citizenship Act of 1964 and the Constitution of 1990. As a result they could neither acquire land ownership nor could avail government benefits. Although amendments were introduced in the Citizenship Laws of the land in November, 2006, which permits people born and residing in Nepal before the 1990s to acquire citizenship, it has been alleged that many Madhesis and Dalits are still deprived of citizenship. According to a report published by IRIN (Humanitarian News and Analysis: a Service of the UN Office for the Coordination of Humanitarian Affairs) in 2007, 40 per cent of the Madhesis still do not have citizenship or voting rights.

Secondly, the NIOs allege that the Nepali government has been undermining their cultural traditions, as has been evident from the fact that the government has been attempting to introduce compulsory Nepali language, both at work and in the education system. Nepali is the only medium of competitive examinations for various governmental positions in Nepal. The Madhesi demand of introducing Hindi has not yet fructified.

Thirdly, the level of discrimination against the NIOs has been visible from the fact that, despite the NIOs population constituting nearly one-third of the total Nepali population, their share of representation in government employment is merely 9.9 per cent, and also that in the year 2007, only 15 per cent of the 330 Nepali Parliamentarians were Madhesis. According to A.C. Sinha:

"There are a number of ways through which Nepal has denied them a genuine representation in its parliament. For example, demographically, terai constituency is much larger than that of the constituencies in the hills. Second, division of the constituencies has been done from north to south ostensibly with a view to including hill people and excluding dominance of the terai people, and not from east to west, which is natural and which favours the Madhesis."

Fourthly, issues concerning economic exploitation of the community have also been raised. A fact of the terai region or for that matter the Madhesis that, it contributes 70 per cent of the agricultural production of Nepal, 65 per cent of the total GDP, and 76 per cent of the country's total revenue. However, despite such extensive contribution of the region the infrastructure here is considered to be much poorer as compared to North Nepal. Additionally, accusations have also been made as to how in the name of land reforms, major land holdings of the NIOs were given to the peoples' from the hills.

Fifthly, A.C. Sinha has also pointed out that the NIOs in Nepal, like that of the INOs in India, receive very little academic attention. According to him, the academicians and writers of the hills, make all out efforts to distant themselves from the Madhesis. And one best example of this deliberate down playing is visible in Dor Bahadur Bista's 252 paged book titled, '*People of Nepal*', which has only 12 pages talking about the NIOs who reside in the terai region.

Considering these identity questions, the NIOs have started taking matters in their own hands. This is evident from the fact that numerous political parties and non-state actors have emerged in the terai region addressing the Madhesi cause. Some of these are: Nepal Terai Congress, Madhesi Mukti Andolan, Madhesi Janadhikar Forum, Terai Madhesh Loktantrik Party, etc. There are also various armed groups in the terai region, who have been aspiring to achieve divergent goals, for instance, a separate sovereign Terai state, opposition to religious extremism and Maoism, retention of constitutional monarchy and multiparty democracy, etc. Some of these armed groups are Janatantrik Terai Mukti Morcha, Terai Cobra, Nepal Defence Army, Chure Bhawar Ekta Samaj, etc. (Nayak, 2010)

Conclusion

Consequently, it has been visible that both India and Nepal seems to be treating the INOs and NIOs in typically the same manner in which the colonial masters treat their subjects. Therefore, the need of the hour is to address those issues in the Indo-Nepal relations which need to change with the passage of time, i.e., among other things, some of the provisions of the Treaty of Peace and Friendship, especially Article 7 might need re-examination keeping in mind the interest of both the communities residing in their respective countries.

However, in all this, an interesting fact here to note is that, in both the communities, i.e., the INOs and the NIOs despite their being internal tensions on the basis of language, religion, caste, class, ethnicity, have in fact emerged as a unified entity, fighting for one common demand of rights and respectful identity. In this regard, Shrawan Acharya has rightly pointed out that;

In a democratic society conflicts are inherent and are not necessarily destructive. One has to realise that assertive movements have important social processes which can be effectively harnessed not only to address the grievances of the groups but also to enhance social solidarity amongst the contending groups.

References

1. Acharya, Shrawan, 2009, Consolidating Nepali Identity: *A Cultural Planning Perspective, in Indian Nepalis: Issues and Perspectives*, T.B. Subba, A.C. Sinha, G.S. Nepal & D.R. Nepal (eds.), New Delhi, Concept Publishing Company.
2. Devi, Nira, 2009, History of Nepali Settlement in Assam, in Indian Nepalis: Issues and Perspectives, T.B. Subba, A.C. Sinha, G.S. Nepal & D.R. Nepal (eds.), New Delhi, Concept Publishing Company.
3. Hutt, Michael, 2009, Where is Home for an Indian Nepali Writer? in Indian Nepalis: Issues and Perspectives, T.B. Subba, A.C. Sinha, G.S. Nepal & D.R. Nepal (eds.), New Delhi, Concept Publishing Company.
4. IRIN, February 08, 2007, Nepal: Background of the Terai's Madhesi People, (Online Web), Accessed: October 02, 2014, URL: http://www.irinnews.org/report/70027/nepal-background-of-the-terai-s-madhesi-people
5. Ministry of External Affairs (Government of India), Treaty of Peace and Friendship (July 31, 1950), (Online Web), Accessed: September 25, 2014, URL: http://mea.gov.in/bilateral-documents.htm?dtl/6295/Treaty+of+Peace+and+Friendship
6. Nayak, Nihar R., 2010, Madhesi Movement in Nepal: Implications for India, Institute of Defence Studies and Analysis, (Online Web), Accessed: October 01, 2014, URL: http://www.idsa.in/event/MadhesiProblemandImplicationsforIndia.html
7. Sinha, A.C., 2009, Introduction, in Indian Nepalis: Issues and Perspectives, T.B. Subba, A.C. Sinha, G.S. Nepal & D.R. Nepal (eds.), New Delhi, Concept Publishing Company.

8. Sinha, A.C., 2009, Shared Destiny: Indians of Nepalese Origin (INO) and Nepalese of Indian Origin (NIO), in Indian Nepalis: Issues and Perspectives, T.B. Subba, A.C. Sinha, G.S. Nepal & D.R. Nepal (eds.), New Delhi, Concept Publishing Company.
9. T.B. Subba, 2009, The Last Word So Far..., in Indian Nepalis: Issues and Perspectives, T.B. Subba, A.C. Sinha, G.S. Nepal & D.R. Nepal (eds.), New Delhi, Concept Publishing Company.
10. Thapa, Tapasya, 2009, Being and Belonging: A Study of the Indian Nepalis, in Indian Nepalis: Issues and Perspectives, T.B. Subba, A.C. Sinha, G.S. Nepal & D.R. Nepal (eds.), New Delhi, Concept Publishing Company.
11. Upreti, B.C., 2009, The India-Nepal open border: Nature issues and problems, in Himalayan Frontiers of India: Historical, geo-political & Strategic Perspectives, K. arikoo (ed.), Oxon, Routledge Contemporary South Asia Series.

Bibliography

About the Editor

Dr Mohammed Badrul Alam is a citizen of India and had his education at a number of institutions including Utkal University, Bhubaneswar, Odisha; Jawaharlal Nehru University, New Delhi; and Cornell University, New York, USA; from where he earned M.A, M.Phil and Ph.D degrees respectively. He has taught for over a two decades in the United States, Japan and India at various educational institutions. Since January 2006, Dr Alam has been Professor (and Head of the Department since January 2013) at the Dept. of Political Science, Jamia Millia Islamia University, New Delhi, India. Dr Alam is the author of several books including, *Perspectives on Nuclear Strategy of India and Pakistan* (2013), *Indo-US Relations: Dimensions and Emerging Trends* (2013), *Contours of India's Foreign Policy: Changes and Challenges(2014)*, as well as numerous articles, monographs and books reviews published in international journals. He is a recipient of number of prestigious awards including Fulbright Fellowship, Shastri Canadian Foreign ministry award, DAAD Fellowship, Salzburg Global Fellowship, Baden-Wuerttemberg Fellowship, Visiting Scholar at East-West Center, etc. His research interests include: Study of Diaspora, US-India relations, Nuclear issues in South Asia and the Study of Indian elections.

Contact Address:

Dr Mohammed Badrul Alam,
Professor and Head, Dept. of Political Science,
Faculty of Social Sciences, Jamia Millia Islamia University, Okhla,
New Delhi. 110025. India. Office Tel: 011-26981717, extn: 3530,
Cell No: 9313397023, E-mail:**mbalam786**@gmail.com

Epilogue

Index

B

F

G

I

J

N

R

T